OUR MEDIA, NOT THEIRS

Our Media, Not Theirs

The Democratic Struggle Against Corporate Media

Robert W. McChesney
and John Nichols

An Open Media Book

SEVEN STORIES PRESS / NEW YORK

Series Editor: Greg Ruggiero
Sections of this book originally appeared in Nichols and
McChesney's *It's the Media, Stupid* (Open Media/Seven Stories
Press, 2000).

ISBN: 1-58322-549-8

Cover design and photograph: Greg Ruggiero

Cover photo: Washington, D.C., police descend on microradio
activists as they prepare to march to FCC and NAB headquarters
to demand increased community access to the airwaves.
Washington, D.C., Dupont Circle, October 5, 1998.

College professors may order examination copies of Seven Stories
Press titles free for a six-month trial period. To order, visit
www.sevenstories.com/textbook, or fax on school letterhead to
(212) 226-1411.

9 8 7 6 5 4

Printed in Canada.

EDITOR'S NOTE

Our Media Not Theirs is a fully revised and updated version of Robert McChesney and John Nichols' book, *It's the Media, Stupid* (Seven Stories Press, 2000). Some sections of the text, including Ralph Nader's and Barbara Ehrenreich's forewords, appeared in the original 2000 edition. Most of the text, however, including Noam Chomsky's foreword, is new material written during the summer of 2002

Greg Ruggiero

Contents

The World We Share

BY BARBARA EHRENREICH

WHATEVER CONCERNS MOTIVATE you as a citizen—education, tax policy, health care, gay rights, campaign finance reform—there is no escaping the media. Run a candidate for office, and you'll have to hope her message doesn't get lost when it's squeezed into the increasingly microscopic sound-bites favored by TV news. Stage a protest demonstration, and you must worry about whether it will get any coverage—or whether the coverage it gets will turn out to be so warped that you'll wish the media hadn't covered it at all. Or maybe you just want to educate the public about an issue you're all fired up about. Where are you going to turn if not to the media? There's just no other way to communicate with large numbers of other people—to make a point, raise an issue, and begin to flex your muscles as a free citizen of a democratic nation.

The media are as inescapable and ubiquitous a presence in our lives as the environment. In fact, they are, to a large extent, the mental and cultural environment we inhabit every day, bringing us the first voices we hear in the morning, the opinions we absorb while driving, the stories and images that entertain us after work. Insofar as we are intelligent social beings, the media are the world we share.

But the media are more than just an "environment" or a kind of neutral space where ideas, images, and opinions compete for our attention. In the last few years, the media have become a contentious issue in their own right. There's a groundswell of public concern about violence in the media, which may be useful for capturing the attention of channel-surfers, but almost certainly seems to have a morally desensitizing effect on the viewer. There's a growing worry about the impact of relentless media-transmitted advertising, especially on children, but ultimately on all of us as the advertising slops over into the "content" of a program or an article. And we are just beginning to understand all the ways the news media, in particular, subtly shape public policy and debate: Sensationalized crime coverage, for example, lays the groundwork for grotesquely punitive criminal justice measures like "three strikes and you're out." Grossly inadequate coverage of foreign news leaves us increasingly clueless in an era of globalization.

The problem has always been what to do about it. We can write cranky letters to the editor; we can turn off our TVs. But these are tiny gestures. How can we really affect something as pervasive and powerful—vast, and at the same time, intimate—as the media environment we live in? Here's where Robert McChesney and John Nichols come in. What they show in *Our Media Not Theirs* is that control of the media is becoming a political issue in countries all over the world—a subject for debate and potentially for legislation. It can happen here too, if we are willing to take the next step beyond griping: We can build a grassroots movement to counter the sleaze, the distortions, and the mind-numbing materialism of our unaccountable and corporate-dominated media.

Imagine the kind of media that a democratic society deserves: Media that bring us a wealth of diverse opinions and entertainment options; media that are held responsible for providing us with the information we need to function as informed citizens; media where ideas flow in both directions, and where ordinary people routinely have a chance to voice their concerns. If you like that picture, put yourself into it today by joining the struggle for media reform. McChesney and Nichols have shown us what is possible; now it falls to all of us to realize that potential with our activism.

In an Honest Debate

BY RALPH NADER

NOT TOO LONG ago, I opened a press conference in Salt Lake City by looking into the television cameras and talking about the fact that the people, not the multinational communications corporations, own the airwaves.

That's one way to make media an issue. But—as Bob McChesney and John Nichols point out, it's not the only way. In countries around the world, trade unionists, indigenous people, political activists, and ordinary citizens have put media on the agenda. Now, argue McChesney and Nichols, we the people of the United States need to make media a part of the national debate in the land where the founders guaranteed freedom of the press because they knew democracy required rich and diverse sources of information and ideas.

McChesney and Nichols are right.

We all need to start talking about the fact that the people of the United States own the broadcast airwaves; they're the landlords. The radio and the television stations are the tenants. The corporations that own those stations should be paying the Federal Communication Commission (FCC) for the airwaves and some of that money should be recycled into developing television for the people. The rent money should be paying for audience-run networks that serve the people, that serve democracy, that treat serious matters in engrossing ways.

We all need to start talking about the fact that multinational corporations should not be allowed to dictate to the government the limits that will be placed on competition in the broadcast and print media sectors. We all need to start talking about the power that the people have to use existing antitrust and broadcast regulations—as well as new laws and new technologies—to break up monopolies and open up a true, wide-ranging democratic dialogue in this country.

There are corporate supremacists who say that issues of media ownership and content are too complex, too abstract to be issues for political debate. But the big corporatists, and those who make apologies for them, are not talking to the people.

When I bring up media issues with citizens in Salt Lake City and Atlanta, Detroit and Nashville, Los Angeles and Denver, I always find that the people get it. They get it 100 percent.

People know the media are betraying their public trust. Whether it's what's on the TV—the exploitation, the commercialism—or the news and public service programming that isn't on the TV, people know that what they're getting is not what they want or need. When I bring the discussion down to a question of what is and what isn't being covered on the evening news in their own neighborhoods and communities, when I go through how the local news breaks up the thirty minutes—the packaged crime news, the sports, the weather, the phony chitchat—it all connects with what people instinctually know about the disproportionate allocation of television news time.

When anyone talks about what's wrong with media today, and about how citizens should have the power to make meaningful change, people get excited. People like the idea of controlling some of what they own, and they're pretty shocked when they hear that the government gives away the airwaves to the radio and the television conglomerates.

In an honest debate, the side that argued for the status quo as regards media wouldn't get five percent support. That's why we need to open up that honest debate. It won't be easy. But this book will help. You hold in your hands a key to unlocking the corporate media chains that have shackled real freedom of the press and real democracy in this country for all too long. Use it!

Renewing Tom Paine's Challenge

BY NOAM CHOMSKY

Two hundred years ago, Tom Paine issued a call to "recover rights" that had been lost to "conquest and tyranny," thereby opening "a new era to the human race." The call to action that follows renews Paine's challenge. The rights that an aroused citizenry must recover, in the present case, are among those most essential to a truly functioning democracy: the right to information and to free and open discussion, not filtered by the state-corporate nexus that has effectively shaped the major media into instruments of class power and domination.

Recovering rights has never been an easy course. Paine died with little honor in the country he had helped to free from British rule, condemned as an "infidel" who had "done much harm." As his call to recover rights was published in 1792, James Madison expressed his concerns about the fate of the democratic experiment. He warned of "a real domination of the few under an apparent liberty of the many," deploring "the daring depravity of the times" as private powers "become the pretorian band of the government--at once its tools and its tyrant; bribed by its largesses, and overawing it by clamors and combinations." Thomas Jefferson feared the rise of a "single and splendid government of an aristocracy, founded on banking institutions, and moneyed incorporations" that would enable the few to be "riding and ruling over the plundered ploughman and beggared yeomanry." His thoughts were echoed by Alexis de Tocqueville, who perceived the dangers of a "permanent inequality of conditions" and an end to democracy if "the manufacturing aristocracy, which is growing up under our eyes,... one of the harshest that has ever existed in the world," should escape its confines. A century later, during a period not unlike today's, America's preeminent social philosopher, John Dewey, called for a recovery of basic rights to reverse the decline of democracy under the rule of "business for private profit through private control of banking, land, industry, reinforced by command of the press, press agents, and other means of publicity and propaganda," casting over society the shadow called "politics."

The vision of democracy that has inspired such concerns, and the popular struggles to advance the hopes and realize their promise, has been challenged in thought as well as deed. Madison's own attitudes towards democracy were ambivalent. During the Constitutional Convention, he urged that power should be vested in "the wealth of the nation," the "more capable set of men," who recognize that it is the responsibility of government "to protect the minority of the opulent against the majority." To perform this necessary task may be difficult, he anticipated, with the likely increase in "the proportion of those who will labor under all the hardships of life, and secretly sigh for a more equal distribution of its blessings." Meaures to combat their "leveling spirit" were basic principles of the constitutional order of which he was the leading framer. There should be no conflict with high principle, Madison believed, because the men of property who would hold power would be "pure and noble," each an "enlightened statesman" and "benevolent philosopher." Reality was harsher, as he soon came to appreciate. Hence his forebodings a few years later.

Similar illusions animated Wilsonian progressivism. Wilson's own view was that an elite of gentlemen with "elevated ideals" should govern in order to sustain "stability and righteousness." The intelligent minority of "responsible men" must control decision making, Walter Lippmann held. The dean of twentienth-century American journalism and a respected progressive democratic theorist, Lippmann was convinced that for democratic forms to function for the general welfare, public opinion must be shaped, and policy set and implemented, by this intelligent minority—self-designated, and owing their authority to their services to authentic power, a truism kept in the shadows by the elite intellectuals who find these ideas attractive. The general public, "ignorant and meddlesome outsiders," must "be put in its place," Lippmann added. Their place is remote from the centers of power. They are to be "spectators of action," not participants, though they do have a "function": The public is to act "only by aligning itself as the partisan of someone in a position to act executively," in periodic exercises called "elections." One of the founders of modern political science, Harold Lasswell, instructed the intelligent minority to be cognizant of the "ignorance and stupidity [of]...the masses" and to dismiss "democratic dogmatisms about men being the best judges of their own interests." They are not; we are.

The masses must be controlled for their own good. As societies become more democratic, and force is no longer available as a means of social control, the "responsible men" must turn to "a whole new technique of control, largely through propaganda," he urged.

The ideal is what the academic democratic theorist Robert Dahl calls "polyarchy," not "democracy." Like Tom Paine, those who seek popular democracy "do much harm," according to prevailing elite doctrine.

Not surprisingly, the world of private power agrees. The modern public relations industry was strongly influenced by Wilsonian progressives who advocated "the engineering of consent," a technique of control employed by the responsible men for the benefit of their flock, the ignorant masses, whose minds must be "regimented" much as an army regiments their bodies. The stupid masses must be trained to abandon any dangerous and destructive ideas about controlling their own lives. Their task is to follow orders while focusing their attention "on the more superficial things that comprise much of fashionable consumption." They are to adopt a "philosophy of futility," business leaders explain, abandoning their fate to the gentlemen of "elevated ideals" who manage the political system, and to the concentrations of unaccountable private power that are the "tools and tyrants" of government. Their lives are to be restricted to a narrow private sphere, where consumption of commodities and individual wealth maximization are the reigning values. Much of the right-wing fervor behind the drive to destroy Social Security and public schools, and to block efficient and popular programs of public health care, reflects the understanding that such programs rely on values that must be extirpated: the natural and deep-seated values of sympathy and solidarity, the conviction that one should care about what happens to the child or disabled widow on the other side of town. These pernicious ideas must be driven from the mind. People must be atomized and separated if they are to be ruled by the responsible men, for their own good.

These conflicting visions are in constant tension, and there is considerable ebb and flow in the struggle to recover, sustain, and extend rights and freedom. Victories by the ignorant and meddlesome outsiders inspire fear, often panic, among business leaders, who warn of "the hazard facing industrialists in the rising political power of the masses" and call for increased vigor in "the everlasting battle for the minds of men." Liberal intellectual elites ponder the threat of the "excess of democracy" as normally passive and apathetic populations seek to enter the political arena to press their demands, forgetting their proper place in the democratic order. Deeply concerned by the "excess of democracy" of the 1960s, the Trilateral Commission intellectuals, representing liberal internationalist sectors of the industrial world, urged "more moderation in democracy," perhaps even a return to the days when, according to Harvard political scientist Samuel Huntington, "Truman had been able to govern the country with the cooperation of a relatively small number of Wall Street lawyers and bankers." To reverse the excess of democracy, they advised, it will be necessary to overcome the failures of the institutions responsible for "the indoctrination of the young," perhaps even to institute government regulation of the press if its leaders do not impose "standards of professionalism," curtailing the occasional departures from orthodoxy and obedience.

The "crisis of democracy" perceived by the Trilateral analysts became more severe in the years that followed as large-scale popular movements developed from the ferment of the 1960s, interfering with elite control: feminist, environmental, solidarity, antinuclear, and others. These democratizing tendencies have been countered by important developments in domestic and international society. One fundamental element of the neoliberal programs of the last quarter-century is to restrict the public arena, undermining the threat of democracy by transferring decisions to unaccountable private tyrannies, under the slogan of "minimizing the state." The basic idea was captured by David Rockefeller, who founded the Trilateral Commission and shares its general liberal internationalist perspective. He expressed his approval of the trend towards

> lessening the role of government, something business people tend to be in favor of. But the other side of that coin is that somebody has to take governments' place, and business seems to me to be a logical entity to do it. I think that too many business people simply haven't faced up to that, or they have said, "It's somebody else's responsibility; it's not mine."

Crucially, it is not the responsibility of the public.

The program of "minimizing the state" is nuanced, however: State functions are to be modified, not minimized. The state must at least continue to serve its "tools and tyrants," ensuring that the world is well-ordered for their needs, and at home, maintaining the traditional mechanisms for social-

Robert W. McChesney & John Nichols

izing cost and risk to protect "the minority of the opulent" from market discipline.

The financial liberalization that is a central component of neoliberal programs also undermines democracy, as has been well-understood for half a century. It creates what some international economists call a "virtual Senate" of investors and speculative capital, who hold "veto power" over governmental decisions and can punish "bad policies" that might benefit the population rather than improving the climate for business operations. Leaving nothing to chance, those who wage "the everlasting battle for the minds of men" have also established influential think tanks and other devices to constrain the limited public space allowed by corporate media. Consolidation of media and restriction of any public service function is a natural concomitant of these programs, quite apart from independent factors that are leading to oligopoly in many sectors of the economy, controlled by a small number of conglomerates linked to one another by strategic alliances and to the powerful states on which they rely, and over which they cast their shadow.

The public is aware of the growing "democratic deficit." One of the topics addressed below is the coverage—or perhaps "coverup" would be more apt—of the November 2000 elections in the corporate media. It is also worth noting that on the eve of the election, well before the Florida shenanigans and Supreme Court intervention, three-quarters of the population did not take the process very seriously, regarding it as a game played by financial contributors, party leaders, and the PR industry, which crafted candidates to say "almost anything to get themselves elected" so that one could believe little they said even when it was intelligible.

On most issues citizens could not identify the stands of the candidates, not because they are stupid or not trying, but because of conscious efforts to direct voter attention away from issues to "qualities." Many issues of great importance to the public could not even enter the electoral agenda because popular attitudes are so strongly opposed to the elite consensus: Among them are issues related to international economic affairs, including the "free trade agreements" that the business press, more honestly, terms "free investment agreements." Even a decade later, the position of the U.S. labor movement on NAFTA and the conforming conclusions of Congress's own research bureau have yet to be reported outside of dissident sources—for good reasons: They predicted rather well the harmful effects of these agreements on working people in the three countries concerned and proposed constructive alternatives. These might have received considerable popular support had they been made available, but are opposed by the elite consensus that sets the bounds for the electoral arena and media debate. A Harvard University project that monitors political attitudes found that at the time of the November 2000 elections, the "feeling of powerlessness has reached an alarming high," with more than half saying that people like us have little or no influence on what government does. The figures have risen steadily through the neoliberal period, not just in the United States but internationally, including Latin America, where the spread of formal democracy has been accompanied by a steady decline of faith in democracy.

Powerlessness need not translate into despair, however. As in the past, popular forces are organizing on a significant scale, highly decentralized in the familiar American style, with its weaknesses and strengths. McChesney and Nichols provide much evidence that we may be in "the early stages of a serious social movement," for which democratization of the media will be a central focus of discussion, activism, and reconstruction. They make a powerful case in support of these priorities, and suggest paths that can be followed to lay these foundations for recovering rights, and carrying forward the endless struggle for freedom and justice.

Introduction

"A popular Government without popular information or the means of acquiring it, is but a Prologue to a Farce or a Tragedy or perhaps both. Knowledge will forever govern ignorance, and a people who mean to be their own Governors, must arm themselves with the power knowledge gives."

—JAMES MADISON

IT WAS SUPPOSED to be our media. In the age of enlightenment at the close of the eighteenth century, when thinkers began to imagine casting off the tyrannies of monarchs and inherited rather than elected governance, they understood that the essential tool of newly enfranchised citizens would be information. Thus, when James Madison and his comrades in the Revolutionary cause framed the Constitution of the new United States, they enshrined protections for a free and freewheeling, diverse and dangerous press that would serve as the foundation upon which American self-government and freedom would over the next two centuries be slowly—often painfully—built. There was never any question of original intent. "Our liberty cannot be guarded but by the freedom of the press," warned Thomas Jefferson. The media was to serve as a stern watchdog over those in power and those who want to be in power, in both the public and private sectors. "The functionaries of every government have propensities to command at will the liberty and property of their constituents," Jefferson explained. "There is no safe deposit for these but with the people themselves, nor can they be safe with them without information. Where the press is free, and every man able to read, all is safe."

But is all safe? Does anyone seriously suggest any longer that the media provide all citizens with detailed accurate information and a range of informed opinions on the important issues of our times? Does anyone claim with credibility that the media is today the underpinning of America freedom and liberty? Would Jefferson and Madison see in the media monopolies of the twenty-first century the free press without which they knew there could be no democracy?

Of course not.

What was by design and necessity to have been *our media*—a brilliant blossoming of divergent, disagreeing and disagreeable voices, organized with the purpose of informing and convincing an electorate, arrayed in the service of that electorate and the democracy they would forge—has become *their media*. And much of what ails our democracy, our nation, and our world can be traced to this bastardization of the intentions of revolutionary democrats like Tom Paine. Paine dreamed of a nation that encouraged an "unceasing circulation of (ideas), which passing through its million channels, invigorates the whole mass of civilized man."

Far from invigorating the whole mass of us, the media system as it operates in the United States today fails to provide basic support for citizenship. It fails to protect or promulgate a public good. It is not a media system of our creation, by our hand or in our interest. That is because what we are subjected to today is not our media. It is their media.

Who are they? A handful of enormous conglomerates that have secured monopoly control of vast stretches of the media landscape. The oligopolistic structures they have created make a mockery of the traditional notion of a free press, where anyone can launch a medium and participate in the marketplace of ideas. And the monopolies grow ever more omnipresent with each passing year. Decades ago, A.J. Liebling wryly observed: "In America, freedom of the press is largely reserved for those who own one." We would update his line only by removing the word "largely."

Who does their media serve? They deliver first and foremost for their stockholders—major media in the United States can be enormously profitable. To maintain that profitability, they serve the major corporate interests that bankroll so much of the media with fat advertising checks. To avoid regulation in the public interest, they serve a political class that returns the favor by giving media conglomerates free access to the public's airwaves while routinely removing barriers to the expansion of corporate control over communications. To the extent that those who own major media in America today see themselves as being bound by public service duty, that duty is toward the affluent consumers who are served by round-the-clock business coverage that speaks to a tiny investor class.

The problem with their media system is that it exists to serve their interests, not ours. Profit trumps civil society every time. No wonder civil society is in crisis. Consider the diminution of basic values of community, service, and charity that we see as media-driven hypercommercialism pervades every nook and cranny of our culture. Consider the dramatic levels of disengagement that result when what passes for journalism leaves citizens uninformed. Consider the ugliness of elections in which serious coverage of the issues has been replaced by campaign ads chock full of the insulting lies and half-truths that have become the lingua franca of political discourse. Consider the way in which elected leaders—who are no longer chased after by a watchdog media—refuse any longer to address issues that vast majorities of Americans say require a governmental response: access to health care, affordable housing, crumbling schools, inadequate transportation, a fouled environment, and a prison-industrial complex that locks away those who suffer from ailments that can and should be cured.

The argument is broadly made that we as citizens must take greater responsibility for advancing the public good and, certainly, there is a grain of truth in this view. But what about the media? Why don't more of us demand that the media display the level of responsibility that Madison and Jefferson intended?

The response that comes from apologists for major media usually suggests such questions are unpatriotic. After all, this theory goes, media conglomerates earned their success--and power—the American way: By winning the robust competition in the marketplace. This "free-market" defense of media has one flaw, however. It is not based in reality.

The claim that American media is the result of market competition won by a handful of multinational corporations is one of the Big Lies that media firms desperately propagate. Like a lot of their programming, it's a load of crap. Our media system is the direct result of government action— laws and regulatory policies--that established not just the playing field but the winners of the game. In the case of radio, television, cable, and satellite TV, governmental agencies grant monopoly rights to frequencies and/or franchises to private firms at no charge. Whoever gets these licenses is essentially guaranteed a profit. The value of this form of corporate welfare, over the past seventy years, is mind-boggling. It is certainly in the hundreds of billions, if not trillions, of dollars. Nearly all of our huge media giants today are built on the backs of this corporate welfare, though you would never know it by listening to their rhetoric.

Even films, music, and traditional print media depend upon government regulation for their existence. Copyright, which is a government sanctioned and enforced monopoly, is the foundation for most of these industries. Without this clear government intervention into the market to prevent competition, these industries would look radically different—not just to investors but to consumers. Or consider this: Tax codes that explicitly permit advertising to be written off as a legitimate business expense feed the commercialism that has overwhelmed media and society. And beyond writing tax codes that promote the commercial carpet-bombing of our homes, the government is itself a major purchaser of media content, and a major advertiser.

Put the pieces of the puzzle together and you will realize that there is nothing natural about media industries as they currently exist. They did not win an honest competition in the free market; they won a government lottery in which the overwhelming majority were denied the right even to buy tickets.

The battle is not between private media and government regulation. Today's private media system is the direct result of aggressive regulation and massive subsidies made by the government. The question is what will tomorrow's media system look like. And it will be answered as we decide the sort of regulation the government will provide—and in whose interest and according to what values that regulation will be asserted. Media corporations want more of the same: greater concentration of ownership, bigger monopolies, less responsibility to inform or enlighten and more profits. Most Americans, if they were given a choice, would opt for something different.

The problem in the United States is that, while regulatory policies have been and are being made in the public's name, they are not being made with the public's informed consent.

Indeed, it would be difficult to imagine a more corrupt example of corporate-government cooperation than what passes for communication "policy making" in Washington, DC. Huge corporate lobbies duke it out to get the best deals from politicians and regulators, all the while the commercial news media give the matter not one bit of attention. The debate over the Telecommunications Act of 1996—a dramatic reshaping of media ownership rules and one of the most dramatic corporate welfare schemes in the nation's history—rated just one short story on an evening news broadcast. Indeed, the only place where you will find consistent coverage of media policy making in the press is in business and trade publications, where it is framed as an issue for wealthy investors and executives. You will only rarely find media policy debates framed as issues of concern to consumers, and forget about a frame that considers media policy as an issue for citizens in a democracy. Most Americans are therefore entirely ignorant about the government policy making that shapes the media that we are all in contact with for the vast majority of our waking hours each day.

But don't we see commentators on Fox television complaining about the media? Doesn't Rush Limbaugh complain about the media on his nationally syndicated radio show?

Media criticism does exist in America. But by and large, it is not citizen-based criticism designed to make media a better source of information in a democracy. Instead, it is a cynical manipulation of the discourse designed to silence even the mildest dissent from the conservative, militantly pro-corporate dogma that has come to pass for news in an era when "reporters" brag about the size of their American-flag lapel pins.

No one should be surprised that the only form of media criticism that gets ample play in the commercial news media is criticism of corporate media for deferring—on rare occasions—to the pluralist values that most Americans embrace. Thus, we hear a lot about how the media has a left-wing or liberal political bias. The leading media feature prominent reviews and discussions of such claims—to such an extent that Bernard Goldberg's book *Bias* became a media-promoted bestseller about media bias. Readers of Goldberg's book discovered it was based on evidentiary standards so anecdotal, inconsistent, and paltry as to be pathetic. But those who tell us not to believe the liberal media have no qualms about appearing pathetic. They are on a mission.

When cable television commentators prattle on about liberal bias in the media without even acknowledging the irony of their circumstance, they do so not to win an ideological debate but to discredit any journalist who might still attempt to tell both sides of the story. The liberal-bias industry mushroomed during the Reagan years as a response to reporting on the president's foibles. As with media supporters of George W. Bush today, Reagan's backers did not want to have to address concerns about their man's competence so they suggested that any critical reporting was the result of liberal bias.

The truth, of course, is that there is no liberal bias in the media. World-class scholars, such as Edward S. Herman and Noam Chomsky, have made substantial arguments about the media's structural bias toward the corporate and political status quo. Analysts with Fairness & Accuracy in Reporting, and scholars at dozens of journalism schools, have confirmed this critique in study after study. Yet while a Bernie Goldberg or Ann Coulter can march into any television study in America to screech about liberal bias that does not exist, Herman, Chomsky, and others who would offer a more rational critique are regarded by the media in much the same way that Soviet dissidents were by *Tass* or *Pravda*.

The bottom line: The corporate media are more than willing to entertain the idea that their main problem is that they are too critical of big business, the military, and people in power, and too sympathetic to the dispossessed. It reconfirms their self-image as some sort of feisty Fourth Estate. They are unwilling to even broach the idea that that they sit atop a system that was set up in a corrupt manner and that works to advance the interests of corporate American and limit democracy.

No wonder conspiracy theories are so popular in America; no wonder, when the makers of James Bond movies look for believable villains these days, they eschew Eurotrash bad guys for more credibly threatening villains such as the Rupert Murdoch-like media baron of 1997's *Tomorrow Never Dies*.

Don't get us wrong; we're not claiming there's a conspiracy. That gives the masters of corporate media and their servants in stations of political and regulatory power too much credit. Corporate media firms and trade associations do not even worry about subverting the popular will of a people they have effectively depoliticized with daily infusions of nonsense news about celebrity crimes and congressmen chasing interns. They could care less about their critics—on the left or the right. They are worried about making the most money possible. Thus, big media firms aim their lobbying arsenals not to block out the public, but simply to remove the few remaining barriers to their own expansion. The main fight the corporations and trade groups have in Washington, DC is with one another. But it is never about values, just money. The best way to understand how the big debates about media policy and regulation take place today is to recall a great film, *The Godfather, Part II*. One classic scene in the Oscar-winning 1974 picture depicts–all the American gangsters sitting on the roof of a hotel in Havana carving up a cake shaped like Cuba. (The time period is the 1950s, back when the Mob ruled Cuba.) The gangsters each got a symbolic slice of the country. They would all jockey with each other for larger slices, but they agreed that only they were eligible to get a slice. It was their country.

The giants of corporate media engage in similar calculations and contrivances today, with similar results. Just as the mobsters of the 1950s could claim Cuba as their country, so the masters of the multinational firms that control communications in the United States can claim that it is *their media.* And it belongs to them because—as in Cuba, where the dictators deferred to the Mob—media policy decisions are made in contemporary America in deference to the demands of media conglomerates. The federal government has a cake shaped like the United States, or, increasingly, the globe, and the corporate communication giants are all fighting behind closed doors to get the largest slice. And they all agree that it is best for all of them if the public plays no role whatsoever in the process. There is an old axiom that "if you are not at the table, you are not part of the deal." That is what has taken place here. The system is set up for the benefit of the bottom lines of multinational media corporations, as opposed to the top line of democracy.

It is a rotten system, as corrupt and destructive as the one the mobsters constructed, and we—the citizens—must change it.

That's the point of this book. After many years of writing, arguing, and advocating against an increasingly undemocratic media, we are convinced that the time has come to build a movement that seeks to replace their media with a media that serves the great mass of Americans—*our media*. We know that it is mandatory that citizens blast open debates over media policy so that decisions that shape the media landscape are made not in secret, but with the *informed* public consent that our media system is supposed to be built upon. The ultimate objective of all our arguments is to open the way for the establishment of a more diverse and competitive media system, with a much larger nonprofit and noncommercial component.

We understand this is not an easy fight. The corporate media are powerful. They have world-class PR, and they have gotten very good at spinning the lie that they are "giving the people what they want." The struggle to remake media begins by spreading recognition that major media gives the people what they want only within the range that major media can maximize profits. So all sorts of things people clearly want—like less advertising and higher quality journalism—are not provided because they are not profitable. When they think about it, Americans will fully understand that the existing market is not a flawless indicator of public desires, because it can only address what makes the most short-term profit for the media giants. That understanding opens the door for a renewed respect for the role that public policy making can and must play in shaping media systems that serve citizens.

The need to promote an understanding of the urgency to assert public control over the media system has never been greater. The problem has gotten so severe that the media system has become a major barrier to the exercise of democracy and to the discussion of any of the mounting social problems that face us. And there is no reason to think the media can self-correct; all the pressure is working against reform in the public interest.

Some will say, "But, hey, what about the Internet? Won't that break open the media system for us so that we do not need to worry about media policy making? Can't we just set up a Web site and go toe-to-toe with the media giants?" There is an element of truth to this claim—and the Internet is certainly changing a great deal about our lives. There is some extraordinary material online, but the Internet has yet to be proven successful as a platform to launch commercially viable competition to the media giants; again and again, the market trumps the democratic potential of the technology. This tends to marginalize dissident Web sites. And the

Robert W. McChesney & John Nichols

Internet is hardly some autonomous force in society. Legislative, regulatory, and judicial determinations regarding copyright, antitrust, and access issues will decide exactly how progressive a medium it will become. In other words, if we want the Internet to deliver, we will need to craft policies addressing the broader issues of media reform in order to foster that prospect.

Even with the Internet, for instance, the damage done by the current media system to democracy in recent years has been dramatic. We do not use the word "damage" casually. It is our contention that a bottom-line obsessed, massively monopolized, and increasingly irresponsible media is no longer just unreliable. Their media are fostering our crises.

To give some sense of the scope of the problem, consider the three most important stories in recent memory—the dysfunctional election of 2000, the September 11 attacks and the ensuing War on Terrorism, and the revelation that American corporations have engaged in massive frauds against their employees, retirees, stockholders, and taxpayers. How has the media handled these tests of its mettle?

Since so much of focus here is on democracy, let's begin with the 2000 presidential election. Al Gore won the national popular vote by 600,000 votes. It is now clear that a plurality of the Floridians who went to the polls to cast ballots on November 7, 2000, intended to vote for Al Gore. Yet George W. Bush is president. What is important to understand is that he is president at least in part because major media spent much of November and December 2000 rushing to anoint Bush president rather than digging until they found out who actually won the election. If the media can't stop a stolen election, who can?

When the September 11 terrorist attacks struck, a select-ed-not-elected president began an assault on domestic civil liberties and a sweeping War on Terrorism that appears to have no endgame. The media should have met the president's power grabs with fierce skepticism as the track record of chief executives is clear: In nearly every major war the United States has fought over the past century, the administration in power has lied through its teeth to generate public support, because it feared the people would not approve of war were they told the truth. Yet the U.S. news media has been entirely compliant is supporting "America's New War," offering scarcely any hard interrogation of officials, the sort of interrogation that would be directed at the leader of any other nation that attempted to lead the planet into an ongoing, ill-defined, and seemingly limitless war. As this has been proclaimed by President Bush as an endless war against evil-doers everywhere, one that will put us in a full war economy for a generation, this lack of criticism or rudimentary evaluation is a stunning abrogation of responsibility for a free press. When you add in the assaults on domestic civil liberties contained in Attorney General John Ashcroft's USA PATRIOT Act, and a penchant for secrecy on the part of the chief executive that would make Richard Nixon cringe, the media should be raising red flags on a daily basis. Instead, it is chirping along to the script provided by White House political director Karl Rove. No wonder serious international analysts compare U.S. media coverage of the war to that which might be expected in an authoritarian society where free press protections do not exist.

The U.S. media has done no better on stories that do not relate to September 11, the biggest of which has been the ongoing series of revelations about corporate corruption that began with the blowup of Enron. Arguably one of the greatest political scandals in a century, the Enron catastrophe is the direct—and predictable—result of what happens when massive corporations pay off politicians to get deregulation rulings that permit them to fleece workers, consumers, and taxpayers. The most striking feature of the Enron affair is how much of the company's sleazy activity was legal, and how most of the nation's political establishment—regardless of party or even ideology—was in bed with Enron swindlers. Revelations about Global Crossing, WorldCom, and other corporations reveals that Enron-style sleaze is rampant throughout industries that depend upon government regulation. It is safe to say that, in some industries, corruption is standard operating procedure. Yet the media, which are owned and operated by firms that rely on the same sort of cozy regulatory arrangements as did Enron, have converted these dramatic revelations into a business story and the political implications have fallen from view. There is every prospect that the problems that led to firms like Enron corrupting government policies will continue full steam ahead. The media have failed to fulfill a basic watchdog function, which means reform—even reform that is so obviously necessary—may be thwarted under cover of a (real) news blackout.

The report card on media is a dismal one. And—like any bad report card, it should be a call to action.

The failures of the media in recent years should underline for all of us the crises that arise—and go unaddressed—when media are more interested in being popular than in being accurate or useful. And it should drive home the demand that we, as citizens, must become media reform activists if we are serious about defending democracy.

This is not news to some Americans. As we travel the United States, we are struck by the extent to which ordinary Americans have recognized that it is no longer enough to complain about the media. Thousands of our fellow citizens have already begun to organize to change the media system. The growth of this media reform movement is one of the striking developments of the past decade; though, understandably, it has passed beneath the corporate news media radar. In the 1980s, for example, media critics did not even broach the idea of media reform as a serious issue; their goal was to help people understand the system so they could engage in self-defense. Even alternative media did not give the issue the time of day. Things are changing, however. Consider the following:

➤ Fairness & Accuracy in Reporting, a media watch group formed in the late 1980s, has blossomed into a major high-quality source for media research and analysis.

➤ Progressive media like *The Nation*, *The Progressive*, *In These Times*, and *Z Magazine* regularly report on media monopoly.

➤ Many national gatherings—from Media and Democracy gatherings to the recent Reclaim the Media Conference—have brought media activists together to discuss strategy and tactics.

➤ In cities like Baltimore, community groups have organized to get liquor billboards out of working-class and minority residential neighborhoods.

➤ Local "media watch" groups have developed in numerous cities, including Chicago, Denver, New York, and Seattle.

➤ Since 1999, Independent Media Centers (IMCs) have sprung up across the United States and the world. Internet-based IMC activists offer alternative journalism, covering stories that are ignored or mangled by the mainstream press. Criticism of corporate media has become a recurring theme for the IMCs—and the communities that have developed around them form a base of media activists.

➤ The group Commercial Alert is growing. It leads the fight against the spread of commercialism into every corner of our lives, especially in traditionally noncommercial public institutions like schools and museums.

➤ People for Better Television is growing. It leads the fight to make commercial broadcasters do public service in order to justify their monopoly licenses.

➤ Organizations like the Center for Digital Democracy have emerged to protect the Internet from corporate and commercial domination.

➤ An enormous grassroots organizing campaign in 1999 and 2000 led the FCC to begin opening the way for the licensing of approximately 1,000 new community-driven noncommercial "microradio" stations in open slots on the FM band.

➤ In 1998, 2000, and 2002, demonstrations took place at the National Association of Broadcasters (NAB) headquarters and national convention, and in front of the FCC's headquarters in Washington, DC. The former were to protest the

NAB's opposition to microradio noncommercial broadcasting; the latter was to protest the FCC's efforts to eliminate the few remaining regulations limiting the size of media corporations.

➤ In 2002, Representative Bernie Sanders (I-VT) introduced legislation to freeze second-class mailing costs for small, nonprofit publications that carry little advertising. The Independent Press Association, the trade association for small independent publications, organized a major lobbying campaign on its behalf. Sanders is also looking to propose additional legislation, and he is not the only member of Congress moving on this front.

We could go on and on. Almost everywhere one turns, media activism is evident. To the untrained eye one might think we were in the early stages of a serious social movement, perhaps even a revolution.

But the closer one looks, the more one sees the difficulties of organizing around media. Corporate lobbyists are paid to keep citizens out of the process, and they earn that money. Consider the fight over microradio. After the FCC announced a cautiously progressive policy in 2000, the National Association of Broadcasters (NAB), the trade association of commercial broadcasters, launched an aggressive counteroffensive to derail it. The handful of huge corporations that dominate U.S. radio broadcasting did not want any competition for "their" listeners. (So much for the Big Lie that the media system is based on competition.) The profit-driven fear of the NAB was legitimate—if the bottom line is the bottom line. Were communities able to organize their own noncommercial local stations, the media giants would have to compete and provide more local content and less commercials in order to keep listeners from migrating. So the NAB did what came naturally. It lied about the FCC plan to members of Congress, claiming that the new microstations would interfere with the existing stations. In fact, the FCC's cautious microradio engineering plan was taken from a plan that had been successfully developed by commercial broadcasters themselves in the early 1990s to put more stations on the air. Thus, when their profits were threatened, commercial broadcasters willingly sought to discredit their own research.

The lies being told about microradio were so blatant that even the NAB could not convince the Republican-controlled Senate to scrap the FCC plan. In the end, the NAB had one if its Congressional stooges add a rider to a budget bill in the middle of the night in December 2000 to block the FCC microradio plan. At first, Clinton vetoed the bill and openly disapproved of the rider gutting the microradio initiative. The budget bill was revised and sent back to Clinton again with the anti-microradio rider attached to it. As the bill was the product of arduous negotiations, President Clinton was of no mind to veto it. Microradio, as a viable alternative on the radio dial, was killed.

Should we read the microradio defeat as evidence that there is no hope for a media reform movement?

That's what the NAB would like. But it is not a rational response

In fact, the microradio fight illustrates the enormous potential of a well-organized reform movement. Broadcasters and their lobbyists prevailed in the microradio battle only because they had the ability to flood members of Congress with lies that supporters of microradio lacked the resources to counter. A media reform movement may never have the financial resources of the NAB, but there are millions of Americans who know the media needs reforming and their numbers are growing. Like Saul Alinsky we believe that when you are fighting organized money, you need organized people.

That is the demand—and the promise—of this book. We argue that Americans need to start taking media issues a lot more seriously if they want to shift the debate on all the issues they care about. We argue that groups that are already organized—trade unionists, feminists, religious groups, teachers, students, civil libertarians, farmers, environmentalists—need to put media reform on their agendas. And we argue that we need to do sustained outreach to the broad unorganized population to educate and mobilize on media reform. From our experiences giving hundreds of talks every year, we can tell you that the soil is fertile. But, as Midwesterners, we know that even in fertile soil seeds still must be planted and fields still must be plowed.

As progressives, we believe in the intrinsic desire of an informed citizenry to work together for a more egalitarian, humane, and sustainable world. We believe that most Americans, were we offered real information and real choices, would prefer to live in a truly democratic nation where political institutions respond to the people's needs, and where the economy is no longer warped by profit-obsessed monopolies. But real information and real choices are denied to most Americans by the current media regime. We want to change that media regime and, in this sense, our call is radical.

But the arguments we forward grow out of mainstream political values. We argue that if one takes the core values of constitutional democracy seriously, it is mandatory that there be informed public debate on media policy. This is Democracy 101. We are more than willing to live with the outcome of informed public debate as long as such debate exists. The more informed and democratic the policy debate, the better the resulting policies. We are actually encouraged when we see the ends the corporate media go to prevent public involvement in communication policy making. It quickly becomes obvious that they fear what would happen if the American people understood how corrupt the process was. They recognize that an informed citizenry would never stand for the media status quo. On this point, we are in full agreement with them.

The only difference is that, while they fear democracy, we want democracy. That's why we are certain that the broad movement we propose will draw support from far beyond the outer boundaries of American progressive activism.

Because the fight we propose is first and foremost a struggle for democratic processes, the potential base of support includes everyone in the population who favors democracy over plutocracy. In short, the traditional distinctions of left and right are not decisive categories. The more accurate split is between up and down, those who benefit materially from the corrupt status quo, and those who do not. Even so-called political conservatives, especially those outside the beltway without million-dollar stock portfolios, dislike the way their children's brains are marinated in commercialism. They despise the corporate welfare that gives tens of billions of dollars worth of public property to corporations every year, and they no longer even participate in political campaigns based on idiotic thirty-second TV commercials. The core reform measures of the burgeoning media reform movement will speak to these Americans because they are all content neutral and viewpoint neutral. They do not call for censorship, nor do they propose the appointment of a Tom Ridge-style federal commissar to "educate" the masses. They call for blasting open the media system with more competition and more noncommercial and nonprofit voices. They call for establishing a genuinely pluralistic media system with a variety of institutions to provide culture, entertainment, and journalism. They seek to dilute the power of a handful of transnational conglomerates that put profit above all else and answer only to Wall Street, while empowering community voices that answer to Main Street.

This is a book with an agenda. We want to fan the flames of the movement for media reform that we believe is taking shape in the United States. In the first chapter, we spell out the problem in more detail. In the second chapter, we look abroad–to explain how, as the U.S.-style, corrupt corporate media system becomes one of the central consequences of globalization, media reform is becoming an international issue. In some respects, the United States is a laggard in the global media reform movement and we have much to learn from studying other nations and working with them. In the final chapter, we return to the United States to discuss the burgeoning domestic media reform movement and the steps that must be taken to broaden its scope and power.

Throughout the book, we return frequently to the premise that democracy requires a truly free press. We are guided by the words of James Madison, who once argued that "all the triumphs which have been gained by reason and humanity over error and oppression" were made possible by free-dom of the press. We believe that a new era of triumphs by reason and humanity over error and oppression is in the offering. What is required to unleash it are the reforms that will give us our media, not theirs.

CHAPTER 1

The Problem with U.S. Media

"The Founders didn't count on the rise of megamedia. They didn't count on huge private corporations that would own not only the means of journalism but also vast swaths of the territory that journalism should be covering."

—BILL MOYERS

"Experimenters have discovered that you can turn a cat into an alcoholic. The normal cat doesn't expect it, but keep adding vodka to the dish and the cat will soon demand spiked milk as an absolute necessity. The fat cats of the American mass media have lost their taste for the mother's milk of normal free enterprise: real competition for a reasonable profit. Thanks to addictive doses of sympathetic governmental policies and two decades of a drive for power, a shrinking number of large media corporations now regard monopoly, oligopoly, and historic levels of profit as not only normal, but as their earned right. In the process, the usual democratic expectation for the media— diversity of ownership and ideas—has disappeared as the goal of official policy and, worse, as a daily experience of a generation of American readers and viewers."

—BEN BAGDIKIAN

"Night after night audiences are terrified and titillated, aroused and manipulated, but not informed. Like an unbalanced diet, which gradually can lead to serious illness, the local TV news threatens the health of our community."

—PAUL KLITE, former executive director, *Rocky Mountain Media Watch*

IT IS IMPERATIVE for Americans who care about democracy to come together and organize a mass movement for reform of the media system.

Two core observations bring us to this conclusion. The first is that the current media system is the direct result of explicit government policies, and that these policies have been made in a corrupt manner with minimal public participation. On this point there is virtually no debate.

Our second observation is that the existing media system in the United States operates is a manner that is highly detrimental to the requirements of a democratic and self-governing society. The system works to advance the interests of the wealthy few, rather than the many. This is a much more controversial argument, if only because it is an extraordinarily sensitive matter, going directly to the heart of how power operates in our society.

Yet as this chapter will illustrate, the case against the U.S. media system as it currently operates forms an overwhelming indictment.

Americans devour media at a staggering rate; in 2002, the average American spent almost twelve hours per day with some form of media. We are also in the midst of an unprecedented technological revolution—based around digital technologies, typified by the Internet—that looks to weave media and electronic communication into nearly every waking moment of our lives. In conventional parlance, these developments are presented as benign; they are, we are told, all about liberating individuals, investors, and consumers from the constraints of time and space while offering a cornucopia of exciting new options and possibilities. This, however, is a superficial and misleading perspective on what is happening. Indeed, when one lifts the hood, so to speak, to see what is driving the media revolution, a very different picture emerges. The engine of change at this point is highly concentrated corporate power, which pulls the strings to dominate our existence so as to maximize return to shareholders. A secondary, yet no less significant purpose, is to protect the corporation's role—and corporate power in general—from being subjected to the public scrutiny and political debate it so richly deserves. This combination is a poison pill for democracy.

Yet in our American democracy the issue of media reform barely registers. The structures of our media, the concentration of its ownership, the role that it plays in shaping the lives of our children, in commercializing our culture, and in warping our elections, has been off-limits. When we examine the reality of media in the year 2002, however, it becomes clear that this circumstance must shift.

The argument for making media an issue can be found, above all, by surveying the contemporary media landscape.

In 2002, the U.S. media system is dominated by about ten transnational conglomerates including Disney, AOL Time Warner, News Corporation, Viacom, Vivendi Universal, Sony, Liberty, Bertelsmann, AT&T-Comcast, and General Electric (NBC). Their media revenues range from roughly $8 billion to $35 billion per year. These firms tend to have holdings in numerous media sectors. AOL Time Warner, for example, ranks among the largest players in film production, recorded music, TV show production, cable TV channels, cable TV systems, book publishing, magazine publishing, and Internet service provision. This first tier owns all the commercial television networks, all the major Hollywood studios, four of the five firms that sell 90 percent of the music in the United States, a majority of the cable TV systems, all or part of most of the successful cable TV channels, and much, much, more. The great profit in media today comes from taking a movie or TV show and milking it for maximum return through spin-off books, CDs, video games, and merchandise. Hence it is virtually impossible to compete as a "stand-alone" movie studio, TV network, or music company, when one's competitors are part of vast empires. This has fueled the massive conglomeration rush of the past fifteen years.

Another twelve to fifteen firms, which do from $2 or $3 billion to $8 billion dollars per year in business, round out the system. These firms—like Hearst, the New York Times Company, the Washington Post Company, Cox, Advance, Tribune Company, Gannett—tend to be less developed conglomerates, focusing on only two or three media sectors.

All in all, these two dozen or so firms control the overwhelming percentage of movies, TV shows, cable systems, cable channels, TV stations, radio stations, books, magazines, newspapers, billboards, music, and TV networks that constitute the media culture that occupies one-half of the average American's life. It is an extraordinary degree of economic and social power located in very few hands. The highly concentrated market makes a mockery of the freedom of press clause in the First Amendment, which was predicated on the ability of citizens to create their own media if they so desire. A person may have the "right" to launch a new movie studio or major daily newspaper, but, except in the rare circumstances of a handful of billionaires, it is a "right" in name only. "The history of survival of start up newspapers in markets that already have at least one daily is not a happy one," a newspaper analyst commented in 2002. "In fact, there is no history. There has never been one survivor."

It has not always been this way. Much of this concentration has taken place in the past few decades, as technology and market imperatives made concentration and conglomeration far more attractive and necessary. Today it is impossible for the small, independent firm to be anything but a marginal player in the industries mentioned above. Most important, the flames of media concentration were fanned by a collapsing commitment on the part of the federal government to serious antitrust prosecution, a diminution of the federal standards regarding fairness, and government "deregulation," most notably the 1996 Telecommunications Act. Congressional approval of the Telecommunications Act, after only a stilted and disengaged debate, was a historic turning point in media policy making in the United States, as it permitted a consolidation of media and communication ownership that had previously been unthinkable.

In 2002, a series of developments suggest that media concentration is becoming even more extreme. For decades, a few key FCC ownership regulations limited the ability of the media giants to expand. These included rules preventing the same company from owning TV stations and cable franchises in the same market, limiting the number of TV stations a single company could own, and restricting ownership of newspapers and TV stations in the same community. The FCC, under the leadership of President George W. Bush's appointed chair, Michael Powell, is expressly committed to decreasing or eliminating these and other limits on media monopoly—including the last barriers to a single corporation gaining dominance of print, broadcast, and cable communications in a single market. The multipronged strategy of the media giants also has a legal component. In 2002, the conglomerates won cases in the federal court system tossing key ownership regulations out as unconstitutional. Only if the FCC or Congress can make a better defense of them will the regulations be preserved.

The result of all this deregulation, should it proceed, will be an explosion of corporate deal making that will make the last decade of unprecedented media conglomeration look like a Wednesday night bingo game at the local old folks home. For the first time, media giants that have controlled TV station empires—Disney, News Corp., Viacom, General Electric—would be able to merge with or acquire media empires built on cable franchises, such as AOL Time Warner and AT&T-Comcast. As Blair Levin, a former FCC chief of staff, puts it, the ruling "allows for a powerful new entity we have never seen before—something that combines both cable and broadcasting assets." Include the ability to merge with the giant newspaper chains and you have a recipe for what Gene Kimmelman of the Consumers Union calls an "earth-shattering" shift in media ownership patterns. "The end result could be the most massive consolidation in media this nation has ever seen," says Kimmelman.

A surface survey of the statistics regarding media ownership, while deeply disturbing in what it reveals, fails to convey the full depth of the concentration of media ownership. Not only are media markets dominated by a handful of conglomerates with "barriers to entry," making it nearly impossible for newcomers to challenge their dominance, but they are also closely linked to each other in a manner that suggests almost a cartel-like arrangement. Some of the largest media firms own parts of the other giants; Liberty, for example, is the second largest shareholder in News Corporation and among the largest shareholders in AOL Time Warner. Moreover, the media giants employ equity joint ventures—where two competing firms share ownership in a single venture—to an extent unknown almost anywhere else in the economy. These joint ventures work to reduce competition, lower risk, and increase profits. By 2002, the nine largest media giants had an equity joint venture with six, on average, of the other eight giants; often a media giant would have multiple joint ventures with another firm. In sum, this is a tightly knit community of owners, dominated by some of the wealthiest individuals in the world. Indeed, thirteen of the hundred wealthiest individuals in the world—all of whom are worth over $4 billion—are media magnates.

Such concentration of media ownership is clearly negative by any standard that cherishes free speech and diversity in democratic culture. But concentration in media ownership is not the sole cause of the problems with the media, and in some cases it is not a significant factor at all. Concentration is important to a large extent because it magnifies the limitations of a commercial media system, and makes those limitations less susceptible to redress by the market. However, this sounds very abstract, so let's cut to the bone: The two main problems fostered by concentrated media are hypercommercialism and denigration of public service. These are really two sides of the same coin. As massive media corporations are better able to commercially saturate society, their ability or willingness to provide material with editorial and creative integrity declines. It is not that

Robert W. McChesney & John Nichols

the individuals who run these firms are bad people; the problem is that the system of business in America is designed for profit making, not public interest, and thus we have a media system set up to enrich investors, not serve democracy.

No better example of how this process works can be found than in the U.S. radio industry. This was the one sector where ownership limits were explicitly deregulated by the 1996 Telecoms Act and what happened there should give a sense of where we are heading as ownership deregulation becomes the rule everywhere. Since deregulation of ownership in 1996, well over half of all U.S. stations have been sold. A few massive giants, owning hundreds of stations—as many as eight in each market—have come to dominate the industry. Six years ago, the law permitted a single firm to own no more than twenty-eight stations nationally; today Clear Channel alone owns some 1,200. As profits shoot through the roof, low-budget standardized fare has nearly eliminated the local content, character, and creativity that were once features of this relatively inexpensive electronic medium. Local news-gathering operations have been gutted, with many media groups now employing one announcer to read the "news" for as many as eight stations. "A huge wave of consolidation has turned music stations into cash cows that focus on narrow playlists aimed at squeezing the most revenue from the richest demographics," the trade publication *Variety* observed. "Truth be told, in this era of megamergers, there has never been a greater need for a little diversity on the dial."

The radio example points to the one other crucial group, aside from media owners, that gets treated with love and affection by corporate media executives: the corporate advertising community. Businesses spent over $230 billion in the United States on advertising in 2001—some 2.4 percent of the GDP—and much of this money ended up in the hands of some media firm. Though journalists and civics teachers bristle at the notion, those media that depend upon advertising for the lion's share of their income—radio, TV, newspapers, magazines—are, in effect, part of the advertising industry. Throughout the 1990s, the media giants used their market power to bend over backward to make their media attractive to Madison Avenue and pummel customers with their ads. By 1999, the four major TV networks, for example, were providing nearly sixteen minutes per hour of commercials during prime time, an enormous increase from just a decade earlier, and the problem only grew worse in the years that followed. A conglomerate like Time Warner was able to sign a $200 million advertising deal with General Motors that "crosses most of the entertainment company's divisions," so that "GM will have a first-look option on all automobile marketing opportunities within Warner Bros. operations." Not content with traditional advertising, media firms are now working on "virtual ads," whereby "a marketer's product can be seamlessly inserted into live or taped broadcasts." With ads so inserted during actual programs, viewers will be unable to avoid the commercials through zapping. Advertising has also been plugged into new venues, such as video games. But this does not capture the full spread of commercialism. In television, for example, the new growth area for revenues is selling merchandise that is shown on its programs. It barely caused a ripple when Tommy Hilfiger hired the Viacom-owned cable channel VH1, rather than an ad agency, to produce a series of TV ads, because VH1 is so effective at selling. In sum, the entire U.S. media experience increasingly resembles an infomercial.

Nowhere is the commercial marination of the American mind more apparent than in the case of children, where the advertising assault was increased exponentially in the 1990s. There are now four full-time cable channels (owned by the four largest U.S. media firms) bombarding children with commercial programming twenty-four hours per day. Advertisers have targeted the youth market as arguably the most important in the nation. Girls between the ages of seven and fourteen spend some $24 billion per year and influence parental decisions worth another $66 billion. Commercial indoctrination of children is crucial to corporate America. One study revealed that when eight-year olds were shown two pictures of identical shoes, one with the Nike logo and the other with the Kmart logo, they liked both equally. The response of twelve-year-olds was "Kmart, are you kidding me?" This desire to indoctrinate fuels the commercial drive into education and suggests that the moral foundations for coming generations may be resting on a dubious base. Nobody knows what the exact consequence of this commercial blitzkrieg upon children will be, but the range of debate extends from "pretty bad" to "absolutely terrible." The only thing we know for certain is that the media giants and advertisers who prosper from it do not care and cannot care. It is outside their frame of reference.

In this light, it is worth considering the status of the longstanding conflict between "church and state" in media, this refers to the ability of journalists and creative workers to conduct their affairs without having output determined by what serves the immediate interests of advertisers, or owners for that matter. In conventional wisdom, the U.S. media system has been at its best when the divider between "church and state"—especially, though not exclusively, in journalism—has been pronounced and respected. That way media users can regard the articles and news and entertainment programs they read, see, and hear in the media as reflecting the best judgment of media workers, not the surreptitious bribe of a commercial interest. Nowhere has the collapse of editorial integrity been more pronounced than in magazine publishing. As the late Alexander Liberman, legendary editorial director of Condé Nast, noted in 1999, advertisers "have too much power. They determine, if not specifically, then generally what magazines are now." A series of scandals in the late 1990s affirmed what has been suspected: Advertisers have tremendous control over the editorial copy in U.S. magazines, and editors who are discomfited by this had best find employment elsewhere. "They're glitz bags," Norman Mailer said of magazines in 1999. "They are so obviously driven by the ads that the ads take prominence over the stories."

Hollywood films have so thoroughly embraced commercial values that *Variety* now writes of the "burgeoning subfield of Product Placement Cinema." Conglomerate control of films and music has opened the floodgates to commercialism and has proven deadly for creativity. "A movie studio is part of this huge corporate cocoon," Peter Bart, editor of *Variety* and former head of Paramount, writes, "and therefore, theoretically, a studio should be willing to take bigger risks because one bad movie...won't erode the value of the [parent company's] shares. But the way it works out, the studios are if anything more risk averse. They are desperate to hedge their bets. It's the nature of bureaucratic self-protection.... The pressure is reflected in the sort of movies that get made... the sort of pablum that studios chewed on for ten years, that's gone through endless rewrites, has been pretested by endless focus groups, and is successful—if insipid." Or as an executive at Time Warner's "independent" studio New Line Pictures puts it, "We're very marketing-driven as a company. I'm instructed not to greenlight a project if I can't articulate how to sell it." As Bart concludes, this is "not exactly a recipe for art."

This said, we are not attempting to make a blanket indictment of everything produced by the corporate media system. We are not suggesting that every article or broadcast segment is foul, nor that they are all tainted, nor even that some material that is tainted cannot also be good. There are extremely talented people employed in the commercial media system, and the pressure to satisfy audiences does indeed sometimes promote excellent fare. But corporate and commercial pressures greatly undermine the overall quality of the system and skew it in ways that are not at all the result of audience demand. In the world of corporate media, the key is to attract the preferred target audience while spending as little money as possible. In the battle for consumer attention, this strongly promotes a rehashing of tried-and-true formulae, as well as the use of sex, violence, and what is termed "shock" or "gross-out" fare. In a world where people are surrounded by innumerable media options (albeit owned by numerable firms), sex and violence are proven attention getters.

Corporate control and hypercommercialism are having what may be their most devastating effects in the realm of journalism, and as journalism is the oxygen of democracy, it is here that we must devote considerable attention. There is no need to romanticize the nature of U.S. professional journalism from the middle of the century into the 1980s; in many respects it was deeply flawed. Yet whatever autonomy and integrity journalism enjoyed during the era of Bob Woodward, Carl Bernstein, and *Lou Grant* is now under sustained and unyielding attack by corporate owners in the hunt for profit. No more striking evidence for this exists than the results of a 1999 Pew Research Center poll of journalists concerning their profession. Until the 1990s, journalists tended to be stalwart defenders of the media system, and most scholarship emphasized journalists' hypersensitivity to criticism of their field. No more. The Pew poll found that "at both the local and national level, majorities of working journalists say the increased bottom-line pressure is hurting the quality of coverage." "This past year," David Halberstam wrote in 1999, "has been, I think, the worst year for American journalism since I entered the profession forty-four years ago." Bob Woodward, the Watergate investigator who has enjoyed one of the most successful and prestigious media careers of the era, says that in these days of hypercommercialism and hypercompetition, "No one is the keeper of the conscience of journalism."

The brave new world of corporate journalism manifests itself in many ways. The primary effects of tightened corporate control are a serious reduction in staff, combined with pressure to do vastly less expensive and less controversial lifestyle and feature stories. Where there is "news," it often takes the form of canned crime reports that foster unrealistic and unnecessary fears. This is the magic elixir for the

Robert W. McChesney & John Nichols

bottom line. Sometimes the new world of corporate journalism is typified by blatant corporate censorship of stories that might hurt the image of the media owner. But the maniacal media baron as portrayed in James Bond films or profiles of Rupert Murdoch is far less a danger than the cautious and compromised editor who seeks to "balance" a responsibility to readers or viewers with a duty to serve his boss and the advertisers. In media today, even among journalists who entered the field for the noblest of reasons, there is an internalized bias to simply shy away from controversial journalism that might enmesh a media firm in a battle with powerful corporations or government agencies. True, such conflicts have always been the stuff of great journalism, but they can make for very bad business, and in the current climate business trumps journalism just about every time.

During the 2000 presidential race, for instance, major television stations argued against what one might think would be their own self interest. In their moves to exclude Green Party candidate Ralph Nader from three presidential debates, they guaranteed that controversial issues involving corporate power—including media conglomeration—would not be raised. Yet the exclusion of Nader also guaranteed that the debates would become duller-than-dirt agreeathons in which Al Gore and George W. Bush essentially invited viewers to turn off their televisions.

The most common and noticeable effect of the corporate noose on journalism is that it simply allows commercial values to redirect journalism to its most profitable position. As a result, relatively vast resources are deployed for news pitched at a narrow business class, and suited to their needs and prejudices; such news has come to dominate newspapers, specialty magazines, and cable television. Likewise, news for the masses increasingly consists of stories about celebrities, royal families, athletes, natural disasters, plane crashes, and train wrecks. Political coverage is limited to regurgitating what some politician says, and "good" journalism is practiced when a politician from the other side of the aisle is given a chance to respond. During the Florida recount following the 2000 election, television networks featured nightly food fights between backers of Gore and Bush, but left the real reporting on disenfranchisement of minority voters, structural flaws in the voting systems, and corrupt practices within the offices of Florida Governor Jeb Bush and Secretary of State Katherine Harris to the British Broadcasting Corporation (BBC) and other foreign broadcasters.

The approach to "reporting" practiced by America's corporate media today is not journalism; it is stenography. Perhaps the strongest indictment of corporate journalism is that the preponderance of it would be compatible with an authoritarian political regime. So it is that China has few qualms about letting most commercial news from the United States inside its borders; it can see that this low caliber of journalism is hardly a threat to its rule. It is the BBC, with its regrettable penchant for covering politics seriously, that draws the commissar's ire.

There is also intense pressure for journalism to contribute immediately and directly to the bottom line. One Tennessee TV station received adverse publicity for offering to do TV news "puff pieces" on local businesses in exchange for $15,000 payments. It is important to note, however, that the mistake made by that Tennessee station was not the spirit of the offer—it well reflects the pattern across the news media—

but rather the baldness of it. Firms also use the news to hype their other programming, as in 1996 when *NBC Nightly News* made the Summer Olympics its most covered news story that year, even though none of the other networks had the Olympics ranked on their top-ten lists. Why? Because NBC was airing the Olympics that summer—and reaping the attendant financial rewards. The fall of 1999 saw a huge debate erupt in newspaper circles after the *Los Angeles Times* devoted the entire editorial space in an edition of its 164-page Sunday magazine to articles, photos, and graphics describing downtown Los Angeles' new Staples Center sports arena. The newspaper did not reveal at the time of the magazine's publication, however, that it would be dividing the $2 million in revenues generated by the section with the owners of the arena. So dark was the scenario that the former publisher of the *Los Angeles Times*, Otis Chandler, sent a letter to the staff describing the new management's move as "unbelievably stupid and unprofessional."

Above all, however, the *Los Angeles Times* was blatant. It allowed the corrupting linkage between advertisers and the media to be clearly identified. More often than not, a measure of subtlety keeps controversies under wraps.

All told, this creates a crisis for democracy. Alexis de Tocqueville rightly celebrated the role that a free and diverse media plays not only in greasing the wheels of electoral systems but in maintaining the very structures of civil society. The nineteenth-century surveyor of the American public landscape went so far as to say of news organizations, "They maintain civilization." Who would seriously attempt to make such a statement about media in an era of round-the-clock Gary Condit coverage?

The current caliber of journalism is decidedly unsatisfactory for a democratic society. Democratic journalism should provide a ruthless accounting of the powers-that-be and the powers-that-want-to-be, both in government and politics and in the extremely powerful corporate sector. Democratic journalism should also provide background information and a full range of viewpoints on the main social and political issues of the day. We cannot expect each news medium to provide all of these elements of a quality journalism, but in combination, a democratic media system should make this caliber of journalism readily available to the entire population. It may be true that the media are not entirely responsible for the apathy, cynicism, and depoliticization that mark U.S. electoral politics today; in fact, media executives sometimes use this lack of interest in politics to justify their declining attention to public affairs and their continuing coverage of trivial and mindless stories. However, it is also true that the lack of journalism has fanned the flames of depoliticization and contributed to U.S. electoral politics becoming a commercial contest sponsored by a small group of billionaires, in which most Americans rationally assume they have no role to play, or stake in the outcome. Presidential elections now draw, at best, no more than half of the electorate to the polls. They have become media entertainments, complete with graphics and play-by-play reports but bereft of any suggestion that citizens should—or could—actually play any more of a role in this extravaganza than they do in the Super Bowl or the Academy Awards.

Not only is political coverage in American media increasingly empty and meaningless, there is also less and less of it. Indeed, while the amount of air time allotted the Super Bowl and the Academy Awards has increased in recent years—as prices paid for properly placed advertising skyrockets—coverage of the most fundamental workings of our democracy is getting squeezed. And without apology. Asked by the *Dallas Morning News* about slackening coverage of the 2000 presidential campaign by America's television networks, former ABC White House correspondent Sam Donaldson answered, "We are doing a very minimal amount of coverage at ABC. Outside of *Nightline* and our Sunday show, ABC News, in my opinion, has simply forfeited the field." Let's not pick on ABC, however; all the broadcast networks are cutting back, according to the watchdog group Alliance for Better Campaigns. During the 2000 presidential primary season, the Alliance reported, the networks were giving the presidential campaign 20 percent less coverage than they did in 1988—the last time the U.S. saw serious contests for the Democratic and Republican presidential nominations. Ex-CNN president Rick Kaplan told the *Philadelphia Inquirer* that the major broadcast networks had been "derelict" in their coverage of the 2000 campaign. "They're making their news divisions less important than they were. They're just getting out."

To be fair and accurate, journalism is flawed not merely due to corporate pressures to generate profits or to satisfy the political desires of the owners; the problem goes deeper than that. Much of the problem with contemporary journalism is due to the codes of professional journalism that emerged a century ago, and that remain of paramount importance in understanding journalism today. Professional journalism was a revolutionary break with the idea that the journalism of a medium—usually a newspaper at that time—would and should invariably reflect the political viewpoints of the owner. Partisan journalism, the bread and butter of Jefferson, Jackson, and Lincoln, could only be defended in an environment where there were competitive markets, and a wide range of opinion. In the highly concentrated newspaper markets that emerged by the twentieth century, partisan journalism appeared more like uncontested propaganda than anything else. In this environment, the large newspaper publishers pushed for professionalism. Their journalists would all be trained to be nonpartisan so the matter of who owned all the media and the lack of market competition were now irrelevant. As research has shown repeatedly, however, the professional code "smuggled in" the political biases of the owners, but made them now appear as nonpartisan, even objective truth.

With this in mind, let us return to the three great news stories of recent times that we mentioned in the introduction, each of which goes to the heart of a core democratic function of the free press. The first, the 2000 presidential election, was about whether the American people could hold a fair election for the highest office in the land. The second, the War on Terrorism, concerns how this nation arrives at the most important decision any society can make: to enter and conduct a world war with no end in sight. The third, the revelation of Enron's ability to squeeze billions from taxpayers, workers, and consumers by buying off politicians right and left for its dubious deregulation schemes, speaks to the ability of journalism to hold government—and the firms it regulates—accountable for corruption.

Let's start with the War on Terrorism. When a democracy considers whether to engage in war, the free flow of information is of dramatic significance: How can parents decide that they favor sending their sons and daughters off to fight when they lack adequate information about the causes, goals, and strategies of the proposed fight? How can citizens decide whether it is appropriate to reorder national economic priorities in order to fund an ongoing "War on Terror" when they do no even know the targets of that war? From World War I to Korea and Vietnam, presidents have lied to the American people because they believed that if the American people knew the truth, they would not support the move for war. The track record of the U.S. news media in the twentieth century is one of regularly going along with fraudulent efforts to get the nation into one war or another by the administration in power. These are considered the dark moments in the history of U.S. journalism. What is most striking in the U.S. news coverage following the September 11 attacks is how it followed this lamentable pattern. The most essential debate—the one about whether to go to war—never really occurred in Congress or the media. Tough questions were ignored. Why should we have believed that a militarized approach would be effective? Why was the United States entitled to determine—as judge, jury, and executioner—who is a terrorist or a terrorist sympathizer in this global war? What about international law?

Most conspicuous was the complete absence of comment on one of the most striking features of the war campaign—something that any credible journalist would be quick to observe were the events taking place in Russia or China or Pakistan. There are very powerful interests in the United States that greatly benefit politically and economically by the establishment of an unchecked war on terrorism. This consortium of interests can be called, to use President

Eisenhower's term, the military-industrial complex. It blossomed during the Cold War when the fear of Soviet imperialism—real or alleged—justified its creation and expansion. A nation with a historically small military now had a permanent war economy, and powerful special interests—private-sector defense contractors chief among them—that benefited by its existence.

For journalists to raise issues like these did not presuppose that they opposed government policies, merely that the policies needed to be justified and explained, so the support would be substantive, not ephemeral, the result of deliberation, not manipulation. Such has not been the case. Much of mainstream U.S. journalism was bluntly propagandistic in the weeks and months following September 11. As a result, most Americans supported a war, even though they knew next to nothing about the region where U.S. soldiers would be fighting, the historical context of the battles, or the role that past military adventurism might have played in stoking the resentments that feed international anger at the United States.

It is important to be clear about why the coverage has been so deplorable. It is not directly due to concentrated media ownership, or meddling CEOs, although the very firms that are now saluting "America's New War" are also going before the Bush Administration asking for ownership deregulation that will make all of them much larger and more profitable. The main reason for this distorted coverage is due to the way in which so-called "professional" journalism is practiced in the United States. To avoid the taint of partisanship, and to keep costs low, professionalism makes official or credentialed sources the basis for news stories.

Reporters report what people in power say, and what they debate. This gives the news an establishment bias. Even when there is disagreement, the range of debate extends only as far as does the disagreement of those with a vested interest in limiting the scope of the discourse.

When a journalist reports what official sources are saying, or debating, she is considered "professional." When she steps outside this range of official debate to provide alternative perspectives or to raise issues those in power prefer not to discuss, she is no longer considered "professional."

In matters of international politics, "official sources" are almost interchangeable with the term "elites," as foreign policy is mostly a preserve of a wealthy and powerful few— C. Wright Mills's classic power elite. At its worst, in a case like the current war on terrorism, where the elites and official sources are united on the core issues, the nature of our press coverage is uncomfortably close to that found in authoritarian societies with limited formal press freedom.

Many working journalists would recoil at that statement. Their response would be that professional reliance on official sources is justifiable as "democratic" because the official sources are accountable to people who are elected by the citizenry. The problem with this rationale is that it forgets a critical assumption of free press theory: Even leaders determined by election need a rigorous monitoring, the range of which cannot be determined solely by their elected opposition. Otherwise the citizenry has no way out of the status quo, no capacity to criticize or advance the political culture as a whole. If such a watchdog function grows lax, corruption invariably increases, and the electoral system decays. If journalism that goes outside the range of elite opinion is dismissed as unprofessional or partisan—and, therefore, justifiably ignored—the media merely lock in a corrupt status quo and can offer no way out. If journalists must have official sources on their side to pursue a story, it gives people in power a massive veto power over the exercise of democracy.

This problem becomes acute in a political environment like the United States, where electoral laws and campaign costs have made politics a fiefdom for the superwealthy and those who represent the superwealthy. Over ninety percent of the "hard money" contributions to congressional and presidential campaigns come from the wealthiest one percent of Americans. By relying on official sources, our journalism does not pose a democratic challenge to plutocracy, but rather cements the plutocracy in place.

But the best example of the plutocracy protection principle that now defines U.S. journalism is the Enron scandal that unfolded in late 2001 and 2002. The story of Enron's collapse was shocking only because, although evidence of Enron's shady operations had been cropping up since at least the mid-1990s, the rah-rah corporate journalists of our era were falling all over themselves to praise Enron as the exemplar of the New Economy. Enron was regularly featured on *Global Finance* magazine's annual list of the "world's best global companies." Even as the collapse of Enron approached, *Fortune* magazine hailed the corporation as its "most innovative company in America."

Only when the company approached bankruptcy did it rate as anything akin to a news story—and not much of a news story at that. The corporate media had special incentive not to push the Enron story too far. Were discussion of Enron and energy policies to lead to any sustained examina-

    Robert W. McChesney & John Nichols

tion of the way communication policies are produced behind closed doors in Washington—arguably the most off-limits story in U.S. journalism in our times—it would find a thick stench that would rival anything Enron has done. But that wasn't the whole of why the media missed the real story.

Although it is clear that the Enron affair is a stunning example of supreme political corruption, the coverage increasingly came to concentrate upon the business collapse of Enron, and the chicanery of Arthur Andersen, rather than the sleazy methods, legal as well as illegal, in which the company used the political system to make billions of dollars ripping off consumers, taxpayers, and workers. In another era, the Enron collapse would have been provoked a bigger political crisis than the Teapot Dome scandal, which shook the presidency of Warren Harding and forced dramatic action by Congress. Still, all indications are that the Enron scandal will not turn into a political crisis that will end political careers and lead to major political reform; the opposition Democrats are in no hurry to push the story to its logical political conclusion because so many of them would be implicated as well. Thus, there is no debate among official sources about the proper response to the political corruption issues raised by the Enron case. Without those official sources, "professional" journalism is restricted to a discussion that begins and ends within the limits of what those in power pursue, and the balance of the population has no one representing *its* interests. What about those who simply want the whole truth to come out? What about those who want the system changed so this sort of corruption is less likely to occur in the future? They are out of luck. This is disastrous for liberal democracy, as it suggests to citizens that even dramatic revelations of corporate and political corruption will not lead to change. If the press system cannot produce coverage that leads to peaceful and credible reform of corruption, it only means the problems will get worse and the costs of an eventual resolution significantly greater.

Finally, consider the manner in which the press reported President Bush's "victory" in the 2000 election. It is now clear that the majority of people in Florida who went to vote for president in November 2000 intended to vote for Al Gore. Indeed, buried in the footnotes of a recount conducted by the major news media in 2001 was the revelation that using any method that sought to quantify the actual sentiments of the actual voters the result was the same: Al Gore won Florida. And winning Florida was supposed to cinch the presidency. But Al Gore isn't president. Why is that? Or, to put it another way, why didn't the press coverage assure that the true winner would assume office? After all, if the free press cannot guarantee the integrity of elections, what good is it? The primary reason is due to sourcing: Throughout November and early December of 2000, the news media were being told by all Republicans that the Republicans had won the election and Al Gore was trying to steal it. The Democrats, on the other hand, were far less antagonistic and showed much less enthusiasm to fight for what they had won. Hence, the news coverage, reflecting what their sources were telling them, tended to reflect the idea that the Republicans had won and the Democrats were grasping for straws. When Greg Palast broke the story in Britain in November 2000 that the Florida Republicans had systematically and illegally excluded thousands of poor Floridians from voting—in itself, certainly enough to cost Gore the state—no U.S. mainstream news medium dared pick it up, even though the story was painstakingly well documented. Why? Most likely because journalists would have been out on their own, since the Democrats had elected not to fight on this issue. Once the Supreme Court made its final decision, the media announced that our national nightmare was over—neglecting to note that, according to most polls, Americans would have been perfectly willing to have the process go on in order to identify a clear winner. The media had helped anoint a president. The only losers were the irrelevant and powerless souls who clung to the belief that whoever gets the most votes should win the election, and that the press should tell the whole truth and let the chips fall where they may.

Having played the role that it did in picking the president, the media was in no position to criticize the Bush Administration. This explains at least some of the willingness of the mainstream U.S. news media to suspend criticism of President Bush almost *in toto* after September 11. Having foisted the moronic child of privilege upon the American people, it became necessary in a moment of national anguish to remake him as another Lincoln, albeit one who preferred lifting weights to reading books.

When the recount report containing data that seemed to confirm that Gore had won Florida was released two months after September 11, what was striking was how almost all the press reported that the results were mixed or that Bush had won. Major newspapers and television networks reached this "conclusion" only through the Olympic-style gymnastic twist of analyzing the data from the standpoint of what the Gore campaign had requested in November of the year before. The identity of the actual winner of the actual election in Florida—i.e., the person who most of the voters preferred—seemed not to interest the press one whit. In a manner of thinking, the press had no choice but to provide this interpretation. If the media conceded that Gore, in fact, had won the race in Florida, it would have made people logically ask, "why didn't the media determine this when it mattered?" Moreover, a concession that the United States had an unelected president would make the laudatory coverage of President Bush after September 11 look increasingly like the sort of paeans to "maximum leaders" expected from the news media in tinhorn dictatorships. As soon as the leaders are not the product of free and fair elections, they lose credibility; with that development, the "professional" reliance on official sources, which is wobbly by democratic standards to begin with, collapses.

In years past this criticism of the U.S. media would have been met by howls of indignation from journalists, professors, and citizens of every stripe. Ours was a truly free press, they would argue, celebrating the majesty of the freedom in American history. Today that response is muted; the asininity and degradation of our media culture is palpable and hard to digest even for the old true believers. Or, perhaps, especially for the old true believers who have seen their faith in what good the media might do erased by the reality of what it does. Yet the system still has many who defend it, albeit with less enthusiasm and righteous fervor than in years gone by. One defense is that the media system is based on the pursuit of profit, so firms are compelled to "give the people what they want," or face economic ruin. There is an element of truth to this claim, but it should not be exaggerated. Media markets are hardly competitive in an economic sense, and because of that firms have a great deal more power to force people to choose from what they deem most profitable. Moreover, media markets often are set up with advertisers, not people, as the primary partner; in such cases the needs of the citizenry fade from view beneath the commercial imperatives of Madison Avenue. This is especially true in the newspaper industry, where the drive to attract affluent readers has led in many cities to a radical decline in serious coverage of poor and working-class neighborhoods as resources are shifted to the coverage of suburban areas where the readers that advertisers want tend to congregate. Moreover, even a purely competitive market media system, and one without any advertising, would be far from perfect. Markets are predicated upon one dollar, one vote, rather than one person, one vote. Hence, rich individuals have many more votes than people who are poor. The market in this sense is more plutocratic than democratic. While the market can play an important role in a democratic media system, it should never comprise the entirety of a democratic media system.

Another defense of the existing order is that this is the "natural" American system; if someone is dissatisfied with it, that person should shut up or move to another country, preferably on the other side of the world. The "love-it-or-leave-it" theory, aggressively advanced by the likes of millionaire radio personality Rush Limbaugh, holds that the First Amendment has authorized two dozen profit-seeking transnational corporations to rule U.S. media with ample government subsidies but with no public "interference" otherwise. This is an argument that does not stand up to any historical scrutiny. It is true that the First Amendment prohibits congressional interference with a free press; however, it does not therefore authorize concentrated corporate and advertiser domination of the press. Imagine a parallel phenomenon in the practice of religion: If a handful of faiths were using their accumulated resources and their lobbying influence with government to gain dominance in the spiritual life of the land while forcing faiths with different ideas and values out of the public sphere, would First Amendment absolutists argue that this was the intent of the "freedom of religion" protection? If they tried to do so, they would be stymied by the courts, laughed out of any serious debate, and appropriately labeled as self-serving theocratic totalitarians.

The First Amendment belongs to all Americans, not just the billionaire investors in a handful of giant media firms, and it is based on the notion that democracy demands a press that serves us all. We are not arguing for government censorship of the commercial media—in fact, we oppose efforts in that direction—but we think efforts to reduce the power of Wall Street and Madison Avenue, and to increase the role of Main Street and every other sector of the population, in the running of our media system are entirely consistent with the meaning of the First Amendment.

Some also defend the status quo by asserting that the corporate media do not have much effect upon anyone; thus, complaints such as the ones we have raised amount to much ado about nothing. This perspective holds that media consumers are savvy in the ways of the media, and can interpret commercial messages critically. It's true that few citizens swallow everything the media dish out. In the old Soviet Union, few citizens believed what they read in *Pravda* or

Izvestia, but that didn't mean the society would not have been well-served by massive reform of the media system. And to suggest that the corporate media have no effect upon us seems to be untenable; after all, there are limits to how far we can expect citizens to "read into" media messages. Nor do we suggest that all that media produces should be met with deep skepticism; we recognize that the system offers much material that is useful and entertaining. Our claim is simply that the media system produces vastly less of quality than it would if corporate and commercial pressures were lessened.

There is one new argument in defense of the media status quo, the argument that the Internet will set us free. Ironically, it seems that the same people—like George Gilder—who just a few years ago were telling us how great the media system was in the United States are now suddenly conceding that it is, indeed, dreadful, but that there is no reason for concern. The Internet, they tell us, allows us to escape this failed media landscape. How? The theory goes something like this: Because anyone can start a Web site at a relatively nominal expense, and because anyone online can access any Web site, then the giant media firms are dinosaurs from another age, and their monopolistic control will be doomed once the Internet comet fully smashes into the earth. Happy days are here again. Heaven on earth. Digital nirvana. And all we have to do is sit back, wrap our mitts around our mouse, and let the private sector do its thing. It doesn't get any easier or better than that, does it?

As with the other defenses of the media status quo, there is an important element of truth, or half-truth, in this euphoric vision of the Internet as a magical democratizing technology. The Internet, and digital communication more broadly, are radically changing our lives. In a few years, the world we live in is going to look quite different from the world of just a few years ago. Moreover, the Internet is forcing a reconfiguration of the media industries, as the shift to digital communication means that the traditional distinctions between media and even communication sectors are disappearing. Nevertheless, the hope that the Internet is going to overturn the media system and open up unlimited space for new voices—not to mention marginal, dissident, or noncommercial voices—has been proven to be unfounded. In particular, many of the utopian visions of what the Internet might do have clashed with the reality of the digital divide between "wired" CEOs and millions of impoverished Americans who lack access to telephone lines, computers, and all the other "tools" needed to ride the Internet highway. This hardly means that there will not be exciting and important use of the Internet by activist and noncommercial interests—nor that, with concerted effort, the divide between Internet haves and have-nots might be closed. What it does mean, rather, is that the Internet—ruled by commercial values—has already been turned to purposes far less noble than those imagined by digital utopians.

The core problem with the "Internet will set us free" argument was that it mistook the existing power of the media giants as being based on technology, when in fact that power is also based on the market. While it is true that anyone can start a Web site, it has proven nearly impossible for anyone to start a commercially viable Web site unless they are owned by or affiliated with an existing media giant. The evidence suggests that the Internet was going to enhance

Robert W. McChesney & John Nichols

concentration among media firms, as well as their overall size. One survey found that far from being "a democratizing force, allowing a large number of relatively equal market contestants to compete on a level playing field," the Internet instead gives the dominant sites "an accelerating advantage over their competitors." Even Microsoft, with its billions of dollars in hard cash, effectively abandoned producing content for the Internet after squandering a few hundred million dollars on the endeavor in the late 1990s.

The explanation is simple: the media giants have several tremendous advantages as they colonize the Internet. They have existing digital programming to put on the Web, while it is exceedingly expensive for new competitors to produce such fare. The giants can bring advertisers over to their Web sites as part of their contracts with their traditional media. They can heavily publicize their Web activities over their traditional media, in a manner that would be cost prohibitive for any Internet media start-up that did not have a traditional media outlet. The media giants also have tremendous leverage with Internet service providers, search engines, and portals to get premier position on the screen. And, to top it off, the media giants have invested heavily in Internet content ventures to keep a finger in the pie. The media firms know that their ultimate survival depends upon their dominating cyberspace, so they are willing to assume losses there far longer than would any rational investor without other media holdings. In combination, these factors are overwhelming. Moreover, as cyberspace is colonized by the media giants, it appears to be fanning the flames of hypercommercialism inherent in the traditional media system. Media Web sites often feature e-commerce as a means of generating revenues, and to attract advertisers, the crumbling notion of editorial integrity from commercial pressure has been compromised even further.

And where does this leave us? Facing more concentrated media ownership than ever; deteriorating standards of journalism; hypercommercialized culture and entertainment; a declining civic life in a shrinking democracy; and slim hope on the Internet. Depressing, no?

And that's not the half of it. The system seems almost impervious to change. Consider how powerful the media and communication lobbies are in Washington, DC, as they routinely use the campaign contribution scalpel to remove politicians' backbones. By virtually every measure, the corporate media, telecommunications, and computer lobbies, and trade associations are among the most powerful in the nation. The corporate media not only have piles of money but also control access to the public, something that politicians covet. One of the favorite lobbying techniques of the NAB and other big-media advocacy groups is to bring local station managers to Washington to meet with members of Congress. Imagine the effect of sitting a congressman down with the person who has the power to decide whether his face ever again graces television screens in his hometown. Talk about influence! And that's just the beginning. In 1999, the NAB went so far as to use the wives of members of Congress in their televised public service announcements. As one report noted, "It is a quiet way of further ingratiating itself with lawmakers." Finally, the corporate media are in the position of being able to provide the press coverage of any debates over media policy and hence define what the public will be exposed to on the issues. This trump card ought to make the corporate media the envy of the business community.

The purpose of this book is to not to wallow in how bad things are getting, but to begin exploring how to reverse the trend with workable strategies for activism, organizing, and direct action. So long as this is a legitimate democracy, things do not have to be this way, and we have the power to both change the system—and build independent alternatives to it. Public policy could effectively restructure our media system such that it has a significant and viable nonprofit and noncommercial component. Once media is made a bona fide political issue, as soon as it is "in play," the forces favoring media reform will prevail. We may not democratize it completely, but we will advance. (That is why the media giants work so incessantly to ensure that media issues never see the light of day.) So getting media reform on the public agenda is the first and greatest obstacle we face. And here we run up against the ultimate defense of the media status quo, after all the other arguments have been discredited. This is the notion that there is simply no other way for media to be operated in a democratic society, so it is not even an issue worth considering. This line of analysis tells us that any change from the status quo must be, by definition, a change for the worse. This is a powerful and paralyzing notion, and it carries considerable weight in the United States, not only for media reform but for social reform in general. But by looking outside the United States we can see the fraudulent nature of this claim, for it is in these other lands that democratic forces are mobilizing to oppose the sort of hypercommercial, concentrated corporate media system we have in the United States. The lessons from abroad provide a powerful sense of how Americans can—and, we would argue, must—creatively and constructively approach media reform in the United States.

Robert W. McChesney & John Nichols

CHAPTER 2

Global Media and its Discontents

"Broadcasting is too important to the functioning of a democracy for decisions to be left entirely to the broadcasters."

—TONY BENN, British parlimentarian

"Our democracy depends on the free flow of ideals and information. When that flow is blocked, and our access to information is controlled by the few and the wealthy, our ability to make informed choices suffers, as does our democracy. This is exactly what is happening as media conglomerates continue to increase their share of the communications market unfettered by government regulation or control... [A] healthy democracy demands an informed electorate. We need policies that limit media concentration and ensure a rich exchange of ideas. We believe that diversity of expression must be promoted through tax incentives to assist community groups, cooperatives, or entrepreneurs to invest in community media, and that newspaper owners should not also own broadcasting corporations."

– Platform of Canada's
New Democratic Party, 2001

"There cannot be a democratic country, democratic society without freedom of the press."

—JOSE RAMOS-HORTA, Nobel Laureate,
Minister of Foreign Affairs for East Timor

AMERICA PUBLIC LIFE features little in the way of debate about the role a truly free and diverse media could play in shaping a truly free and diverse democracy. In other countries, however, media is treated as a core issue. Indeed, if there is a measure of the seriousness with which a nation ponders its potential to address fundamental issues, then that measure may well be found in the depth of its discussion about media and democracy.

Surely that is the case in East Timor, the Pacific island state that proudly bills itself, "The World's Newest Democracy." In August 2001, East Timor emerged from a quarter century of brutal repression at the hands of Indonesian military rulers and held a historic round of free elections for its Constituent Assembly. More than two dozen political parties jockeyed for position in a competition where there was a powerful sense the winners would not merely govern but would in fact define the scope and character of a freshly minted democracy.

In this election contest, issues of media and democracy were not abstractions. The Indonesian military had limited democratic discourse at every turn and, after the East Timorese voted overwhelmingly for independence in 1999, the offices of the region's only daily newspaper were sacked and burned during a rampage by the Indonesian soldiers and militias allied with them. In East Timor, political leaders and citizens well understood that media was a serious political issue. The different parties developed detailed policy statements and platforms on issues of broadcast diversity, concentration of media ownership, and the role that the new government of East Timor ought to play in fostering the free flow of information and the open debate that is fundamental in a democracy. The party that swept those elections, FRETILIN (The Frente Revolucionaria do Timor Leset Independente), produced a manifesto, "Towards the Restoration of Independence and the Freedom of our People, " that touched on issues ranging from health care to housing to the role that the new nation would play in the world. A full section in the manifesto explained that to restore freedom, it would be necessary to "democratize mass media": "The democratization of mass media must deserve privileged attention in a national development policy; it must aim at extending freedom of expression and the press," the manifesto declared. "The FRETILIN Administration will stand for an objective and independent media in search of factual truth. The Administration will pursue efforts to extend radio and TV networks nationwide and guarantee a timely access to information to every citizen. FRETILIN will pursue a national policy favoring the diversification of media operators as a way to fight private or state monopolies and defend the freedom of the press."

Within months of the election, a FRETILIN-led government produced a new Constitution that did, indeed, include a substantial section guaranteeing "freedom of the press and other mass media." Far more detailed than the U.S. Constitution's First Amendment, the document enacted in East Timor states, "The monopoly of the mass media shall be prohibited." The document also outlines the rights of journalists declaring, "The state shall guarantee the existence of a public radio and television service that is impartial in order to, *inter alia*, protect and disseminate the culture and the traditional values of the Democratic Republic of East Timor and guarantee opportunities for the expression of different lines of opinion."

"These rights are fundamental to a true democracy," explained Virgilio da Silva Guterres, the president of the East Timor's journalist association, in a recent statement detailing the explosion of new and diverse media in a place where there is little mystery about necessity of a truly free press in the development of a truly free country.

Virgilio da Silva Guterres was, of course, correct to view East Timor's bar on media monopoly, its guarantees of the rights of journalists, and its promise of a vibrant and diverse public broadcasting service as "fundamental to a true democracy."

Yet that statement would surely draw debate, perhaps even ridicule, in the United States, where media monopolies are expanding at a breakneck pace and where public broadcasting services are being squeezed to the point of dysfunction by politicians who, with strong encouragement from private broadcast lobbies, have successfully strangled public funding for public broadcasting.

Between the experience of the expanding democracy of East Timor (where the 2001 assembly elections drew a ninety-three percent turnout) and the rapidly waning democracy of the United State (where barely thirty-six percent of eligible voters were expected to participate in the 2002 Congressional elections), there is a world of difference. Still, around that world, wherever there is a real debate about democracy, there is an understanding that media is a serious political issue.

It should come as no surprise then that when we look at what is happening to debates about media abroad, we see a growing willingness on the part of democratic forces to organize for media reforms that challenge the patterns of globalization and corporate domination. These calls for media reform are also proving popular with voters, if not with the business class. In this chapter, we outline the nature of the emerging global commercial media system and the currents of the democratic resistance to it. We believe that there are hopeful and powerfully instructive lessons for Americans in these global developments.

First, let's look at the developments to which movements for media reform are responding. Since the 1980s, a global commercial media market has developed. As a result of deregulation of national media markets, new communication technologies, and heavy pressure from the U.S. government and the international business community, the face of media has undergone striking change in virtually every country on the planet. Whereas media systems were formerly best understood as national phenomena, with a minor role played by media imports, today it is more appropriate to regard media as a global system with national variants.

The global media system is the province of fewer than one hundred firms that provide the significant portion of the world's media fare. There are two distinct tiers to this hierarchy. The first tier is comprised of about ten transnational media conglomerates (including AOL Time Warner, Disney, Bertelsmann, News Corporation, Viacom, Sony, and Vivendi Universal) that each collect between $10 billion and $35 billion per year in annual media-related revenues. These firms tend to be dominant players in numerous media sectors and to do business all across the world. The remaining eighty or ninety firms are smaller, tend to concentrate more upon one or two media sectors, and are more likely to be national or regional powerhouses. A great chasm separates the first-tier media firms and those near the bottom of the second tier. AOL Time Warner, for example, has annual sales some fifty times greater than the fiftieth largest media firm in the world.

The transnational media giants, as one leading media analyst notes, "are increasingly setting their sights on global expansion." In 1999, for example, Disney completely reorganized its corporate structure to expand and strengthen its "global presence." Disney's enthusiasm is understandable; experts project that the major Hollywood studios, which currently earn around one-half of their income outside the United States, will see that portion rise to two-thirds in the next five to ten years. An examination of the top ten grossing films in each of the eight largest national markets after the United States in the summer of 1999 reveals that Hollywood films, each produced by a first-tier media giant, accounted for seventy of them.

Still, the global media system should not be perceived as one where U.S.-based transnational conglomerates dump their standard fare on new audiences. On the contrary, the media giants localize their content whenever feasible, and almost always enter new markets in a partnership with local firms and investors. Sony's Hollywood-based studios have been most aggressive in producing films and localized TV content, doing so across Europe, Latin America, and Asia. Rupert Murdoch's News Corp., however, is the flagship firm for establishing major joint ventures with local firms across the globe, especially with regard to cable and satellite television. By 1999, even India's massive domestic film industry had been penetrated by joint ventures with News Corp.'s Fox studios and several other Hollywood giants.

The balance of the largest media firms are meeting the challenge and going global with a vengeance. Liberty Media and Microsoft have both made major investments in global cable systems. Even second-tier global media firms find it necessary to move beyond their national or regional markets in order to grow—and to avoid being taken over by more aggressive competitors.

Nor is this pattern of global growth and concentration exclusive to the largest, mostly U.S.-based firms. Deregulation of national media ownership restrictions has both opened up national markets to outsiders and permitted domestic giants to grow ever more powerful. Spanish media and telecommunication firms, for example, "are invading Latin America in search of its corporate treasures." Major national media markets like Mexico, Brazil, and India are each increasingly dominated by just a few massive media firms, and these firms all work closely in joint ventures with the transnational media giants. In no sense can the massive capitalist media firms of the developing world like Mexico's Televisa or Brazil's Globo be characterized as "oppositional" to the global corporate media system; they are integral players in that system.

This is not just a process taking place in what has been called the Third World. In Britain, the television and newspaper industries have undergone a tremendous consolidation in recent years, and U.S.-based firms are now prominent players in these oligopolistic markets. Indeed, most nations have vastly more concentrated ownership of media than the United States, if only due to their smaller populations and geographic sizes. And the process is far from over.

The European Union, for example, is working to help European media firms become not only regional, but global, powers. As a result of deregulation, the *New York Times* observed that "Europe's television industry is suddenly in the grip of an American-style consolidation." In addition to first-tier media giants like News Corp. and Bertelsmann, European TV is falling into the hands of a few regional giants like Canal Plus, SBS, and Fininvest. These firms hope to use their European base as the foundation for eventual expansion into the United States, either directly or through joint ventures.

One other development is working hand in hand with global media concentration: the rise of a highly concentrated global advertising industry. For the past decade the advertising agency industry has consolidated at a rate even greater than that of the media industry, and is now dominated by three to six global giants that dwarf the remaining players. These giants tend to have subsidiaries in every major market, and they increasingly represent corporate clients who need global marketing campaigns. These ad agency titans find that the global media giants are best positioned to provide them with the global reach their clients need and demand.

In 2001 and 2002, many of these burgeoning media giants have fallen on hard times. From Vivendi Universal and Kirch to AOL Time Warner and News Corporation, stock prices have plummeted as earnings collapsed. In most cases, however, the underlying media activities were still profitable; the problem was that these firms had vastly overpaid in a number of extravagant deals during the halcyon days of the Internet expansion in the late 1990s. The upshot may well be some fire sales and a reshuffling of assets among the big boys, but no alteration in the logic operating of the system.

So far, what we have presented in this chapter may not be widely known, but it is hardly controversial. The pages of business and trade publications teem with this information on a daily basis. And were we to leave the discussion at this point, investors might be the only audience with a direct interest in the subject. However, we are not discussing the widget market here, or some other incidental commercial undertaking. We are discussing the means of communication and information distribution—the lifeblood of journalism and culture—and, accordingly, the foundation of democracy. As we discussed in Chapter 1, the most striking way to conceive of the negative implications of the global commercial media market is quite simple: As the power of the largest firms grows, they use that power to commercialize content to the greatest extent possible and, if necessary, to protect their political interests, and they denigrate any notion of public service that might interfere with either of those aims.

This attack on public service assumes many forms. Deregulation and the rise of the commercial media market have cast the future of public service broadcasting in grave jeopardy. Traditional public service broadcasters, such as the BBC, have begun to look like square pegs in a world of round holes. They are increasingly pressured to adopt the practices of commercial firms in order to establish their efficiency and worth, but as they go commercial, they lose their *raison d'étre*. They even get chastised for being publicly subsidized competitors to the now dominant commercial media. The *Economist* calls this the "conundrum" of public service broadcasting: "If it goes upmarket, nobody watches it, so it is hard to justify state finance. If it goes downmarket, it ceases to look like public service broadcasting, so it is hard to justify state finance." There is a crucial change assumed in that formulation, however. At its best, public broadcasters sought to provide high-quality, noncommercial fare to the entire population regardless of what the commercial media were doing. This made it possible for them to develop mass audiences while providing noncommercial standards. In this new era where corporate media giants ride roughshod over governments, public service broadcasters are expected to concede popular programming to commercial interests, and to concentrate upon that for which there is not much of a market. A vicious cycle is created, wherein underfunded public broadcasting outlets are unable to compete for viewers, are told to turn to commercial support, and ultimately are threatened with privatization.

Until public broadcasters are again provided with the resources and mandate to provide noncommercial programming to large audiences, they are on a dead-end street. They may survive as quasi-commercial entities, but they will not survive as genuine public service broadcasters. An example from New Zealand is illustrative. After the government sold off most of Radio New Zealand's stations to private investors, complaints began to arise that the system's respected news-gathering operation was too costly to maintain. The catch-22 situation was summed up by the New Zealand parliamentarian Jim Anderton: "Radio New Zealand News is under pressure for the simple reason that it is not supplying news to anyone other than Radio NZ. It is effectively a single radio station trying to support a nationwide network of newsrooms. No wonder it's in a squeeze."

The defense of public broadcasting—and its reformation along less bureaucratic lines—is one of the cornerstones of media reform movements worldwide. There is a growing sense that we are on the verge of losing a unique and indispensable cultural resource. It is a concern well expressed by an Australian senator during a debate over funding the Australian Broadcasting Corporation: "Starving the ABC of its funds means that the ABC cannot afford to purchase the rights to a whole spectrum of content, including sport, and especially cannot afford to produce its own content."

As in the United States, a striking and important consequence of the global commercial media market has been the attack on journalism, and the reduction in its capacity to serve as the basis for an informed, participating citizenry. Let us be clear here: We are not blaming the global media system for all the flaws in journalism. Establishing a media system that fosters a freewheeling, independent, wide-ranging, and vibrant journalism and political culture is no easy matter, though it is something that all democratic societies should aspire to develop. National press systems prior to—and in conjunction with—the global commercial system were and are sometimes adequate at this job, but many were failures. Frequently, the media have been owned by wealthy individuals or firms that have clearly censored journalism to support their usually reactionary politics, as is the case in Turkey today. Both public and commercial broadcasters in many nations have often been handmaidens of the dominant political parties and interests. In places like Mexico, Peru, and Brazil the dominant commercial broadcasters have tended to be in bed with the dominant pro-business political parties, and to use their media power aggressively and shamelessly to maintain the favored parties in power. Editors and reporters from dissident media who courageously bucked the system and reported on those in power have often found themselves arrested or on the receiving end of a beating or a gunshot. These practices continue today across the world.

Consider the case of Venezuela, where elected President Hugo Chavez's populist advocacy on behalf of programs to aid his country's impoverished masses conflicted with the neoliberal agenda of privately owned newspapers and television stations. The press coverage accorded Chavez by this privately owned "free press" would have earned Josef Goebbels' or Joe Stalin's deepest admiration. When business, corrupt unions, and factions within the military deposed Chavez in a coup in April 2002, the banner headline of one of the nation's largest newspapers announced that it was "A Step in the Right Direction." The columns of the press and broadcast commentary blamed Chavez for the shooting deaths of demonstrators on the day of the coup and quickly relegated the ousted president to the dustbin of history. "They say history elevates or buries men; for you it has reserved a pit beside the Venezuelan leaders infamous for their atrocities," the newspaper *El Nacional* declared. Similar sentiments were expressed in enthusiastic editorials that appeared in the *New York Times* and other U.S. papers. Though popular with press barons, the coup proved less appealing on the streets of Caracas and other Venezuelan cities. Even though reports of Chavez's removal was spun as great news, the streets filled with citizens demanding the restoration of their elected president to office. As the protests grew, the media simply stopped covering the news. Newspapers ceased to publish, the state television station was pulled off the air, and privately owned stations started showing a steady stream of soap operas.

Only when the protesters took over the state television station did Venezuelans begin to receive news of what was happening in their country. A British academic, Jon Beasley-Murray, prepared in an analysis of events in Venezuela for the North American Congress on Latin America. "State television had, amazingly, come back onto the airwaves," wrote Beasley-Murray, who was in Venezuela during and after the coup. "The people who had taken over the state television station were clearly improvising, desperately. The color balance and contrast of these studio images was all wrong, the cameras held by amateur hands, and only one microphone seemed to be working. Those behind the presenters' desk were nervous, one fiddling compulsively with something on the desk, another shaking while holding the microphone, but there they were: a couple of journalists, a 'liberation theology' priest, and a minister and a congressman from the previous regime. The minister spoke first, and very fast. She gave a version of the violent end to Thursday's march that differed absolutely from the narrative the media had put forward to justify the coup that had followed: The majority of the dead had been supporters of Chavez (not opposition protesters), and the snipers firing upon the crowds were members of police forces not under the regime's control. Moreover, the former president had not resigned; he was being held against his will at a naval base on an island to the north. The current president, Carmona, was illegitimate head of a de facto regime that was product of a military coup. Thousands of people were on the streets outside the presidential palace demanding Chavez's return. A counternarrative was emerging."

"The congressman appealed directly to the owners and managers of other television stations to portray what was happening in Caracas," the account continued. "No change [appeared] on those other channels, however, most of which had returned to their regular programming. And then the state channel went off the air."

Beasley-Murray titled his analysis, "The Revolution Will Not Be Televised"—referencing a famous song by Gil Scott-Heron. And just as the agitating poet and songwriter predicted, the revolution succeeded in spite of the media's blackout. When Chavez returned to power, he did not sanction the media. But the citizens of Venezuela—who had relied on the Internet, cell phones, and other new technologies to spread the word of their protests—had learned a powerful lesson about where their mainstream media stood on the question of democracy. And the cheerleading from American newspapers and television commentators served as a reminder that the sympathies of those who enjoy the freedom of the press in the U.S. do not lie with those who seek to preserve basic freedoms and democracy in other lands.

In theory the rise of the global media giants was regarded as a plus to many countries; these organizations, it was thought, would use their money, power, and prestige to bring neutral, professional, nonpartisan journalism to nations desperate for such fare. Indeed, to the extent "globalization" affects national media regulation to undermine censorship of the news, that is a good thing. The sad truth, however, is that the caliber of the journalism provided by these giants tends to be deplorable. When a journalist actually attempts to maintain a higher standard, she quickly learns that she does not fit into the new media landscape.

Until 1986, award-winning writer Robert Fisk was the Middle East correspondent for the *Times* of London. He left, he says, because of the quality of journalism—or is it lack of quality?—demanded by *Times* owner Rupert Murdoch. "I would not accept the Murdoch ethos. Over and over again, I was writing against the paper's presumptions. I was in the odd situation where the *Times* didn't want me to leave but they would find themselves embarrassed at the content of what I wrote. *The Times* is an example of what has happened to much [of] journalism in Britain and Europe, which has become dominated by the microjournalism of television and radio newscasts of one minute each."

It should come as no surprise then that reporters and editors connected to the media giants are only rarely the ones who show up as the arrested and murdered reporters on the annual list published by the Committee to Protect Journalists. The media giants are not interested in pursuing dangerous stories that cost a lot of time and money to investigate, promise little financial payoff, and can antagonize governmental authorities with whom the media barons desperately want to stay on good terms. Most indicative of this trend has been the manner in which the largest media firms in the world have fallen over themselves attempting to please the government of China. Disney's and News Corp.'s campaign to please the Chinese rulers by watering down their journalism and operations has been chronicled elsewhere. Time Warner and Viacom entered the fray in the fall of 1999. What these episodes make clear is that no viable system of journalism can be expected from a system under the thumb of massive self-interested commercial organizations.

The most visible manifestation of the rise of the global commercial media has not been its journalism but its broader popular consumer culture, as its fare is drenched in commercialism. Report after report chronicles the rapid and stunning shift in culture around the world, especially among middle- and upper-class youth, as the commercial media system subsumes each nation's television system. This is a generation that is under pressure from the media it consumes to be brazenly materialistic, selfish, and depoliticized: devoid of social conscience. To the extent one finds these values problematic for a democracy, we all should be concerned.

The commercial media system is the ideological linchpin of the globalizing market economy. Consider the case of the Czech Republic. Only a decade ago the young generation led the "Velvet Revolution" against the communist regime under the slogan "Truth and love must prevail over lies and hatred." Ten years later even the *Wall Street Journal* acknowledged that the Czech Republic had turned into a demoralized morass, where "an unnerving dash to the free market" had created a society awash with greed, selfishness, corruption, and scams.

The type of political culture that accompanies the rise of the corporate media system worldwide looks to be increasingly like that found in the United States: in the place of informed debate and political parties organizing along the full spectrum of opinion, there will be vacuous journalism and elections, dominated by public relations, big money, moronic political advertising, and limited debate on tangible issues. It is a world where the market and commercial values overwhelm notions of democracy and civic culture, a world where depoliticization runs rampant, and a world where the wealthy few face fewer and fewer political challenges.

It is because of this context that many people around the world are organizing to reform their media systems to better serve the democratic needs of the great mass of citizens. These movements are many and they are varied. They take place at the local, national, regional, and global levels. They remain largely uncoordinated and yet all share basic values regarding media. They understand that the corporate media system is in many respects the advancing army of a global economic system that is hellbent on producing profits regardless of the social and environmental implications. This global "free market" economic system has produced considerable benefits for some (usually very wealthy) people, and notable benefits for many more (usually the middle and upper-middle classes), but it has come at a very high cost. Social inequality is increasing in nearly every nation, as is the divide between rich nations and poor nations. For working-class and poor people, especially women, the results of the global "free market" can be disastrous.

Because of the obvious linkages between the corporate media system and the global economic system, media reform is seen by a growing number of activists around the world as a necessary part of any democratic political platform; rarely is it seen anymore as a "single issue" reform activity. In country after country, media reform is being integrated into the platforms, the campaigns, and the parliamentary initiatives of political parties that refuse any longer to operate in denial of the role that media plays in a democracy. This is absolutely essential for success; although media activism can and must assume many forms, it is when that activism is advanced by political parties and related mass movements that media reform can most effectively be linked to broader issues of social justice. This, of course, is the fundamental step that is required for the development of the broad-based support necessary for success. The importance of political parties as vehicles for pushing media reform issues into the public discourse is arguably the single most vital lesson from abroad for Americans to learn concerning media reform.

It would, of course, be unduly romantic to suggest that the development of the global commercial media market has been paralleled by a political response of equally definitional force. Challenges to monopoly and commercialization have yet to reach critical mass in any nation, let alone on an international scale that might cause the media giants to tremble—as, for instance, the campaign against genetic modification of food has caused multinational conglomerates such as Monsanto to quake in recent years. Indeed, one of the great tragedies regarding media activism is that, as the processes of globalization, conglomeration, and commercialization sped up in the early 1990s, many traditional parties of the left abandoned the critiques of commercial media that had, historically, been among their core values.

Take as an example the British Labour Party. Throughout much of its history, the Labour party was an explicitly socialist grouping that nurtured a healthy skepticism regarding media giants within Great Britain and beyond its borders. Targeted for trashing by the "Tory press" from its earliest days, the party displayed little caution in proposing tough controls on media monopoly, and campaigning for a strong, publicly funded broadcasting authority. It also showed a penchant for direct action on the newsstands. On and off during its early history, the Labour party published its own mass-circulation daily newspaper, the *Daily Herald*, which, like the German Social Democrats' *Vorwärts* and the French Socialists' *L'Humanite*, competed directly and at times quite successfully with publications owned by the press barons. In the 1970s and 1980s, Labour cabinet ministers such as Tony Benn were in the forefront of a brief flurry of serious discussion about the role that the government might play in guaranteeing ideological diversity in print and broadcast media. Benn recalls sparking an intense national debate in the 1970s by declaring that "broadcasting is too important to the functioning of a democracy for decisions to be left entirely to the broadcasters." Benn's battle cry resonated with Labour party activists and media watchdogs who developed Britain's innovative Campaign for Press and Broadcast Freedom in 1979. Through the 1980s, the Labour party maintained an openness to the proposals of the Campaign for Press and Broadcast Freedom, which emphasized the need for strengthening the BBC, diversifying ownership of broadcast and print media, and challenging the supremacy of media conglomerates. As late as 1992, the Labour party continued to advocate for what by American standards would be considered radical reform of the media landscape. Its 1992 campaign platform contained a lengthy section on "The Media," which stated, "Labour wants a wider choice for listeners and readers in the broadcast and printed media. Promoting greater diversity and tackling concentration of ownership will ensure wider choice." That commitment was followed by specific proposals for full funding of the BBC, development of monopoly controls to prevent concentration of ownership of newspapers and broadcast outlets, and a host of other plans.

As the 1990s wore on, however, Labour became increasingly comfortable with big media. The political rise of Tony Blair and his "New Labour" allies saw the party that once decried corporate media as little more than a vehicle for recounting "the frivolous doings of the idle rich" move to the right of the Conservative Party of Margaret Thatcher and John Major on media issues. Labour's abandonment of its traditional stance created such a "topsy-turvy affair," according to British journalists Dan Glaister and Andrew Culf, that in 1996, "a Conservative government laid down a twenty percent threshold restricting newspaper groups from diversifying into television, while Labour united with right-wing Tory rebels to scrap the limits altogether." Effectively, Labour became the defender of media conglomeration and monopoly. Around the same time, Blair flew to Australia to meet with Rupert Murdoch, who soon after switched his mass-circulation *Sun* newspaper from an ardently Thatcherite Conservativism to a position of fervent support for Blair's "New Labour." By 1999, Blair was carrying Murdoch's water, using his role as British PM to advance Murdoch's business ambitions in both Italy and China.

With the rise of the Blair-generated "Third Way" ideology—characterized by its advocacy for market "solutions," free trade, and a diminished governmental role in regulation of the economy in general and corporations in particular— the old parties of the left have for the most part abandoned their commitment to challenging private media monopolies and to using governmental policies and spending to promote the sort of ideologically diverse media that sustains democracy. Germany's Gerhard Schroeder and a host of other leaders of social democratic parties have joined leaders of historically liberal parties, such as the American Democrats and the Canadian Liberals, in embracing a neoliberal, market-driven, corporation-defined, privatizing vision of government that Gregor Gysi, leader of Germany's rapidly growing Party of Democratic Socialism, accurately describes as an "unhistoric" politics in which "social justice and ecological sustainability are strangers."

"The old line parties have abandoned the playing field. They have stopped fighting for social and economic justice, choosing instead to seek the favor of the corporations the people want them to be battling," says Svend Robinson, a New Democratic Party member of the Canadian parliament. "I don't know if there is any place where this is more evident than in battles over media monopoly, corporate conglomeration, and foreign control of our media."

As the old parties have made their peace with markets, corporate capital, globalization of the economy, and the media that these patterns produce, they have left a void. In country after country, that void is being filled by new political groupings that, as part of a broader critique of neoliberalism, are making noise about the dangers posed to democracy by corporatization of the discourse. Just as Green parties—many of which have embraced media reform proposals—forced nations to look anew at questions of environmental protection and sustainability in the 1980s, so these new-line parties are forcing media issues onto the agenda. "This is an issue that's emerging all over the world. It's a huge concern. People are genuinely alarmed that at the same time we're witnessing growing concentration of ownership of media we're also seeing massive cuts in publicly owned media. It's a double whammy," says Canada's Robinson. "This neoliberal, right-wing takeover of the media is something that people are aware of, and they don't like it. But the old-line parties aren't willing to address the issue. This is what is going to distinguish new-line parties all over the world—a willingness to talk frankly about issues of media control and to propose an alternative to what's happening. It's inevitable. After you've had somebody say to you for the thousandth time, 'How come we never hear about these issues in the media,' you start to realize that the media itself is the issue."

A number of the parties that have taken the most aggressive stances regarding media issues—as part of broader programs that challenge corporate conglomeration and market-driven globalization—refer to themselves as members of "The Third Left." The name is intended to suggest an advancement from the narrowly focused political or economic critiques historically associated with pre-Marxist and orthodox Marxist movements toward an approach that comfortably links feminist, green, and traditional left values in a new model of politics. Critical to the message of these red-green groupings around the world is a determination to present a clear vision of the more humane, sustainable, and functional society that these parties would use political power to develop. "We work for a society in which all people have equal worth and the same right to a good life, " declares the program of Sweden's Left party, which has experienced a steady growth in its electoral strength as opinion polling has identified the party as that country's third most popular political grouping. "We want to live in a world

Robert W. McChesney & John Nichols

where people solve conflicts by peaceful means and live in harmony with nature. In community and cooperation a living culture is created which strengthens people's identity and self-esteem and provides society valuable inspiration and criticism."

An awareness of the relationship between ideologically diverse media and real democracy is a constant among Third-Left parties, as well as the green, nonsocialist left, and even non-left-wing groupings that have begun to embrace media issues in countries around the world. "From the point of view of democracy, it is essential that all political decision making is preceded by a genuine and interactive discussion in which all interested parties and even temporary coalitions are openly and impartially heard. In addition to political decision making, essential economic decisions should also be as public as possible," argues the platform of Finland's Left Alliance, a party that has maintained a Third Left vision as part of that country's governing coalition. "The openness and public nature of decision making can only be guaranteed with the aid of free, pluralistic, and diversified communications. In an open society, communications must go in all directions, which is why we need the possibility of interactive communications in addition to the mass media. In a democratic society the freedom of communication and the diversity of the media represent in principle a positive direction in development, because the fragmentation of the media and the public gives people a wider freedom and choice than before. Advanced information technology offers increasing possibilities for contacts and interaction between people and different NGOs. In a world of diversifying media, society ensures that ownership is not excessively concentrated, and that diversity and variability as well as the accessibility of the media and public communication services are supported by taxes wherever necessary."

Sweden's Left party has made media reform central to its politics, emphasizing at every turn that "Prerequisites for democracy are freedom of speech and press freedom..." and arguing that "in a living democracy it is necessary to have a broad and independent choice of media. Everyone should be able to express their opinions in one form or another. All opinions should be able to reach the public." The Left party pushes aggressive and innovative media reforms, including abolition of all advertising on radio and television and a program of subsidies for print media designed to guarantee enriched democracy by the broad availability of publications expressing distinct and sometimes unpopular views. The party, which in 1998 national elections saw its vote double to twelve percent of the total, does not simply talk about big ideas and grand visions, however. It has joined with labor groups to boycott a television station that refused to honor a Swedish law barring the airing of advertisements aimed directly at children, it has developed sophisticated newspapers, magazines, and Web sites to advance its ideas, and its members have been active players in the creation of radio programming designed to serve Sweden's growing immigrant community, women, and young people.

Sweden's experience with the Left party and the ban on TV advertising to children points to an important lesson: Once the left gets media reform in play, the traditional parties can no longer serve the interests of the corporate media with abandon. Moreover, media reform is an issue that has appeal across the political spectrum. Most of Sweden's parties now support the ban on TV advertising to children—it is popular with voters. Greece and Norway have enacted similar bans, and other European nations are contemplating doing so as well.

The coalition building that is at the heart of these evolving parties—like the fall 1999 anti–World Trade Organization (WTO) protests in Seattle, the spring 2000 anti–International Monetary Fund (IMF) and World Bank protests in Washington, the summer 2001 protests at the G8 summit in Genoa, Italy—recalls popular front models of the 1930s. In refreshing contrast to traditional liberal parties, "inside-outside" approaches characterize their challenge to global media. No longer do party strategists and "consultants" form policy positions in isolation. Parties of the left and even of the center, are raising media issues because their positions are informed by the groundbreaking work of media unions, watchdog groups, academics, and grassroots activists. These activists, who had a hard time getting a hearing from old-line parties, frequently find that newer, less bureaucratic, and more politically open parties are enthusiastic about incorporating media issues into their agenda. Thus, in Brazil, media activists found an easy ally in the Workers Party of Luis Inacio Lula Da Silva, which used its powerful grassroots networks to organize demonstrations outside the headquarters of Brazilian media conglomerates that the activists identified as having failed to provide serious coverage of the political process in that country. In the new political dynamic of post-apartheid South Africa, the comprehensive stance on broadcasting policy advanced by the Congress of South

Africa Trade Unionists (COSATU) has influenced the approach not only of the African National Congress and the South African Communist Party, with which the unions have long maintained close ties, but also of smaller parties of varying ideologies.

In Canada, New Zealand, and Australia, relatively new political parties have worked closely with unions and activists to make media an issue—with dramatic and instructive results. As part of a reshaping of the Canadian New Democratic Party to better respond to the debate over globalization, the party has made media reform issues a central focus of its agenda. The party platform now attacks media conglomerates by name and places the struggle for democratic media in the context of broader struggles over globalization: "One company, CanWest Global—a major contributor to the Liberal Party—now owns forty percent of our print media as well as television stations in eight provinces reaching eighty-eight percent of English-speaking Canadians." The platform goes on to declare:

> Our cultural identity has been put in jeopardy by an American media tide, globalizing economic forces, and the new communications technologies. The Liberals have done nothing to stem this tide. In fact, their trade deals have turned our culture into a commodity—opening the door to split-run magazines today and other U.S. attacks tomorrow. Severe funding cuts have undermined our public broadcaster, the CBC. And media barons have been able to buy up our newspapers, television, and radio stations, severely limiting the scope of information that reaches the

public.... In a global information society, the voices of our artists, writers, creators, and citizens need to be strengthened, not undermined. Media ownership must be balanced with strong independent voices to ensure the free flow of ideas and the health of our democracy. And governments must make it clear that our cultural identity is not for sale by ensuring that trade deals include protection for our culture. New Democrats are fighting for investments and policies that protect Canadian culture.

New Zealand's Alliance party, formed in 1991 as a coalition of greens, Maori rights campaigners, and refugees from the Labour party (which had drifted from its socialist moorings) became a home even for frustrated former journalists. After a nineteen-year career in broadcasting in New Zealand and Australia, which culminated in her appearing from 1987 to 1996 as host of a popular national talk show on Radio Pacific and the Newstalk ZB networks, Pam Corkery stepped away from the microphone and into the political fight over media. Elected to the New Zealand parliament on the Alliance slate in 1996, she became the party's spokesperson on communications, information technology, and arts and culture. Corkery's experience in radio, television, and print media, along with her passionate opposition to privatization of public broadcasting services, marked her as the parliament's most effective advocate on media issues. She used her platform to campaign with an energy and a focus that shook up the debate in that country—even forcing the Labour party to rethink its movement toward neoliberal positions on privatization and broadcast policy.

Early in her parliamentary career, Corkery declared the fight to assert popular control over the media to be "at the very least, a human rights issue." Working with Alliance Party leader Jim Anderton and other Alliance leaders, Corkery helped to build a powerful "inside-outside" movement that has seen the Alliance raise issues of media monopoly on the floor of the parliament and on the streets of Auckland, Wellington, and Christchurch with unions, Maori and Pacific islander organizations, and grassroots media activists. In particular, this coalition has dogged Tony O'Reilly, the former Heinz Soup executive who began building a media empire in Ireland and has now extended it to South Africa, New Zealand, and other countries. After purchasing the *Auckland Herald* newspaper, O'Reilly began to gobble up recently privatized radio stations, laying off staff, cutting news operations, and threatening to break a deal to have the privatized stations buy news from Radio New Zealand. The storm that the Alliance and New Zealand's media unions raised over the question of whether one man should control so much of a small nation's media led to hearings, debates, and investigations. It reopened the whole question of privatization and, eventually, prompted leaders of the Labour party to indicate that they would oppose any further media privatizations.

Reaffirming a vision that the airwaves are public property that citizens of a democracy have a right and a responsibility to regulate, Anderton and his allies in the Alliance called during the 1990s for a radical restructuring of New Zealand's broadcasting: limiting foreign ownership of television and radio stations, developing new government-funded television and radio networks and stations to serve minority communities, eliminating all forms of advertising during hours when children view television to combat "intrusive and cynical manipulations through commercial messages," and massively increasing support for and funding of existing public-sector broadcasting. "We do not believe that private media are essentially interested in New Zealand popular cultural expression, nor is it reasonable to expect them to be beyond a certain regulated level," explained the Alliance leader's policy declaration. "It is therefore essential that significant broadcasting organizations in both radio and television should remain in public ownership."

Not satisfied merely to defend the public broadcasting sector, the Alliance worked with media unions, indigenous peoples, artists, academics, and activists to develop proposals to reshape media in New Zealand. Even after the coalition dissolved in 2002, Anderton and Greens in the New Zealand parliament continued to raise media issues—as do a growing number of Labour party parliamentarians who have come to recognize the appeal of the critique Corkery and others developed.

The small yet energetic Australian Democrat party, which is a force in that country's Senate, has developed perhaps the most sophisticated political response yet seen to concentration of media ownership, domestic content issues, monopoly, and commercialism.

The Australian Democrats are not a traditional party of the left, nor would they fit comfortably into the Third-Left category occupied by Sweden's Left party, Finland's Left Alliance, or Iceland's Alliance. Yet they certainly meet the "new-line party" standard established by Canada's Svend Robinson. Founded in 1977 as a reform party with a strong environmentalist bent, the Australian Democrats made a name for themselves—especially among young voters—by taking tough stands in support of environmental protection, nuclear disarmament, aboriginal rights at home, and human rights abroad. In the 1990s, the party emerged as a solid supporter of sustainable development and a determined watchdog over Australian media. Working closely with the national "Save the ABC" movement, which was developed by media unions and consumers to oppose privatization proposals and funding cuts designed to undermine the Australian Broadcasting Corporation, the Australian Democrats became the most outspoken parliamentary defenders of that nation's popular yet embattled public broadcasting service.

Though they remain a small party, the Australian Democrats have registered significant victories in fights over the structure of media in their country. In 1997, working with unions and media activists nationwide, the Australian Democrats succeeded in convincing the government to abandon proposals that would have weakened existing limits on media cross-ownership by domestic and foreign conglomerates. Their work in conjunction with "Save the ABC" activists forced the government to scrap plans to restructure public broadcasting in a manner that would have meant cuts in services. They also gained support for the establishment of a federal government inquiry into patterns of media ownership. By the spring of 2000, the Australian Democrats were leading the fight to provide government funding for development of ABC's online and digital television projects. The goal, the Democrats explained, was to assure that ABC is not forced into commercial arrangements

with private concerns that might seek to dilute its independence and profit from its good name.

Legislative victories are only one test of the Australian
Democrats' success, however. The real measure of their
impact may well come in the shifting of attitudes toward
media issues within Australia. By making media a central
focus of their national campaigns and by forcing debates on
subjects such as media ownership, foreign content on television, digital technology, and related issues, the Australian
Democrats have pushed media issues into the political
debate and—in what may be their greatest triumph—onto
the front pages. For instance, appointments to the
Australian Broadcasting Corporation Board are no longer the
perfunctory distribution of political plums that they once
were, not with the Australian Democrats using each new
round of appointments to raise questions of political
favoritism, backdoor deals, and special-interest influence.
Since the 2001 national elections, the Democrats have been
in the forefront of a fight to prevent conservative Prime
Minister John Howard's government from erasing rules limiting cross-ownership of media. The struggle on this issue
has yielded a useful proposal for the U.S., where similar battles are taking place: a requirement that media proprietors
seeking exemptions to the rules barring cross-ownership of
broadcasting outlets and newspapers must maintain separate newsrooms.

The most exciting developments in media activism may
well be at the global level, though these remain nascent. The
global justice movement that has been organizing across
national lines against the neoliberal economic deals and
organizations like the WTO, the IMF, and the World Bank,

has made media one of the main targets for change. (It is this spirit that fuels much of the national activism described in this chapter.) At the World Social Forum in Porto Alegre in February 2002, where 70,000 people from across the world gathered to generate an alternative to neoliberal capitalism, media was one of the defining issues. The United Nations is convening a World Summit on the Information Society in December 2003, and leading scholars and activists are already working to make the need for autonomous, well-funded nonprofit and noncommercial media a major area for discussion. Among global democratic activists, there is an emerging consensus that unless the road to democratic renewal includes structural media reform, that road will be a dead-end street.

All of this is important for people in the United States for two reasons. First, it highlights the increasing importance of media reform politics around the world; the United States is, if anything, somewhat of a laggard in this regard. There are useful and necessary lessons to be learned. Second, it points to what is ultimately the global nature of media reform struggles. The issues are similar everywhere; the reform proposals are all variants of a handful of themes. The forces of darkness—large, profit-driven media corporations and their spoon-fed politicians and regulators—work their commercial schemes everywhere. This is a global struggle.

This notion that a diverse and independent media is vital to democracy is by no means recent. But it has too rarely been expressed on a regular basis in the corridors of political and governmental power. Once the issue is raised, however, the debate shifts. Suddenly, questions that seem technical, obscure, complex, or inconsequential take on a new mean-

Robert W. McChesney & John Nichols

ing. No longer are citizens willing to cede to industry lobbyists and their political pawns control of the debate over ownership of the means by which a democracy discusses fundamental questions.

So says Bharati Ray, a former top administrator of the University of Calcutta, who now serves in the upper chamber of the Indian Parliament. Over lunch in her modest quarters near the great governmental buildings of Delhi, she listened with open delight to a review of the evidence of mounting media activism and its embrace by parties of the left. One of the most articulate advocates for the Indian left, she was genuinely pleased to learn that issues that concerned her, so many Indians, and the Indian left in general—the latter a group with a long history of critically addressing commercialization, media monopolies, and foreign ownership of media—were being raised in other lands.

But then Ray scowled. "Why are we unaware of these developments?" she asked. "Why do we not know more of this activity?" Ray knew the answer, of course. She was well aware that few reports on international media activism are featured on the evening news. Yet the veteran teacher was not accepting excuses. "We must begin immediately to discuss what is being done around the world. We must come together. We must hear what others are doing so that we may imitate them. We must tell others what we are doing so that they may imitate us," she said. "Once we all begin to realize that we are not working in isolation, that we are a part of a great response to globalization, I think that the potential for the forces of democracy to succeed will be very great indeed."

Indeed.

CHAPTER 3

Building the U.S. Media Reform Movement

"There is nothing that obtains so general an influence over the manners and morals of a people as the press; from that as from a fountain the streams of vice or virtue are poured forth over a nation."

—THOMAS PAINE

"The inappropriate fit between the country's major media and the country's political system has starved voters of relevant information, leaving them at the mercy of paid political propaganda that is close to meaningless and often worse. It has eroded the central requirement of a democracy that those who are governed give not only their consent but their informed consent."

—BEN H. BAGDIKIAN

"By the end of the millenium five men controlled the world's media. And the people rejoiced, because their TVs told them to."

—MICHAEL MOORE

IN JANUARY 2002, the *Nation* magazine published its annual media issue in which the two of us contributed an article that opened with this line: "If we are serious about media reform, this is the moment to stop spinning our wheels and build a movement." While we do not underestimate the difficulty of such an endeavor, we argue that the base for such a movement is now so broad, and the necessity for it so urgent, that it is time to make the leap from criticism to campaigning. To our delight, we are finding that we were not alone in having reached this conclusion.

Most activist movements struggle for years, sometimes even decades, before finding tribunes in the Congress. Since our *Nation* article appeared, however, we have been finding a surprising number of open doors on Capitol Hill. In addition to long-time critics of media monopoly, such as Senate Commerce Committee chair Ernest Hollings, who has long advocated for reform, we are hearing serious talk of a need for legislative action coming from U.S. Senator. Paul Wellstone (D-MN), U.S. Representative Jesse Jackson Jr. (D-IL), and U.S. Representative John Conyers (D-MI), the ranking Democrat on the House Judiciary Committee. Still, the willingness of these legislators to write legislation advancing media reform has been overshadowed by the excitement of the House member who actually called us: U.S. Representative Bernie Sanders, the Vermont independent who is often at the forefront of raising new issues on Capitol Hill.

Yes, Sanders said, he was ready to author reform legislation. But as a veteran organizer himself, he said he was even more excited about helping to build the sort of popular movement that would make passage of such legislation possible. Sanders proposed that we come to Vermont in late April and join him for a series of town meetings at which we could gauge the level of support for turning media criticism into media activism.

Only when we arrived in Montpelier, Vermont, on a cold and wet Sunday night, did we fully recognize the historic significance of what Sanders had proposed. The Unitarian

Meeting House near the state Capitol was packed beyond capacity. More than 200 people filled the pews and stood along the walls—some of them having traveled from as far away as New Hampshire and upstate New York. At the appointed hour, the congressman stepped to the podium and declared in a booming voice, "Good evening, I'm Congressman Bernie Sanders and I want to welcome you to what I believe is the first Congressional Town Meeting ever organized to address the issue of corporate control of the media."

The crowd erupted in thunderous applause.

Over the next four hours, as Sanders and his constituents joined us in an animated discussion of how to turn anger into action, the notion of building a broad-based media reform movement in America began to seem more and more realistic. The next night, in Burlington, more than 400 people showed up for a meeting that was even louder and more energized. Sanders said it was the biggest crowd he had seen at a town meeting in years, and it was one of the most enthusiastic ever. In one sense, the two town meetings in Vermont were frustrating: It was clear that many of the people in the room were ready to mail their membership cards in to a movement that did not yet have a name or address.

By any measure, however, this was a sweet frustration. While we have a great deal of basic organizing to do, it is certainly easier to begin that organizing knowing that there is a vast citizen base ready to sign on for the long haul.

The fundamental challenge at this point is not convincing people that something should be done about media structures that do more harm than good. The challenge is to convince people that something *can* be done. That simple leap of faith, if it is taken by enough Americans, will provide us with a base that is strong enough to challenge corporate control and radically reshape the media landscape in the United States.

We already know that when citizens begin to entertain the notion that media can be an issue—rather than something that simply happens to us, and to our democracy—they get excited. When the political imagination is freed, the supposed apathy of the electorate can be replaced with a level of engagement that suggests the promise of U.S. democracy might yet be realized.

So how do we free the political imagination? How do we widen the parameters of the debate to include topics that have been left off the table for generations? How do we make media a national issue? To begin to find answers to these questions, let's consider how the environment has become a political issue in the United States and globally over the past thirty-five years. Our confidence regarding the prospects for a media reform movement in America is informed in no small measure by our association with one of the leading architects of the modern green movement, former U.S. Senator Gaylord Nelson of Wisconsin. Nelson suggests that Americans would be wise to see media reform as having movement-building potential not unlike what the nascent cause of conservation once evidenced.

In the 1960s, Gaylord Nelson was a voice in the political wilderness, an environmentalist who was often treated by his fellow U.S. senators as a nag on issues of clean air and clean water, and who struggled to get serious media attention for what he felt was the most fundamental of all issues: the sustainability of human life on the planet. Nelson's successful effort to make the environment an issue provides a case study in both the frustrations and the opportunities that attend any struggle to broaden the public discourse. It is notable that today, Nelson points to mounting frustration with big media—particularly as it relates to the question of media's role in a democracy—as the sort of issue that could well energize citizens. When Nelson came to the United States Senate in 1963 as the former governor of a small progressive state, he imagined that he could quickly force environmental issues onto the national agenda. The times seemed right. Rachel Carson had published *Silent Spring*, there was a mounting awareness of and concern about pollution of America's air and water, and there were sure signs of a rising level of civic engagement that could be turned to the task of saving the earth.

Nevertheless, making a public issue—even of something so fundamental as the environment—proved to be a far more difficult task than Nelson had expected. His hopes of convincing then-President John Kennedy, who showed an interest in the subject, to make it a focus of his administration were dashed by an assassin's bullet. His subsequent attempts to get Kennedy's successor, Lyndon Johnson, to make the environment a priority were met with little enthusiasm. On the floor of the Senate, and in his dealings with the federal bureaucracy, Nelson encountered more than his share of closed doors. "People would say to me: 'We've got so many other things to deal with—Vietnam, civil rights, poverty, all these important issues—why do you keep going on about clean air, clean water, the population explosion?'" Nelson recalled. "I had to explain to them that a focus on the environment didn't come at the expense of those issues. But the environment had to be an issue; there had to be space for this issue because it simply could not wait any longer. The earth was in danger, real danger. We couldn't put the issue off any longer." Nelson persevered. He introduced bills, organized hearings, spoke in more than thirty states, signed up allies, kept lists, worked with nascent environmental groups and individual activists. "I had the idea of trying to get the environment on the national political agenda. It wasn't there in the 1960s," Nelson said. "Nobody campaigned on it. Hell, as recently as 1968, in the Humphrey-Nixon race, neither candidate made a single speech on the environment. They didn't think it was an important enough issue to talk to the public about. It wasn't seen as a 'vote-getter.' Can you imagine that? Today, no politician would dare say that. But at the time, that was what we were up against."

Nelson's tireless activism left him with the impression that the people were far ahead of the politicians, however, and in 1969, flying home from an antiwar "teach-in" on a California campus, he hit on the notion that would in a matter of months make the environment a front-burner issue. With a handful of allies, he called for a national "Earth Day" in April of 1970, on which he said he hoped that rallies and teach-ins would be organized to educate people about the importance of environmental issues, and about what they could do to advance them. Run out of Nelson's Senate office with little more than a green symbol and a few enthusiastic college students to power the "movement," Earth Day mushroomed into a national phenomenon drawing more than 20 million people to events across the country, earning blanket national and international media coverage, and turning the heads of every politician in the nation, including President Richard Nixon, who quickly signed a series of sweeping environmental protection measures. "I wouldn't have gambled on trying to create a grassroots movement if I didn't think there was support at the grassroots," says Nelson. "I had been across the country. I knew that everybody was impacted by some environmental issue. Every industrial community had an orange cloud. Every community had a polluted lake, a beach that was closed, a wetland that had disappeared. All kinds of things were going wrong. Everybody felt something was going wrong in their local area. And they noticed that the politicians were doing nothing. This was their first opportunity to demonstrate their interest and they demonstrated it in spades. The politicians looked at it and said: 'What the hell is this?' If nothing else, politicians have to be good at sensing what the people are concerned about and they did. It worked."

Nelson proved, as have countless other American activists from John Brown to Elizabeth Cady Stanton to Mother Jones to Martin Luther King Jr., that it is possible to force an issue into the nation's political discourse, even an issue that the political and economic elites would prefer to keep off the radar. The environmental movement shared a damning feature with the cause of media reform: There were no powerful monied interests that would benefit by its success. All the money was either agnostic or firmly opposed to reform. And as Saul Alinsky has pointed out, when faced with organized money, the only recourse is organized people. To determine whether the environmental movement could generate enough popular support to overcome organized money, Nelson said it had to answer three questions affirmatively. It is therefore appropriate to ask whether the media reform movement can do likewise.

The first question is: *Does the issue at hand—in this case, the sorry state of media in America—affect everyone in some fundamental way?* The answer to that question is certainly "yes." In this age of the Internet, round-the-clock cable, and broadcast programming and advertising campaigns that reach even into our children's schools, the average American is in contact with media for almost twelve out of each day's twenty-four hours.

The second question is: *Is there an alternative to the status quo, a remedy that can and should be put in place?* Looking abroad, we can see that the answer again is "yes." Though the exact contours of a U.S. reform program need to be developed, none of the media issues that ought to concern Americans are unique to this country. And none of the responses to corporate media that have been advanced elsewhere would be difficult to adapt to America.

The third question is: *Do people believe they have the power to implement necessary changes and, if not, can they be made to believe anew in their ability to use democracy to set things right?* While we are confident that the answer to this question will ultimately be "yes," the honest answer at this point has to be "no." And for good reason. The sheer corruption of U.S. politics has erected a daunting obstacle. It is difficult to be confident about the prospects for reform when regulators and politicians are frequently in the pockets of big-spending corporate communication lobbies, and—surprise, surprise—there is little coverage of media activism or media policy debates in the corporate news media.

Moreover, activists are well aware that over the past generation the political right has zeroed in on the media as a primary target for their political work. According to Sally Covington's study of leading conservative foundations, they have spent around one-half of their funds to promote pro-corporate right-wing media and media "deregulation." In addition to having deep pockets, these big-bankroll conservatives find they march in ideological harmony with much of the commercial news media, especially on matters of neoliberal economic policy, free trade, and military interventions abroad. At moments like this, as the media cheers on a potentially perpetual war that has yet to be declared— let alone explained in a coherent manner—it feels like the situation is only deteriorating.

This feeling has contributed to a demoralization about the prospects for structural changes in the media system and a channeling of energies toward that which progressives *can* change and improve: their own media. So it has been that much energy has gone into the struggle over the future of the Pacifica Radio network. Many activists have poured their energies into the development of the Independent Press Association, which has grown dramatically to aid and abet scores of usually small, often struggling nonprofit periodicals, which are mostly progressive in orientation. And dozens of community-driven Independent Media Centers (IMCs) have mushroomed up around the world since the first emerged in the 1999 "Battle of Seattle," where progressive forces coalesced to shut down a meeting of the WTO. The Indy Media Centers take advantage of new technology to provide dissident and alternative news stories and commentary completely free of corporate mediation and com-

Robert W. McChesney & John Nichols

mercial interest. Most impressive has been the growing focus of the IMCs on local issues, making them a genuine alternative to established media at a level where that alternative can and has shifted the dialogue. We have seen the positive impact of the IMC movement firsthand—in Seattle and Washington during anticorporate protests, at the summer 2000 Democratic and Republican National Conventions, during the three lamentable presidential debates in the fall of 2000, throughout the Florida recount and places of conflict around the world, from Jerusalem to San Cristobal de las Casas. It is crucial that this decentralized network grow.

Yet as important as this work is, there are inherent limits to what can be done with independent media, even with access to the Internet. Too often, the alternative media remain on the margins, seemingly confirming that commercial media conglomerates have become so massive because they "give the people what they want." The problem with this disconnect is that it suggests that corporate media have mastered the marketplace on the basis of their wit and wisdom. In fact, as we noted earlier, our media system is not the legitimate result of free market competition. It is the result of relentless lobbying from big-business interests that have won explicit government policies and subsidies permitting them to scrap public-interest obligations and increase commercialization and conglomeration. It is untenable to accept such massive subsidies for the wealthy, and to content ourselves with the "freedom" to forge alternatives that only occupy the margins.

How, then, can we force a change in the media systems that dominate the discourse and misinform the debate? By organizing the media democracy movement to make a great leap forward.

The problem for the movement is not that there is a lack of activity. People for Better Television has been formed to enhance regulation of commercial broadcasting. Commercial Alert organizes campaigns against the commercialization of culture. The Center for Digital Democracy and the Media Access Project both work the corridors of power in Washington, struggling to win recognition of public-interest values under the most difficult circumstances imaginable. These groups have won some important battles, particularly on Internet privacy issues. Despite all their good work, however, the "range" of communication policy debate in Washington still tends to run all the way from GE to GM, to borrow a line from FAIR's Jeff Cohen. "The case for media reform is not being heard in Washington now," says U.S. Representative Jesse Jackson Jr. (D-IL). "It is not easy to make the case heard for any reform these days; I'm having trouble getting the case for a right to vote heard. But it is especially hard on media reform. That's why we need to do more. I hear people everywhere complaining about the media, but we have yet to figure out how to translate those complaints into some kind of activist agenda that can begin to move Congress. There has to be more pressure from outside Washington for specific reforms. Members have to start hearing in their home districts that people want reform of the media."

The movement base for making a great leap exists, and is easily identified. Beyond the beltway there are strong currents of activism on media issues. The problem is that it remains largely decentralized and essentially undernetworked. An ad hoc coalition with bases of strength from the

Lower East Side of Manhattan to Morgantown, West Virginia, has worked to provide the basis for microradio broadcasting over the past few years. Across the nation, local organizing efforts have sprung up to challenge alcohol billboards in minority and working-class neighborhoods, advertising in schools, and the dreadful state of local commercial TV news. Innovative lawsuits challenging the worst excesses of media monopoly are being launched by regional groups such as Rocky Mountain Media Watch, and a national consortium that has drawn critical support from the Unitarian-Universalists. Leading media scholars and educators met in October 2002 to form a new national media literacy organization—the Action Coalition for Media Education—one that will remain independent of the media conglomerates that help bankroll the existing groups. Media activists in Honolulu and San Francisco have successfully joined with unions—especially the Newspaper Guild in Hawaii —and community groups to prevent the closure of daily newspapers that provided a measure of competition and debate.

One of our great concerns is that the whole of the current media reform movement is significantly *less* than the sum of its parts. We need to better network our organizations and link our campaigns. With scant resources available, allied groups are often forced to try and outscramble one another in the race for precious little funding. More often than not, we are also forced to defend against new corporate initiatives, rather than to effectively advance positive reforms. We need to energize and build the movement by sharing resources and strategizing to work proactively in ways that cross-support a diverse array of approaches, networks, and campaigns—in and out of the beltway, online, in the reservations, and in the streets. It is in this way that we can best build the coalition—a national media reform coalition—necessary to drive the movement.

We need to continue to educate ourselves and our communities about the issues, and direct a whole lot of energy doing outreach to popularize those issues on the national level. In fact, the primary role of the national media reform coalition must be to demonstrate that media itself is the issue, and one on which members of Congress and federal regulators can and should be held accountable. This is not a radical notion. In Australia, for instance, years of activism have succeeded in placing media concerns on the agenda to such an extent that, when conservative Prime Minister John Howard's government proposed scrapping controls on media ownership, it became a significant issue in recent national elections. Though Howard retained power, he announced immediately after the election that he was backing away from the proposals. "I'm not going to bloody my nose on it," said Howard, as he referred to the battle that would be required to advance corporate media's agenda. Would that an American president would choose "not to be bloodied" by a powerful media reform movement and its newly emboldened political allies!

Making media a political issue in America is going to take an energized coalition to get the issues on the national radar.

How can such a coalition be built? First and foremost, by organizing in our communities. Yes, foundations and other nonprofit organizations have to be a source of seed money for initial development of the movement, but the reform coalition must ultimately be broad-based and member funded—like Greenpeace or, dare we say it, the National Rifle

Association. Activists need to feel both a sense of ownership and attachment to a citizen lobby if we are to have the sort of profound impact that is needed and, we argue, possible. Thus, we need to gather all the current groups struggling to change the media, as well as the foundations and nonprofits willing to support the work of this new movement. "All of the issues we talk about are interlinked. We are fighting against a lot of the same corporations. The corporations, while they supposedly compete with one another, actually work together very well when it comes to lobbying," explains Jeffrey Chester of the Center for Digital Democracy. "We need to link up the activists and start to work together as well as the corporations do for the other side." Will everyone get on the same page? No. But after years of working with these groups in various settings, we have no doubt that most will.

Even if we can draw together all the key media-reform players in Washington and around the country, however, our growing coalition will be little more than a political footnote if we do not quickly reach out beyond the media-reform circle. To fuel a mass movement, we must reach out to and involve organized groups that currently engage in little activity in the way of media reform, but that are seriously hampered by the current media system. Absent for far too long from media reform activism have been the cause's natural allies, organizations that should be sympathetic to media reform and that have been active in other nations. We refer to organized labor, teachers, librarians, civil libertarians, artists, religious denominations, and groups involved with a broad range of civil rights advocacy. To be sure, there has been some movement in this regard. For example, the

Newspaper Guild section of the Communication Workers of America (CWA) union, which represents print journalists and other newspaper employees across the country, is becoming a serious and savvy player in debates over media monopoly and diversity. The National Organization for Women (NOW), many disability rights groups, as well as a number of gay and lesbian organizations, have developed effective and influential critiques of mainstream media coverage of issues concerning their communities—and, increasingly, of the media structures that maintain stereotypes. Both the NAACP and the Rainbow/PUSH Action Network have targeted media as a central focus for their activities—organizing forums, sending leaders to testify before Congress, and raising tough questions about federal policies regarding minority ownership of broadcast outlets. The United Church of Christ has been doing good work for years, and the Unitarians are now supporting some vital media reform initiatives. The American Academy of Pediatrics went so far as to formally resolve in 1999 that commercial television was a public health hazard for children. These groups have to be brought together to strategize and maximize their effect on the national level.

While it may seem like a no-brainer for groups that have long suffered from media neglect to endorse fundamental reform of the media, there are no guarantees that these groups will simply fall into place as coalition partners. Media corporations do not just lobby Congress, they lobby a lot of the groups that suffer under the current system. Some of those groups have been bought off by contributions from foundations associated with AOL, Verizon, and other media monoliths; others—particularly large sections of organized labor—have been convinced that they have a vested interest in maintaining a status quo that consistently kicks them in the teeth. Coalition building requires a tremendous amount of education and old-fashioned organizing that, by necessity in many cases, will involve pressure from the grassroots of major public-interest groups and unions in order to get the national leadership of those organizations to engage. Movement building requires that able organizers—who have already been engaged in the struggle—be provided with the resources to travel, organize, and educate. It's hard work, but it's doable. Consider the successes of the Citizen Trade Campaign and the Jubilee 2000 movement in pulling together diverse coalitions to work on complex international trade and development issues. After watching the dismal coverage of the contested election of 2000, the first stage of the Bush presidency, and the aftermath of September 11, it won't be difficult to make the case for media reform to civil libertarians, religious peace activists, Arab Americans, displaced union workers, and concerned citizens who have been enraged by the media's coverage of international and domestic developments. Millions of American know from bitter experience that a change has got to come, and this is the time to engage to begin making that change.

Recognizing the scope of the issues at stake, some will suggest that even if we succeed in building a true united front for media reform, the movement will be insufficient to take on the media conglomerates, their lobbyists and the politicians they have bought. But we believe such a united front could accomplish a great deal.

Even in these days of right-wing Congressional hegemony, it is important to remember that progressive religious denominations, consumer groups, student organizations, civil rights and women's rights coalitions, the labor movement, farm groups, prison-industrial complex activists, and foreign policy critics together provide a powerful grassroots base from which to pressure for change. If there is a single lesson that came out of the 1999 Battle of Seattle,-it is that the old slogan, "the people united will never be defeated" has more validity than many had ever believed.

Building on the lessons learned by the antiglobalization movement's successes in Seattle and around the world, we need to weave media reform in with the larger platform for democratic change in America today. The demand for social justice is the foundation of such a platform. Economic justice. Racial and ethnic justice. Environmental justice. In the United States today, the richest one percent of the population has as much money to spend as the least affluent 100 million Americans, double the ratio for just twenty years earlier. The political system reinforces this inequality by being, as is now roundly acknowledged, a plaything for big business where the interests of the balance of society have been shoved to the margins, if not forgotten. The corporate media system reinforces this inequality and limits the possibility of democratic reform. It is for these reasons that we need to weave the project of radically changing the media into the braidwork of the larger movement for peace, democracy, and social justice.

Hence we return to the point that emerged forcefully in the analysis of media reform around the world: the importance of political parties to provide necessary leadership to force the issue into the political arena. In the United States, both the upper levels of the Republican and Democratic

Parties are in the pay of the corporate media and communication giants. It is unlikely that any breakthroughs can be expected there until much spadework is done. The logical place to begin such spadework ought to be the small parties and factions of the left in America, as well as at the grassroots of the Democratic Party. The Greens have already begun to take up media reform issues, in no small measure because their presidential candidate in 1996 and 2000, Ralph Nader, has for more than a decade been the country's most prominent and consistent critic of media monopolies and the corporatization and homogenization of the news. The New Party and the Labor Party, Democratic Socialists of America, Americans for Democratic Action, and U.S. Action are also logical vehicles for advancing a media reform agenda. All of these groups need to incorporate media reform issues into their platforms and their public presentations. Ideally, these organizations, which hold similar positions on a host of issues, might adopt a shared vision, perhaps as a step toward building the sort of labor, left, green, feminist, people-of-color coalitions seen in New Zealand's Alliance Party, Iceland's Alliance, and other Third-Left groupings. At the same time, we anticipate that grassroots groups within the Democratic party, which has a membership that is dramatically more left-wing than its leadership, would embrace the cause and make media reform a component of party platforms in states and regions where progressive values can still trump corporate money.

Getting media activists on roughly the same page is essential. All the organizing in the world won't amount to a hill of beans unless there is something tangible to fight for, and to win. What is mandatory for the building of a media reform coalition—and indeed for media reform to ultimately be achieved—are proposals that can be discussed, advocated, and implemented. Media reform needs its equivalents of the Voting Rights Act or the Equal Rights Amendment—simple, basic reforms that everyone can understand, embrace, and advocate in union halls, church basements, and school assemblies. And there has to be legislation, in order to give activism a sense of focus and possibility. While many movements roam the hallways of the Capitol seeking allies, the media reform movement does not. As we have noted, several well-positioned members of Congress have expressed a willingness to introduce separate pieces of legislation around which a media reform movement could be built. The importance of a legislative agenda cannot be underestimated. Grassroots activists are pulled in a thousand directions these days. They invest their time wisely and toward a purpose, they want to be working for goals that—while difficult to achieve in the short term—are at least clearly defined. A legislative agenda allows an activist to stand up at a meeting of a mosque group or a union local and say, "We're all sick of the media, and now we can do something about it. There's a Congressional committee that's preparing to consider a bill to address a lot of what's wrong with corporate media. Let's tell our representatives in Washington that we want them to work to get it passed."

A good deal of citizen outrage at media assumes the form of boycotts and protests that intend to shame the media giants into reforming their ways. Boycotts and protests in recent years have concerned the high levels of infantile sexual content and violence in primetime TV, demeaning portrayals of women, ethnic groups, and gays and lesbians, or simply the lack of cultural diversity in entertainment programming. Likewise, there has emerged a strong movement for media literacy, which attempts to educate schoolchildren and adults about how the commercial media system operates so they may be more informed consumers. With regard to journalism, there is a "civic journalism" movement, which attempts to have journalists reform their practices to produce fare that, in theory, will provide information citizens need to make political decisions. Most of these movements are based upon real problems, but they all shy away from structural criticism that challenges the rule of corporate and commercial interests over the media. They are therefore limited in what they can accomplish. As with the "inside-the-beltway" lobbying groups that focus in particular on regulatory matters, these efforts need to be supercharged by a popular media reform movement that puts the corporate giants and their commercial logic on the hot seat. We saw this happen with the low-power FM (LPFM) movement. It began in the housing projects and inner cities, spread to volunteer-driven grassroots groups, and then to the professional activists—the policy groups inside the beltway. Together, this diverse coalition succeeded in pushing the FCC to end its twenty-two–year prohibition against issuing low-power FM radio licenses.

There is no way around it: Structural media reform is mandatory if we are serious about addressing the crisis of democracy in the United States.

After talking with activists and legislators, reviewing the progress made in other countries, and seriously examining the political realities of America today, we see the following proposals as essential—though certainly not exclusive—starting points for mobilizing a media-reform agenda:

➤ Establish a full tier of low-power noncommercial community radio and television stations across the nation.

➤ Apply existing antimonopoly laws to the media and, where necessary, expand their reach to restrict ownership of radio stations to one or two per owner. Consider similar steps for television stations and moves to break the lock of newspaper chains on entire regions.

➤ Establish a formal study and hearings to determine fair media ownership regulations across all sectors.

➤ Revamp and supercharge public broadcasting to eliminate commercial pressures, reduce immediate political pressures, and serve communities without significant disposable incomes.

➤ Provide for a $200 tax credit that every taxpayer can use to apply their tax dollars to any nonprofit medium, as long as it meets Internal Revenue Service criteria. This tool would allow new low-power radio and television stations, as well as existing community broadcasters, labor union newspapers, and other publications to have the resources to provide serious news coverage and cultural programming.

➤ Lower mailing coats for nonprofit and significantly noncommercial publications.

➤ Eliminate political candidate advertising as a condition of a broadcast license; or require that a station must run for free ads of similar length from all the other candidates on the ballot immediately after a paid political ad by a candidate.

➤ Reduce or eliminate TV advertising to children under twelve.

➤ Decommercialize local TV news. In return for the grant of access to the airwaves, which makes media companies rich, require that those companies set aside an hour each day of commercial-free time for news programming, with a budget based on a percentage of the station's revenues. This would free journalists to do the job of informing citizens, and allow stations to compete on the basis of quality news-gathering as opposed to sensationalism.

➤ Revamp copyright laws to their intended goal: to protect the ability of creative producers to earn a living, and to protect the public's right to a healthy and viable public domain.

Many of these ideas are already popular with Americans —when they get a chance to hear about them. Moreover, the enthusiasm tends to cross the political spectrum. Much of our optimism is based on research that shows how furtively the corporate media lobbies work to keep their operations in Washington outside of the public view. They suspect the same thing we do: When people hear about the corruption of communication policy making, they become appalled. When we as a country understand that it is our democratic right to reform the system, millions of people will be inclined to do so. Hence, our immediate goal in building a new media reform coalition is to get these ideas in play, and to spark discussion and debate.

Once the people of this country recognize that media is an issue and that we have the power to guide the governmental response to that issue, it will be far easier to win the small victories that provide encouragement for the more dramatic struggles that are yet to be waged. "I am convinced that when people start talking about these big issues, these fundamental issues, when they start to understand that they have the power as citizens in a democracy to take on the powers-that-be and change how things are done, then change becomes inevitable," says U.S. Representative Jesse Jackson Jr. (D-IL). "The challenge, of course, is to get people to recognize that they have that power."

The new media reform coalition we envision cannot be simply about building toward a great day of reckoning. It must also have the near term objective of organizing on the pressing policy matters that are currently in play in Washington. As we write, the FCC is considering the elimination of the remaining rules that prevent media consolidation, including bans on owning TV stations and newspapers in the same community and limits on the number of TV stations and cable TV systems a single corporation may own nationwide. The corporate media lobbying superstars are putting a full-court press on the FCC, which is hardly resistant since many of the politicians that appointed them are bankrolled by the same firms! The proposed scrapping of these regulations will increase the shareholder value of these firms dramatically, and will undoubtedly lead to a massive wave of mergers and acquisitions. If the lesson of past ownership deregulation—particularly the 1996 downsizing of radio ownership rules—provide any indication of where this change will take us, we can expect decreased funding for journalism and increased commercialism. All of this is taking place beneath the radar of corporate journalism, unreported, and unexamined—as the 1996

Telecommunications Act was—in classic corrupt fashion. As such, this is a time ripe for an organized assault by a diverse array of citizen groups—the burgeoning media reform movement.

During times of popular political resurgence throughout the twentieth century, media activism has surfaced as a significant force. It was most intense in the Progressive Era, when the rise of the modern capitalist media system was met with sustained progressive and radical criticism from the likes of Upton Sinclair, Eugene Victor Debs, and Robert M. La Follette. It would be difficult to exaggerate what a prominent role the critique of capitalist journalism played across the political culture in the first two decades of the twentieth century. In the 1930s, a heterogeneous movement arose to battle the establishment of commercial broadcasting, and a feisty consumer movement organized to radically limit advertising in our society. In the postwar years, the Congress of Industrial Organizations attempted to establish a national FM radio network, and it was one of the first casualties of the war on independent labor and the left that marked that period. In the 1960s, the underground press provided a vital underpinning for the civil rights and antiwar movements. In the 1980s, a reaction against dishonest and disreputable coverage of Latin America led to the development of a new generation of media watchdog groups. The movements of which we speak were, invariably, born of despair at the failure of print and broadcast outlets to serve what Eugene McCarthy refers to as "the most vital function of the press in a democracy—informing the people." We need no more proof than the current moment to tell us that the time to build a broad movement for media reform has arrived.

We know a thousand frustrations and disappointments lie ahead. Our journey, like that of all true reformers, will be a long one. But consider where it could take us. Consider what the U.S. media landscape would look like if all of the reform agenda we propose were enacted. Corporate dominance over the free flow of information would be curbed, and a truly diverse, creative, multicultural, public-interest media would thrive. Across the country, an amazing variety of well-funded alternative media would emerge, both local and national, many noncommercial and nonprofit. In this new world, the privatized marketplace of ideas would become more of a public commons—a vibrant flowering garden, not the commercialized strip mall we currently endure. Such media would not guarantee the end of injustice, poverty, or oppression, but they would provide a far advantaged basis for our communities to address and confront the important issues of our times.

Is this a utopian vision? Only in the sense that the abolition movement, women's suffrage, trade unions, civil rights, and Social Security were utopian ideals earlier in U.S. history.

Would a platform fight on media issues force the Democratic party to confront its drift to the right, as well as the disconnection between its conservative leadership and its more progressive mass membership? Possibly. But, at the least, it would identify media as an issue on which it is not merely reasonable but necessary to do battle. Struggles of this sort would, as well, draw sympathetic members of Congress into the fray. If Democrats take back the House, the man who will chair the powerful Judiciary Committee is John Conyers. A critic of media monopoly and homogenization, Conyers says, "I think it would be very interesting, very important, to hold hearings on some of these issues." What a remarkable leap that would be—from the first ever Congressional Town Meeting on corporate domination of the media to a House Judiciary Committee hearing on the issue.

Platform debates and Congressional hearings, while important, will not be the central purpose of this movement, however. They are merely tools for promoting the notion that media can be an issue in America. It is the implanting of that notion that we believe will lead to a leap of faith on the part of millions of Americans, who will recognize that mounting a challenge to media monoliths and their political patrons is no more an uphill climb than was mounting a challenge to the corporate polluters of the 1960s and the 1970s, or the WTO of the 1990s. That realization, the essential third component of Gaylord Nelson's equation, is critical to unleashing the sort of broad grassroots action that will finally make media a genuine and ongoing issue in America. "We go around with all this frustration over media. But most of us think it's just something that happens to us," explains Patty Allen, a labor activist who worked twenty-three years on an Oscar Mayer meatpacking line in Wisconsin and got turned on to media issues by Ralph Nader. "When I first heard Nader say that we own the airwaves and that we have a right to demand something better in return, I remember how liberating it felt. I was saying, 'Wow, now that I know this, what do I do? Where do I sign up? When can I demand a change?' I think there's a lot of people like me all over this country who are ready. But we need a sense that we're not just wasting our time."

Media need not be the enemy of our desires for democratic renewal in America. Media can be what Jefferson,

Madison, and especially the most visionary of our founders, Tom Paine, intended: the tool by which citizens ascertain the information they need to be the governors, not the governed. This is the possible future—the future when we can realistically and forcefully demand the reforms that we all know are necessary. We have seen this future taking shape. Toward the close of that first Congressional Town Meeting in Vermont, a man stood up at the end up the evening. "I don't have a question or a comment," he said. "I just want to let folks know that some of us will be getting together Tuesday to talk about organizing a group here in town to work on the media issues we've been talking about here tonight. We can't wait for somebody to tell us when to start this movement. It's going to start with us."

When there are a thousand men and women like our friend in Montpelier, standing up in a thousand towns, and cities across America, we will no longer face the question of whether reform is possible. The only question remaining will be when do we get a chance to start reading and hearing and seeing the reports of renewed democracy that will be the staple of our media, not theirs.

A NOTE ON SOURCES

References for some of the material in this book can be found in our earlier book, *It's the Media, Stupid* (Seven Stories Press, 2000). Other material comes from recent news reports and trade publications. Nearly all of the quotations come from interviews conducted by the authors. For more detailed discussions of these issues, with ample footnotes, see Robert W. McChesney, *Rich Media, Poor Democracy: Communication Politics in Dubious Times* (New Press, 2000) and Robert W. McChesney and John Bellamy Foster, *The Big Picture: Understanding Media Through Political Economy* (Monthly Review Press, 2003).

ABOUT THE AUTHORS

ROBERT W. McCHESNEY is research professor in the Institute of Communications Research and the Graduate School of Library and Information Science at the University of Illinois at Urbana-Champaign. McChesney has written or edited eight books, including the award-winning *Telecommunications, Mass Media, and Democracy: The Battle for the Control of U.S. Broadcasting, 1928–1935* (Oxford University Press, 1993), *Corporate Media and the Threat to Democracy* (Seven Stories Press, 1997), and, with Edward S. Herman, *The Global Media: The New Missionaries of Corporate Capitalism* (Cassell, 1997).

McChesney's most recent book is the multiple award-winning *Rich Media, Poor Democracy: Communication Politics in Dubious Times* (New Press, 2000).

JOHN NICHOLS is Washington correspondent for *The Nation* and associate editor of *The Capital Times* in Madison, Wisconsin. He is the author of *Jews for Buchanan: Did You Hear the One About the Theft of the American Presidency* (The New Press). He is a recipient of the Clarion Award for newspaper column writing and Inland Press Association honors for best editorial writing on an American newspaper.

NOAM CHOMSKY is a world renowned political activist, writer, and professor of linguistics at Massachusetts Institute of Technology where he has taught since 1955. He is author of many books, including Manufacturing Consent (with Edward S. Herman), and the international anti-war bestseller, 9-11.

BARBARA EHRENREICH is the author of many books, including *Blood Rites: Origins and History of the Passions of War*, *Fear of Falling: The Inner Life of the Middle Class*, and *Nickel and Dimed: On (Not) Getting By in America*.

RALPH NADER is a consumer activist and was the 2000 Green Party presidential candidate.

STRIVERS
ROW

During the 1920s and 1930s, around the time of the Harlem Renaissance, more than a quarter of a million African-Americans settled in Harlem, creating what was described at the time as "a cosmopolitan Negro capital which exert[ed] an influence over Negroes everywhere."

Nowhere was this more evident than on West 138th and 139th Streets between what are now Adam Clayton Powell, Jr., and Frederick Douglass Boulevards, two blocks that came to be known as Strivers Row. These blocks attracted many of Harlem's African-American doctors, lawyers, and entertainers, among them Eubie Blake, Noble Sissle, and W. C. Handy, who were themselves striving to achieve America's middle-class dream.

With its mission of publishing quality African-American literature, Strivers Row emulates those "strivers," capturing that same spirit of hope, creativity, and promise

SORORITY
SISTERS

SORORITY
SISTERS

A NOVEL

TAJUANA "TJ" BUTLER

VILLARD · STRIVERS ROW · NEW YORK

Earlier editions of this work were published in 1998 by Lavelle
Publishing, Smyrna, Georgia, and in 2000 by Villard Books, a division
of Random House, Inc.

Library of Congress Cataloging-in-Publication Data
Butler, Tajuana.
Sorority sisters: a novel / Tajuana "TJ" Butler.
p.   cm.
ISBN 0-375-75758-9 (tp.)
1. African American college students—Fiction.   2. African American
women—Fiction.   3. Women college students—Fiction.   4. Greek
letter societies—Fiction.   5. Female friendship—Fiction.   6. Young
women—Fiction.   I. Title.
PS3552.U829 S67   2001
813'.54—dc21   2001035024

Printed in the United States of America on acid-free paper
Villard Books website address: www.villard.com

2   4   6   8   9   7   5   3
First Strivers Row Paperback Edition

BOOK DESIGN BY DEBORAH KERNER

To the four:
Alpha Kappa Alpha Sorority, Inc.
Delta Sigma Theta Sorority, Inc.
Zeta Phi Beta Sorority, Inc.
Sigma Gamma Rho Sorority, Inc.

To all my sorors worldwide,
especially the ladies who grew through
Beta Epsilon and were known to exemplify
intelligence, beauty, charm, class,
leadership, and service to all mankind.
Ladies, I am privileged to be linked to your history.

To my blood sisters and sorors, Kim and Tracy.
I love you two.

To Caren, my third sister. May you forever
share your beautiful voice with the world.

And of course, to my sands,
Angela, Kim, Elisa, Crystal, Monique, and Melissa.
It was inevitable that we would meet.
May we always remain close
and share a sisterhood sincere and rare.

To Rebecca, the Little Sister I gained through
Big Brothers Big Sisters.
My prayers are always with you.

ACKNOWLEDGMENTS

Special thanks to God for guiding me as I make my way through life's course.

Abundant appreciation to my family and friends. To my grandmother Rachel Mack for her love and her prayers. To my parents Raymond and Linda for believing in me. To the "Atlanta Crew": Lanetia, Melinda, Keisha, Margaret, Jerry, Jeremy, Eric, Andrea, Ron, Ricky, and Regina for their support and encouraging words. To everyone at Butler's Antiques: Francis, Suzette, Reggie, and anyone else who was ever drafted to move boxes. I can never repay you. To Mary and Cleotis Westons for your advice. To Martha, Delmar, Rita, and Howard: I love you much. Also, thanks to Bianca Cockram, Ron and Suzanne Akers, Keisha Tillman, Ellis Schaffer, Ed Hebert, and the Reeses: Athena, Alberta, and Alonzo. To Kevin Williams, Phillip Ghee, Angela and Gerald Stephens, Lorenzo A. Works, Eddie DeLeon, Byron Hueston, Cordele Rolle, Marlon Woods, Rodney Carson, Mitch Drone, Allison Moolenar, Linda Marks, and Bill Watson. And to my L.A. family: Roger Lewis, Joe Wilson, Jocelyn Easley, Jamila Hunter, and the Reeds, especially Ernestine and Doran, thanks for being so welcoming. May God continue to bless your family.

To those who have continued to actively support the promotion of *Sorority Sisters* and who have contributed to my growth: Feona Huff (you are awesome!), Alfreda Vaughn (blessings to you and Tyler), Cheryl Blazej, Thomas Dye, Lisa Frederick, Deborah Jones, Norman Payne, Franklin

McGruder, Pam Ragland, Carlton Brevard, Greg O'Kafor, Mike Austin, Alfred Vaughn, Lavonia Smiley, Soror Tanya Watkins, Tony Friarson, Denese Love, Ron Hulmes, McNealy Printing & Associates, Dot Siler (and Alison), Harold Boyd, Thomas Flowers, Ellis Liddell, Kerensa Jackson, Terry Bankston, Dawn Jones. Terry Robinson, Soror Ebony Brown, Wilfred Lee, Larry Scott, Detrick Garvin, Soror LaWanda Page, Ayana Davis, Lynn Ware, Nicole Bailey-Williams, my wonderful editor Melody Guy, Mary Bahr, Bill Green, Dupree, Miller & Associates, and William A. Green. Also to my former interns: Rashauna Crenshaw, Latosha Campbell, Kejar Butler, and Tiffany Batiste-Gilmore.

Also to the writers and small publishers who have inspired and taught me to remain positive and focused, including, but not limited to: Michael Baisden, Breggie James, Eric Jerome Dickey, Thomas Green, Sheneska Jackson, Mel Banks, James Clingman, Camika Spencer, and Jessie Brown.

Best wishes to all the African-American booksellers who gave an "unknown" a chance, including, but not limited to: Clara Villarosa, Emma Rogers, Antoine and Teresa Coffer, Janet Mosley, Amir Tibbs, Carrie Cole, Jackie Perkins, James Muhammad, Charles Muhammad, Janice Doctor, Renecia Glass, Pius Eze, Tariq and Geneva Jones, Jim Rogers, Vera Warren, Jennifer Turner, William and Stephana Clark, Ernestine Carreathers, Rasheed Ali, Mututa, Carla Allison, Robyn Robinson, Michele Lewis, Richard Beasley, Luther Warner, Larry Cunningham, Felicia Wintons, Bill Hart, Tyrone Cousins, Sherri McGee, and Ashraf Tazibo. Keep promoting good literature.

Thanks to all the groups and organizations who have presented me with such thoughtful gifts. Also a special thank you to everyone who supported *The Desires of a Woman: Poems Celebrating Womanhood.*

Because my heart knows what my mind sometimes forgets, insert your name here if I forgot: _____

PART
ONE

Dear Heavenly Father,

Thank you for developing me into a beautiful and talented woman.

Thank you for being my protector and my guide.

And as I make my way along my journey, bless me with the wisdom to make intelligent choices.

ONE

Y ou know how much I care about you," Jason whispered in Cajen's ear. "All of those months I worked so hard just to get your phone number, and now you're gonna question how I feel about you?" Cajen didn't know what to say. She couldn't help but wonder if he was running a game on her, or if he was feeding her the same lines he had apparently used to get with all the other girls on campus he was rumored to be spending time with.

"Why should I believe you?" she asked. "We both know about your reputation, and I can't overlook that." Although she tried to remain strong and not let her guard down, Cajen's heart was racing so fast she knew her effort wasn't working. She hoped her question would not lead to an answer that would break the spell he had her under. She had never been so captivated, and clung to the emotional rush she was experiencing.

"Baby, I ain't thinkin' about nobody else. Right now, you're the only thing on my mind. Believe me, I don't usually work this hard to get to know someone, especially if she's not interested. And you know I couldn't get a decent hello from you about a month ago . . . now I know you're worth the effort," he said, then lightly kissed every inch of her lips, as if they were the most precious possessions he'd ever encountered.

Jason always knew what to say to keep her enchanted. He had a way of touching her just by looking into her eyes. She didn't want to fall for his charm, but it was too late. He was so suave, so smooth. Cajen was hooked, and there was nothing she could do about it. She wanted so much to believe he really cared about her, but he had quite a reputation for being a ladies' man, and he belonged to a fraternity on their school's campus whose members took pride in being known as "nasty," "freaky," and "able to handle more than their share of women."

Jason had been very persistent in trying to get Cajen to notice him. He often showed up outside of her classes and insisted on walking her back to her dorm room. He'd call and leave the cutest little messages on her answering machine. And when they did talk on the phone, he was charming, witty, and never once seemed only to want sex from her. Although the topic did come up, it was never the main focus of their brief telephone conversations.

Once he even had the fraternity's pledges sing "You Are So Beautiful" outside her dorm room window and ask if their big brother "Shaky Jason" could have the honor of taking her to the movies. After that incident and their date, during which Jason was a complete gentleman, Cajen found it easier to ignore the rumors around campus about him being seen with some girl in the student activity center, or seen leaving various girls' dorm rooms at all hours of the morning. But she felt that even if the rumors were true, they would soon stop, because Jason convinced her that she was truly special to him and somehow different from all those other girls with whom he was simply passing time.

Yeah, she thought, I guess Jason really does care for me. She snuggled close and allowed him to hold her tightly as they lay in his dorm bed. Cajen was overwhelmed by Jason. Sometimes she'd feel so emotional when she was with him that she'd lose the ability to hold an intelligent conversation. But conversing was never important because when they were together they spent most of their time being close, with Jason finding new places and new ways to lavish her with kisses.

She had never been in his dorm room this late. It was two A.M. on a Saturday, and Jason's dark room was lit by a purple light that dimly shined out of a lamp on his desk, surrounded by books, folders, and scattered papers, most of which were party flyers. Cajen thought, if he's trying to create an intimate atmosphere, the light is definitely working. She almost forgot she was in a dorm room; it felt more like they were in a secluded, faraway place. Although they were under the covers, Cajen was fully dressed except for her sandals, which were neatly placed by the side of his bed.

Jason worked to intensify the mood. He lifted up her white shirt and attempted to unfasten her bra, but Cajen moved his hands away. She didn't feel comfortable—she felt like they were on one of those TV shows where a boy and girl are in the front room making out while her parents are in their bedroom sleeping. Only their scene was a little different. Cajen and Jason were sharing their intimate space with Ken, Jason's nerdy roommate, who was sleeping in the bed just across the room.

"Why did you stop me?" he asked.

"I want the timing to be right for us. You know what I mean. Ken is right there, and he might hear us." Cajen pulled her shirt down and pulled away. She did want to be with Jason—badly—but this wasn't how she envisioned it. She hoped their first time together would be as special as her first sexual experience. It had been her prom night, and Chris, her first love and former boyfriend of three years, was just as nervous as she was, because it was his first time too. They were in a nice hotel and had champagne and soft music. She would never forget that night, or how "right" it was. But now she was in a musty dorm room with a man she couldn't honestly say she trusted, and she hoped his roommate wouldn't wake up to their intimate, yet not-so-intimate love scene. Jason, on the other hand, didn't seem to be concerned by Ken's presence, because he continued to pull her close and kiss her in such a way that it distracted her from his hands, which worked steadily to undress her.

"Don't you worry your beautiful self about Ken. He won't hear us," Jason promised. "That boy sleeps like a rock, and besides, you and me, we can make slow love and whisper how good it feels into each other's ears," he said, and lightly stroked her ear with his tongue. Hypnotized, she almost didn't notice that her bra was unfastened and that Jason's smooth hands were cupping her breasts. Although her body shivered with desire for him to continue, she asked herself, Why am I doing this? Not yet, not yet.

"Cajen, I want you so bad!" he whispered in her ear. He rubbed her cheeks and looked deep into her eyes. "I need to be with you."

When Jason said that, she couldn't imagine stopping what was about to happen between them. And even though she thought he was moving fast, she didn't know *how* to stop him. She didn't want to stop him. She had no control—it was lost in Jason's charm. As Jason entered Cajen, it didn't matter to her that they weren't in a committed relationship or that his roommate was in the next bed. It didn't even matter that Jason wasn't using a condom.

When Cajen woke up the next morning, she immediately looked across the room to see if Ken was still asleep. Luckily his bed was empty, because she was not ready to face him. He probably went to the campus library, she said to herself, which is exactly where I need to be going today, but I'd rather stay right here. She turned her undivided attention to Jason, who was still sleeping. He was gorgeous, with dark skin, a bald head, sexy, long eyelashes, and the muscular body of a god. She felt safe being close to him. Entranced by his masculinity, she wasn't too mad at herself for breaking her number one rule last night, and assured herself she would make Jason use a condom the next time they slept together.

Cajen couldn't believe she even had a first time with Jason. The only other guy she connected with on campus was her good friend Eric. Eric reminded her a lot of Chris, her first love, which is what attracted her to him. He was a nice guy who would do anything to make her smile. They met when Cajen came to the campus the previous summer, for freshman orientation. They were in the same campus tour group, and hit it off instantly. They exchanged telephone numbers and addresses and kept in touch until school started. Once the fall semester began, they spent every weekend together going to football games, movies, and just hanging out, until she started seeing Jason. Cajen knew that she and Eric would only ever be platonic friends. They never talked about their relationship being more than it already was, and he never tried to kiss her. When they discussed sex, it was different from how she and Jason talked about it. It was more like talking about sex with her girlfriends. But Eric always wanted to spend time with her, and they always had interesting conversations.

Sometimes they'd waste valuable study time discussing their favorite foods, religious beliefs, or dreams for the future.

She didn't feel that way with Jason. They communicated in a different way. She felt intimidated by him, as if he were on some sophisticated level for which she wasn't quite ready. It was that mysterious side of him that attracted her and made her feel so vulnerable whenever they were together. Last night was so intimate, and she hoped such a big step would bring them closer.

Maybe Jason really does care about me and isn't the player everyone says he is. And just maybe he will tell me he wants a commitment, soon. Carried away with her dreaming, she continued. Who knows, maybe we'll get married after he graduates, and we'll have one kid and a dog. Jason would probably want a Doberman or something ferocious like that. I haven't even met his parents yet. I wonder when I'll get the opportunity to meet them. And after I pledge all of my sorors will get to be my bridesmaids, and his fraternity brothers will be groomsmen.

Jason awoke to Cajen staring at him. He looked into her eyes, then kissed her on the cheek. "Good morning, sexy," he said in a deep morning voice, then hopped over, got out of bed, and put on his robe and shower shoes. "I've got a busy day, baby. We're going into Hell Week, you know, and we have to make sure the pledges know their stuff!"

Her daydream interrupted, she reluctantly came back to reality and responded, "Good morning to you too. So why are y'all so hard on the pledges?" she asked. "They are going to be your brothers one day. How can anybody be so hard on somebody they will one day call brother?"

"They might be our brothers one day. Might, that's the key word. No one is guaranteed to cross over into the Greek world. Cajen, everybody, with no exceptions, has to prove themselves to somebody else in order to get what they want. I had to prove myself to you before you let me be with you, and the pledges have to prove themselves to the frat in order to become our brothers."

Cajen half listened to Jason's speech, because she was trying to figure out how she was going to get from his dormitory to hers, which was just across the walkway, without anybody noticing her so as not to feed the rumor mill. She decided the best plan would be to just go for it; to not get too excited about it, and to just walk toward her dorm as quickly as possible. She got out of bed, stretched, and began to put back on the clothes she had worn last night. Cajen Myers had an adorable figure, which complemented every outfit she wore, and was "cute as a button," as she was often told. She wore her hair in a bob that hung above her shoulders, and her bangs were cut just above her eyebrows, which were naturally arched. She had high cheekbones and deep brown eyes that were as warm as her personality. Most of the college men could not help but stare as she walked by on her way to class. She was unofficially declared one of the most desirable girls on campus by unanimous vote of the basketball players, the football players, and all the fraternities. And although women envied her beauty, they couldn't help but like her. Her attitude and personality were addictive. She was smart, witty, and always made a special effort to make everyone she met feel special and good about themselves.

After dressing, she watched Jason prepare for his day and couldn't help but wonder what he was thinking and why he was in such a hurry to get his day started. After all, it was a Saturday. Focused on setting up his ironing board, he didn't look up once. He got out a T-shirt with his fraternity's letters on it and some ripped jean shorts and socks, all the while not saying anything. He pulled out his boots, then paused and looked over at Cajen while shaking his head and smiling. She didn't speak either. Watching him move around, she became paralyzed with disturbing thoughts. What is he thinking? Did he enjoy being with me last night? Does he still feel the same? Will we ever share another night like last night? At a loss for words, she hoped he would break the ice and save her from her troubling thoughts.

Rescuing her unknowingly, he spoke. "Girl, you know something?"
"Yeah?"

"You are so fine . . . and last night was so good!" He walked over to her and without touching her, pecked her cheek. "So, I'll see you later," he whispered in her ear in that sexy deep voice that drove her crazy. He was so cool about the whole thing. He seemed distant.

Maybe I'm overreacting, she thought. Cajen wasn't sure how she was supposed to react. A myriad questions raced through her mind. Does he really care about me like he said? Is he having second thoughts about what we did last night? She decided to act cool as well and not let on how deeply she felt about him and about what had happened between them, because she was sure that's what he was doing—trying to play it cool.

"Yeah, I'll call you later," she responded. "I know you'll be busy with the pledges, so if you're not here, I'll leave a message on your machine. But if you find some free time outside of your big brotherly duties, give me a ring."

Jason flashed her another smile. "All right, sexy!" He grabbed his purple pail that contained soap, shampoo, toothbrush, and toothpaste, and walked toward the door. Cajen grabbed her purse and followed him out. He turned left and headed for the showers, and she went right, to the stairwell and out the door toward her dorm.

TWO

H ow is my beautiful daughter this morning?" Patricia asked. Every Sunday morning since Stephanie Madison had left for college it was their ritual to call each other and gossip about the events of their week.

"Hi, Mommy," she responded in her Mommy-I'm-so-happy-to-be-talking-to-you-because-I-need-to-feel-like-a-little-girl-even-if-it's-only-for-a-moment voice. "I'm just recuperating. I was getting ready to call you myself because I've got to tell you about the crazy weekend I had."

"I can't wait to hear, but first let me tell you about my crazy weekend. Your daddy woke up Saturday morning all out of the blue with the bright idea that he wanted to purchase a Land Cruiser. Tell me what your father is going to do with all that truck! So here we are spending all day Saturday trying to find a black Land Cruiser, in Savannah. And, of course, he wanted it loaded. So we ended up driving all the way to Atlanta to find the perfect sport utility vehicle. And you know how particular your daddy is. We did get a good deal on the damn thing. It's really nice too. But I'll tell you what, when that man gets his mind set to do something, there is no stopping him."

Her father hadn't been home the last few times Stephanie called, which was odd because he was usually in the background yelling comments until her mother passed him the phone. Once Stephanie called on a Saturday night to ask her father's permission to charge a plane ticket, hotel accommodations, and a ticket to see *Cats* on Broadway on the credit card he had given her when she graduated (she always asked if her purchases went over her $500-per-month limit). He wasn't home, and her mother was upset and didn't seem to know where he was. She told Stephanie to charge whatever she needed to and to go ahead and purchase a theater ticket for her friend Sidney, who was going to New York with her. She added that if Howard had a problem with it, then he'd have to talk to her.

"Where's Daddy?" Stephanie asked her mother now.

"Where else! Riding around in that oversized SUV. He left about thirty minutes ago. He's picking up Richard and Will. After they get tired of riding in circles, showing off, they're going golfing. I truly believe that man is going through his midlife crisis. I'm trying to be supportive, but he's driving me crazy. I needed a break from him, so I told him I was going to stay here today and let him enjoy his new toy with his friends. Now I'm going to pamper myself. I've decided that since he'll be gone awhile, I'm going to listen to some jazz, sit back in the hot tub, and relax my muscles. Then I'm going to inspire my mind by reading a few chapters from Susan Taylor's *Lessons in Living*. Have you read her book yet?"

"No, but I do need to get it. I heard that it's really inspirational. And Momma, I hate to tell you, but according to his track record, Daddy has been going through this midlife crisis for a long time. Remember when he had to have a new Lexus when they first came out? Same difference. Momma, Daddy's just a big kid. He's never gonna grow up. You, for one, should know that by now." Although it was obvious, Stephanie was trying to convince her mother that nothing was changing between her and her husband. But they seemed to be growing apart, and although she wanted to help, she couldn't do anything to fix their situation. Patricia acted as if nothing was wrong, but Stephanie knew it was only to protect her. Nevertheless, she often wondered if her father was having an affair. The thought of him being with another woman disturbed her, so when it crossed her mind, she forced herself to think about something more pleasant. She loved both her parents and wanted them to stay together. Once upon a time they seemed the perfect couple. They gave her hope that she would have a sincere and committed relationship in her future, and she needed them to continue giving her hope.

"You're right, Steph. You would think I'd be used to raising that overgrown child by now," her mother joked, in a tone meant to convey that everything was okay. Then she changed the subject, "So tell me about your crazy weekend. What happened? Did you go out with Jeff?"

"Yeah, I went out with him Friday night, but as usual he was rude to the waiter, and all he talked about was himself, basketball, and mutual funds, and at the end of the night, he wanted to get his groove on. Momma, there's more to life than sex, sports, and money, but no one could ever tell that to Jeff. He's so boring and uptight and I'm so bored with him."

"Good!" Patricia said, wishing Jeff out of the picture. She had told Stephanie, many times before this conversation, to move on and stop clinging to him. But she knew Jeff was her daughter's security blanket. She prayed that God would perform a minor miracle and move Stephanie to stop seeing him. "So, when did the excitement start? Come on, tell me the juicy stuff."

"Well, Saturday morning Sidney and I went shopping. Oh Momma, I found the cutest little dress for rush, but I'll tell you about that later. Anyway, we stopped in the record shop to get a new CD, and I saw the man of my dreams. He was clean-cut, extremely handsome, intelligent, and he had the smell of money all over him."

"Stephanie, money is not everything."

"And he gave me this look that could melt ice. Anyway, I smiled at him, and he walked over and asked me what I was doing later. I told him I would be at my apartment sipping on some wine and listening to this new Maxwell CD. He smiled back and said that he had a better offer. . . ." Stephanie always made it a point to be honest with her mother about most things.

"And what did he mean by that, young lady?"

"Shhhh, Momma, just listen. You're always interrupting. To make a long story short, remember that nice restaurant that you and Daddy took me and Jeff to the last time you visited? Remember how nice and exclusive it was—?"

"He took you there?" her mother interrupted, even though she knew her daughter hated it when she tried to predict her stories.

"No. But the restaurant that we went to put that one to shame. He took me to a place called Solomon's, on the outskirts of the city. I hadn't even heard of it before then. Anyway, we had a good time driving to the place in his convertible Porsche. The conversation was good, and he looked so good that I was trying to figure if we'd end up with one kid or two and what their names were going to be. Anyway, we ate dinner and began talking and wouldn't you know it—"

"He's married!?" Her mother interrupted again.

"No, Momma! There you go again. As I was saying, wouldn't you know it, there had to be something wrong with this perfect picture. The man I was supposed to vacation with in Aruba, the man I was supposed to marry and grow old with, let me down."

"What?"

"I never thought in a million years I would experience anything like this."

"What, Steph, what is it? Is your daddy gonna have to get his shotgun out?"

"No, Momma. We were having casual conversation and everything was going well, at least I thought so. That was until the conversation took a one-eighty-degree turn for the worse. Momma, we started talking about sex. Don't ask me how we got on the subject, but he was extremely open about his sexual history. I didn't feel like he was trying to be perverted or dirty or anything like that. You know, he was just talking about how young he was when he lost his virginity and how he wished he had waited a while longer before becoming sexually active—"

"You had sex with the man?" Another interruption.

"No, I did not. Shhhh. I told him I was sure a lot of people felt the same way as he did. I wasn't offended by the conversation at first. And suddenly, out of nowhere, he mentioned that he was not ashamed to talk about his sexuality and how being open and honest were both important factors to building a solid relationship. Somehow, in the middle of that whole spill, he exposed the fact that he was bisexual, but that he planned to marry a woman and someday have a family. However, he did say that until that day came, he would not limit his dating sphere, or something crazy like that."

"What!"

"I lost my appetite. I couldn't even finish my meal. He kept talking, but at that point I was in such a state of disbelief that I hardly heard another word that came out of his mouth. When I finally came out of my trance, he was asking me if I wanted to have a nightcap at his condo downtown. The nerve! I calmly told him that I was tired and had a long day ahead of me and needed to turn in early. Then I politely asked him to take me home."

"So, turns out Don Juan is Don Juana too." Stephanie's mother laughed so hard that she lost her breath. "I'm just glad you made it home safely. I told you to drive your own car on the first date. Did you even get his full name?" her mother asked, showing motherly concern, which was why Stephanie loved her so much.

"David Rodrickson, not that it matters. And I don't see what's so funny! Dating is overrated, and I'm not enjoying it one bit. I just want to find the perfect man and start our lives together. Is that too much to ask? But how am I supposed to find him if I keep running into jerks?"

"Steph, going out and meeting men is fun. Ten years from now you'll look back on this episode and laugh even harder than I'm laughing now. Meeting men who are wrong for you helps you to develop an image of the kind of man who will be right for you. It teaches you what values are important. You learn from dating what you can deal with in a relationship and what you can't. And when you do find the right person, you'll know it. How many times do I have to tell you, stop being in a hurry to find Mr. Right! You have your whole life ahead of you, trust me. Mommy always knows best."

"But I want him now." Although she was pretty honest with her mother, Stephanie never told her of the many short-term relationships she found herself involved in when she thought she was with Mr. Right. After a month or so, she usually realized that even if he had money, he was not the one. Unfortunately, she usually didn't figure it out until after she was intimate with her man of the hour.

"Is it my fault or your father's that you are so spoiled? So tell me about your new dress for rush. I remember my rush. I was so nervous, and what followed . . . I don't even want to go into it, but I'm so glad I had the experience of pledging and being a part of such a positive sisterhood. I know that you'll feel the same. I'm just glad you finally got off your high horse and decided to write your letter of intent. I was beginning to worry there for a while that my only daughter would not be carrying on our family legacy. Your grandmother, all your aunts, and most of your cousins are proud members, and we all hoped you too would someday join."

"Well, your wish is coming true, and maybe they'll accept me," Stephanie said in an uncertain tone.

"What are you talking about, maybe? You are Patricia White-Madison's daughter. They have no choice but to let you in, not to mention the fact that you are the best thing that'll ever happen to that chapter. Oh, Steph, somebody's at the door. I wonder who it could be? I wasn't expecting any visitors. Well, honey, call me after rush and let me know how everything goes. I love you. Oh yeah, and make sure you take a picture in your dress. I want to see how beautiful you look in it."

"Okay, Momma, I will. Talk to you later, and I love you too."

After Stephanie hung up, she stared around at her bedroom. The furniture was contemporary, and the room, as well as the entire apartment, was decorated with the same exquisite taste she had acquired from her adoptive mother. *Why isn't Momma my biological mother? Life would be so much easier if she were.*

Somehow Stephanie could not be as confident as her mother that she would be accepted into the sorority. The reason she held back so long from writing, although her mother never knew, was because she feared that somehow someone would figure out that underneath all of her expensive clothes, expensive car, and expensive tastes, was the true Stephanie, the one who was born to a drug-addicted mother who could not care for her and had put her up for adoption.

Stephanie feared that if any of her friends, or anyone else who was a part of her college community, found out she was not a true "Madison," she would not be able to show her face anywhere, let alone be accepted into such a prestigious sorority.

THREE

Anthony held the door of the Waffle House open while Malena Adams walked out. Right behind her came Philip, who was giving Tammy a piggyback. He moved so fast that they nearly knocked Malena down. Tammy and Philip were so into each other that it was borderline sickening. Malena and Tammy were juniors and had been good friends since freshman year, and they had met Anthony and Philip one night when they went out to the Noncommissioned Officers Club on the army base that was about forty-five minutes from the campus.

It was a beautiful Sunday morning, and the two couples had just finished breakfast, during which they recapped the weekend; they'd enjoyed bowling and going to a comedy show on the army base where Anthony and Philip were stationed. The four of them had been double-dating nearly every weekend for the past year and had grown to be close friends. Whenever Anthony and Philip were on field duty, the two girls would rent movies and spend boring weekends in their apartment watching television and eating popcorn and whatever assortment of junk food they could find.

Malena enjoyed spending time with Anthony, but her attention was shifting toward Ray, an intelligent brother she'd met when she was sneaking a peek at the sorority paraphernalia at the campus bookstore. She found out that he was in a fraternity, and she told him in confidence that she was interested in joining a sorority herself, but she wouldn't tell him which one. They talked for about fifteen minutes in the bookstore. Malena was attracted to him and was floored when he gave her his number and told her that it would make his semester if she called. Since that day she realized that she really wasn't into Anthony, at least not to the same degree he cared about her.

For the past two and a half months she'd spent her weekdays with Ray, studying, talking on the phone, and occasionally meeting him in the school cafeteria for lunch or dinner. They had only gone on a few of what she considered "official" dates—dinner and/or a movie—because she always had weekend plans with Anthony, but she was ready for a change. She liked everything about Ray and wanted to spend more time with him and less with Anthony.

Philip opened the car door for Tammy, who whined, "I guess we won't see each other again until Friday, huh?"

"Yeah, Friday. But we'll talk on the phone every night until then," Philip responded, kissing her cheek.

"I wish we didn't have to be apart," Tammy groaned.

"You act like you're not going to ever see each other again," Malena joked.

"Yeah, Phil man, you're scaring me! I'm beginning to think that you're falling in love or something," Anthony said. "You didn't hear it from me, but every night at nine, just like clockwork, Phil runs down to the phone booth outside the barracks and calls Tammy. If all the phones are being used, he finds the weakest dude on the phone and bullies him until he gets off."

"Now that's love!" Malena said. He and Malena laughed so hard that Philip and Tammy couldn't help but join in.

"But," Malena continued, "don't forget, this weekend will have to be cut short because Tammy and I have rush on Sunday."

Tammy turned around and gave Malena, who was in the backseat of the car, a questioning look. "What does Sunday's rush have to do with Saturday night?"

"We have to get ready for Sunday. You haven't even written your letter of intent yet, and we have midterms coming up . . . at least I do."

"I promise I'll have my letter ready by the weekend. And since when have you been so concerned about studying hard for midterms?"

"Since I saw the rush signs hanging all over campus warning me that

I need to get my act together if I want to pledge and still graduate on time. That's when. Anyway, you two are grown and can do what you want, but Tony and I have already discussed it."

She hated to stretch the truth, but she'd already spent a few extra hours at the library every night during the past two weeks to prepare herself for midterms, and she had written her letter of intent before the semester began. As a freshman she decided she'd wait until her junior year to pledge, and had plenty of time to plan for this semester. It was all part of her bigger plan on the road to success. She hated to lie to Anthony about her availability Saturday, but she already had plans with Ray, and wouldn't dare miss a night with him. Actually, she didn't even want to spend the upcoming Friday with Anthony, because she would be too distracted thinking about Saturday night.

"Whatever!" Tammy said, and rolled her eyes, then abruptly turned around and fastened her seat belt.

Phil and Anthony always took turns driving the forty-five minutes to and from base to campus to pick up and drop off their girls. Today it was Phil's turn, and it seemed to Malena that he was driving slower than usual. He and Tammy were in the front seat kissing and whispering in each other's ears, while she and Tony sat in silence.

When they arrived at their apartment, Malena jumped out of the car. She couldn't get out fast enough, and hoped for a quick good-bye. Ray had gone home over the weekend to visit his family, but had promised he would call her today, whenever he got back, and she didn't want to miss his call. Phil opened the trunk and gave them their overnight bags. Dreading good-bye, he and Tammy stayed by the car and clung to each other. Malena and Anthony walked to the apartment door. She opened the door and dropped her bag in the doorway.

"Are you okay, Malena?" Anthony asked.

"I'm fine. Why wouldn't I be?" she snapped. "Why are you always so concerned about me?" Malena was not a cruel person, but the thought of kissing Anthony good-bye made her feel uneasy. He was a good guy, however, and she hated that she felt that way about him.

"I don't know, I'm just wondering." Anthony gave Malena a concerned look, then changed the subject. "Even though I'll see you Friday,

I'll wish you good luck on your midterms and good luck with rush now. You seem to be on such a mission to be prepared that I know it'll all be good."

Malena sensed sarcasm in his voice. "Anthony, I really am concerned about making sure my grades are stable before I go on line, because from what I understand, pledging has been known to damage GPAs. Don't take it personally . . . we'll make sure to have a good time Friday, because after Sunday I can't be too sure about when we'll see each other again." Not wanting to break his heart, Malena figured she'd get through one more date with him before she went on line. After she crossed, she would tell him that with all the time they'd spent apart and with all of the changes she'd just gone through, she needed time for herself. She knew it was dishonest, but how could she possibly tell him that she'd fallen in love with somebody she barely knew, and that she didn't want to see him again, and that all the time she'd spent with him meant nothing? She couldn't bring herself to be that cruel. She'd give him time, while she was pledging, to realize he didn't really care about her as much as he thought.

"You know I want this for you just as much as you do for yourself, but one part of me really doesn't want to spend all of that time away from you. You know I care about you, right?" His declaration chipped away at her conscience.

"Yeah, I know you do." She couldn't bring herself to lie and say the same. "Thanks for being so understanding, I'll see you Friday, okay?" They kissed good-bye. Anthony walked toward the car confused and Malena went into the apartment feeling guilty. She really liked Anthony. He wasn't the greatest-looking guy, but he was sensitive and supportive and fun to be around. He listened to her when she talked about her dream of one day owning her own public relations firm. Even though he couldn't really relate, he listened to her dreams of pledging and of one day being able to call somebody "Soror." Malena's biggest problem with him was that he was not a dreamer. He was content with his job in the military, and wasn't concerned about going to school so he could move up the ranks quicker. He wasn't even sure when or if he was going to leave the military, and what he would do with his life if he did. Although he had good qualities and values, he wasn't the kind of man she could see herself marrying, or even having a monogamous relationship with. He was not the type of person who would be beneficial in helping her with her master plan to be both economically and socially secure.

Malena walked into the kitchen and checked the answering machine, hoping to hear a message from Ray. There were five messages, and she couldn't wait for Tammy to come inside, so she hit "play." There was a message from Ray. He wanted her to go to a movie with him that was playing on campus that night. It started at nine.

"Of course I will!" Malena responded to the voice on the recorder. "But what will I wear?" She grabbed her overnight bag and went to her room.

While rummaging through her closet, she heard the front door open and close, then she heard Tammy checking the answering machine. After the last message, Tammy knocked on her door. "Can I come in?" she asked.

"Come on."

"So you got a date tonight?"

"Yeah, I'm going out with Ray. I'm just trying to figure out how to be casual and cute at the same time," Malena said. She was shuffling through clothes, but nothing caught her eye.

"What just happened with you and Anthony?"

"Nothing, but I guess you're so in love with Phil that you forgot about our little conversation when we were waiting for them to pick us up on Friday. I told you that Ray and I had something planned for Saturday night.

"Oh Malena, I'm so sorry. I totally forgot."

"Don't worry about it, everything's okay. I guess I'm just not cut out to juggle two men."

"But you've done such a good job for . . . how long has it been, two and a half, three months?" Tammy joked.

"Yeah, about three months too long. It's time to go ahead and let Tony go. I'm beginning to feel guilty. I'm truly beginning to fall in love with Ray. Anyway, after I cross, if I'm accepted, I'm gonna have to somehow break up with him. I faked it all weekend, but to be honest there's nothing there."

"You mean you faked it during sex?"

"No, I mean I faked enjoying his company. We didn't have sex."

"Really." Tammy seemed surprised. "So what did he say?"

"He said he wasn't going to force me to do anything I didn't want to do. And he didn't. He just held me all night."

"He is a good man, you know."

"I do. That's what makes it so hard."

Both Malena and Tammy saw the breakup coming all along, but they enjoyed their couples weekends, and hated seeing them come to an end.

"I'm one year short of graduating. I want to try to work on building a strong relationship with Ray," Malena expressed.

"I thought you said he wasn't ready yet."

"Well, he wasn't at first, but I think he's beginning to think about settling down. He graduates this spring and already has a job lined up with a good company downtown. The only thing left to do is get engaged, right?"

"Malena, like my grandmother always says, 'Don't count your chickens before they hatch.' The relationship is still new. Also, don't forget, Tony's ready and willing to marry you. All you have to do is say the word."

"You think so?"

"You don't see the way he looks at you. He's put you on a pedestal. And according to Phil, he does nothing but talk about you nonstop. He even said he could see himself spending the rest of his life with you."

"Stop making me feel guilty. I think Ray could be the true love of my life. I need to break things off with Tony so he can go on with his life and find someone who will be able to love him back. He deserves that. I'm just gonna have to be woman enough to tell him Friday."

"What? Friday? No. I think you should wait."

"I don't know. We'll see." Malena had already made up her mind, but she didn't want to continue the discussion. "So do you want to go to the library for a few hours? I'll figure out what to wear for my date later."

"I guess so," Tammy said. "Just let me get my study sweats on."

After studying at the library and grabbing a bite to eat, Malena and Tammy arrived at their apartment exhausted. They walked through the door, and each went toward her separate room. The apartment was sparsely furnished with bits and pieces of used furniture they had collected from their families and friends. They had individual bathrooms attached to their bedrooms. Malena walked straight to her room, dropped her book bag, and went to the bathtub. She ran hot water and poured bath beads under the running water. She was going to soak in her bath and decide what she would wear tonight, and how to make sure Ray remained in her life, even while she was pledging. She was also going to go over her plan to somehow break things off with Anthony.

She became totally relaxed while immersed in the warm bath. She had already decided what to do about both Tony and Ray, and was on to daydreaming about what she would name her future PR firm and who her clients would be. She dreamed of representing Jim Carrey, Michael Jackson, Madonna, and Dennis Rodman. "Maybe they're a little too outlandish," she thought out loud. "Maybe I'll deal with milder personalities like Michael Jordan, and Brandy, oh yeah, and Angela Bassett and Whitney Houston."

Tammy knocked on the door and interrupted her dream. "Ray called while I was on the phone."

"Why didn't you tell me?"

"I'm telling you now! I was talking to my mother when he called. Anyway, he said he'll be here to pick you up in thirty minutes."

"What? How long ago did he call?"

"Oh, about five, ten minutes ago," Tammy responded nonchalantly.

"Great!" Malena yelled and quickly got out of the tub. There was no way she'd be ready in time.

She rushed, applying makeup and dressing simultaneously, and made herself presentable by the time he knocked on the front door.

FOUR

Tiara Johnson worked on her letter of intent for two days. She was frustrated and knew she would need help to make it exceptional. But she couldn't ask just anybody for help. Rhonda was her only logical solution. She looked around her dorm room. There were posters of her favorite entertainers hanging on the walls, including the love of her life, LL Cool J. She loved her room because she didn't have a roommate for the first time in her entire life, and she was able to decorate it however she chose.

She got up from her desk, stretched across her bed, and called her Big Sister. Although it was late, she had to call. Tiara had been working on her letter of intent for all night, but couldn't seem to get down on paper what she really wanted to say. Becoming frustrated, she figured her Big Sister, Rhonda, could help her out before she lost her mind. She would make it up to her another time. The phone rang four times before Rhonda answered.

"Hello!" said the groggy voice.

"Rhonda, you just gotta help me! I know it's late but I ain't gonna be able to get no sleep till I finish this letter."

"It's 'I'm not going to be able to sleep,' Tiara. And what do I *just have* to help you with?"

"You're right, but I won't be able to sleep until it's done. I want it to be perfect, flawless. They won't accept nothing that's not above average. You know that."

"Tiara . . . never mind." Rhonda was going to correct Tiara's gram-

23

mar again, but she decided to let it slide this time. Although Tiara had made her Big Sister promise she would stop her every time she "butchered a sentence," it was late at night, Rhonda was tired, and Tiara seemed too excited to care about using a double negative in her sentence structure. Instead of nit-picking, she decided to ask Tiara what she was so worked up about this late at night. "What? Who? Tiara, who are you writing to, and why is it so important that you wake me up at one in the morning to help you complete some letter? As a matter of fact, why don't I call you from work tomorrow?"

"No! Rhonda, you don't understand. I'm working on my letter of intent to become a pledge and eventually a member of your 'distinguished' sorority, but I cain't . . . I mean, I can't manage to find the words to make me sound distinguishable enough to be accepted or even considered. I know what I wanna say, but I don't know how. Maybe I'm tryin' too hard. Rhonda, please stay up and help me. I will be forever grateful. I'll wash your dishes for you the next weekend that I'm home. I'll take Freeman out for a walk to the park, and you know how much I hate walking Freeman in the park. He barks too much. And Rhonda, I'll even—"

"Okay, Tiara, I get the picture. I'll help you, because if I don't I know you'll keep me on this phone all night begging for my help. It will be a no-win situation either way."

"Thank you, thank you, thank you! You're the greatest Big Sister in the world. I'm so glad that I was matched with you."

Tiara never knew quite how to thank Rhonda enough for everything she had done for her since they were matched up through the Big Brothers Big Sisters program back in Gary, Indiana. She was instrumental in shaping Tiara's young adult life, and it was because of Rhonda's intervention that she was in college, and in her dorm room, and writing a letter to become a member of what Tiara considered the greatest sorority in the world—the same sorority of which her Big Sister, Rhonda, was a member. She looked up to her Big Sister, and wanted to follow in her footsteps and someday "be somebody." She also planned to one day be a Big Sister to a little girl and positively influence her life the way Rhonda continued to influence hers.

"I know I'm great, but I do expect you to keep your promise and visit me when you come home. I realize you are a big-time college sophomore now, and coming home to visit your Big Sister may cramp your image, but I'd better be the first person you visit," Rhonda joked, her voice still groggy. "Now let me hear what you've written so far, and we'll go from there."

Tiara read her letter to Rhonda. It did not sound bad. There were a few grammatical errors, and Rhonda helped her rephrase and rewrite important points so the letter flowed smoothly, but the core came from Tiara. Rhonda was proud.

"I'm really impressed with your letter and your reasons for wanting to join the sorority. You've also nicely laid out your intentions to positively represent and help the sorority uplift the community. You have done a great job."

"You really think so?"

"Of course I do. You're really turning into a pretty great young lady, yourself," Rhonda commented. It was true. Tiara Johnson had really matured from the sassy little girl she'd met during their first encounter. Tiara and her social worker met Rhonda at a restaurant so they could become acquainted for the first time on neutral ground, but their first meeting didn't go so well. Tiara was a very bitter little girl and had expressed, without sugarcoating her feelings, that she was not a charity case and didn't "need no Big Sister telling me what I need to do!"

But Rhonda was determined to make the union work, although she wasn't sure what she had gotten herself into by bringing this loud-mouthed, uneasy, attention-starved child into her life. But somehow over the years Rhonda helped to transform a scared caterpillar into a beautiful butterfly. She exposed Tiara to nice restaurants, plays, museums, and the importance of pampering and loving herself. They went to church together on Sundays and read and discussed the Bible and other inspirational books and tapes, like Susan Taylor's *In the Spirit* and Deepak Chopra's *The Higher Self*. From her relationship with Rhonda, Tiara learned how to see herself where she wanted to be and not where she was.

She learned how to dream, and with Rhonda's help Tiara dreamed herself right out of the tiny three-bedroom apartment that housed her, her mother, and five brothers and sisters, and into the college of her dreams. Now Tiara was attempting to dream herself into Rhonda's sorority, which was a big step for someone with her background.

Tiara grew up in one of the roughest projects in Gary, Indiana. Victims of depressed urban life, only some of her classmates managed to graduate and attain blue-collar jobs, and even fewer went to college. However, she knew of many girls in her high school graduating class who were stripping or selling their bodies to make a quick dollar, or were on crack. Several of her male classmates were coerced into selling drugs or illegal firearms. Others were either dead or in jail.

Her mother now dated a drug dealer, and her three youngest siblings all had different fathers. Unemployed, her mother barely kept a roof over their heads and seemed more interested in playing the numbers and chasing after men than she was in her own children. Tiara had overcome a lot, but despite her unfortunate childhood, she felt lucky and blessed to have the opportunity to experience a better side of life here at school.

"I hope your sorors feel the same," Tiara said with hope in her voice.

"I'm sure they will. You have a great chance. Just think positively, say a prayer, and wear something nice to rush. By the way, what's this year's theme?"

"Exclusive Pink Plush Rush."

"I guess my sorors are running out of creative ideas. But I'm sure that when you're accepted, you'll help jazz things up."

"I gotta be accepted first."

"You will. So, Miss Tiara Johnson, are you still giving the men in your life a run for their money? Or better yet, have you found somebody special yet?"

"You know that some things never change. I'm never gonna let a man have my mind, even if it means I gotta be single for the rest of my life. Some of the girls on this campus are so 'gone' over their boyfriends that their lives revolve around them. They cain't even think without asking their men how. It's like they live to serve."

"You're so harsh."

"I have to be. Their men have been seen going to visit other women in dorms all over this campus. And when they finally decide they're tired of being accused of cheating, they leave with no explanation. Then those dumb girls go cryin' to their so-called friends and the next thing you know everybody on campus be talking about their asses until somebody else gets dumped and they have something new to gossip about."

"Watch your mouth, Miss Thing. I thought you were working on cleaning that up."

"My bad, sis. You just hit a subject that pisses me off and I can't be held responsible for my words. I'm working on it. Anyway, I refuse to live like that, even if it means not having a man. So, what's up with that?"

"You mean the relationship thing?"

"Yeah, why do women seem to be the only ones catching he . . . heck from the brothers? And why do the brothers act like they could care less?"

Rhonda and Tiara both knew what Tiara was really asking. She was still trying to figure out why her father left her mother, Tiara, and her two sisters. Tiara never forgot how good things were before her daddy left her mother for a white lady. Polly was her name. She was a thin, stringy-haired blond, poor white trash home wrecker, as far as Tiara was concerned. How dare she come and break up their family and take her daddy away from her? Before her daddy walked out on them, they actually lived in a house. It wasn't in the best neighborhood, but it was a house.

Her father left unexpectedly. Their life was never the same after that because her mother had committed herself to being a housewife and had little education, no self-esteem, and felt that she was not skilled enough to enter the work force. Without a high school diploma, and scared, she did what most uneducated, single mothers do. She signed up to be another victim of the welfare system and moved her family into the projects.

Without her father's presence, her mother lost control of her life and turned into a stranger, whom Tiara had a hard time relating to. Her mother had men coming in and out of the apartment, and before she knew it, Tiara had not two, but five siblings to help take care of. Tamika, who was two years younger than Tiara, was now a senior in high school. Janeece, nicknamed Niece, was a year and a half younger than Tamika. Her three brothers, Lamont, Donnell, and Cayman, were a lot younger. Lamont, nicknamed "Brother," was nine, Donnell was eight, and Cayman, whom they called Man-Man, was six.

Each sibling was named after whatever stuck in their mother's mind during her pregnancy. Tiara got her name after her mother watched a beauty pageant during her ninth month of pregnancy. The winner received a tiara among her many prizes. Her mother wanted her first girl to always be reminded she was as beautiful as that crown looked on the pageant winner's head. Tamika was named after their mother's then-best friend. Janeece and Donnell were each named after guest characters on her favorite sitcom. Lamont was named after the fine man from the auto dealership where she bought her used Chevette. When she was in the doctor's waiting room with her last child, a documentary on Jamaica and the Cayman Islands was on the TV; so she got the name for her last baby boy.

Tiara loved her siblings but hated the ghetto life and hated her father for causing her to experience it. And she figured if her own father was no good, no other man could be any better.

"That's life," Rhonda explained. "There are some jerks out there, true. But all men are not like that. Tiara, you are a smart girl, and you have a life outside of men. You will probably never find yourself in the kind of situation where a man tries to use you up, because you're different. You have a mind of your own, and you will be your own person in a relationship, and I promise you won't end up like them."

"Of course I won't, because I won't allow myself to get wrapped up in anybody. I don't need a man in my life. I got myself and that's all I need. Praise the Lord!"

"You're a trip." Rhonda laughed. "You always manage to crack me up. But Tiara, trust me when I say this. The right man will come your way, it's inevitable. Just don't be so caught up in putting every man off that you miss the right one when he comes along."

"Okay, sis. I hear you, but I ain't gonna be out there looking for him. He'll probably have to run smack-dead into me before I even notice him, so he'd better have a good aim or else he'll miss me."

"He will have a good aim, and he'll knock you head over heels in love."

"This we shall see," Tiara replied.

"Oh, we will, and I'm going to have my popcorn and soda ready to enjoy the entertainment of watching you fall in love. Well, Tiara, I'm gonna let you go, and I'll try to sleep away what is left of this night. I'll be praying for you, and I love you."

"Thanks again for everything, sis. And I love you too. Bye."

Tiara reread her letter of intent. Satisfied with the results, she decided that she should try to sleep too.

FIVE

Chancey didn't want to go back to campus, but it was Monday morning and her first class was at ten. She loved staying at Donald's apartment. It was so cozy and comfortable—a refreshing change from the bare brick walls in her dorm room. Although the school wouldn't admit it, all of the senior football players had exquisitely furnished apartments compliments of the college's alumni football fanatics. Both Don and his roommate were senior starters on the team and were given king-sized water beds and all the trimmings for their bedrooms. They also had a black leather couch and love seat, a twenty-seven-inch television, VCR, a five-disc CD changer in their living room, and an elegant glass dining room table with four black arch-backed chairs. They even had a few paintings to jazz up their walls.

Chancey Wright and Don were in love already, even though they had only been seeing each other for six months. They had met on Chancey's first day on campus. Although Don often swore he had known he was going to make her his wife when they first met, she had a hard time believing him, because when he first laid eyes on her, she was not exactly looking her best. She never forgot how she woke up late that morning and had a three-hour drive to get to the campus. Worried that she would miss her dormitory check-in time, she quickly brushed her teeth, washed her face, dressed, finished loading her car, and took off for campus. She didn't even have time to put in her contacts, so she wore her glasses. Although her mother promised she would be up the following weekend to help get anything else she needed for her room, Chancey hated that her parents had to be out of town on business the weekend she was going away to college. She was not ready to take on the responsibility of moving herself into her new home.

She had parked her car by her new dormitory. After checking in, she began unloading her garment bags of clothes, when a six-foot-four, 260-pound, paper-sack-brown gentleman with the most perfect smile she had ever seen walked up to her, introduced himself, and offered to help carry her things to her room. Chancey was embarrassed that this handsome, overly friendly stranger was offering his assistance to her, a freshman who looked a mess. She was wearing long blue jean shorts and an oversized T-shirt that read WRIGHT FAMILY REUNION. Her shoulder-length brown hair was pulled back into a thick, bushy ponytail, and because it was past time for a relaxer, it looked pretty shabby. She also had on the same glasses that she'd been wearing since she was a freshman in high school. Her tennis shoes were run-over, and, to top things off, her knees and elbows were ashy. However, Chancey was a natural beauty and required little maintenance to look good with her light-brown complexion, striking features, and full lips. Her eyelashes were long, so she didn't need mascara, and her eyebrows were thick and well-shaped.

Although not dressed with the intention of meeting her future husband, she knew that if she unloaded her car by herself, she would never be unpacked in time to get a quick tour of the campus before it got too dark, so she took him up on the offer. While unpacking Chancey's car, she and Don talked as if they had known each other all of their lives. When they finished, he gave her a tour of the campus, treated her to ice cream, kissed her on the forehead, and made her promise that she would not consider seeing any other guy on campus until she gave herself a chance to get to know him better. She promised. And from that day forward they either spent time together or talked on the phone every day.

In fact, they had just spent the weekend together, and she had the opportunity to see his parents again. Emitt and Glenda Robinson had come for the weekend, and Chancey went to Don's football banquet with them. Don won two awards: the Coaches' Award and MVP. Afterward the four of them celebrated by going to a nice bar and grill for appetizers and drinks. Don and Emitt spent most of the time talking about Don's football career, while Chancey and Glenda talked about current events and made plans to go on a shopping spree during Chancey's next visit to Louisiana with Don. His parents were always pleasant, and they really seemed to like Chancey. It was also obvious they cared about their son's future and well-being.

Sunday morning, Chancey and Don met his parents at their hotel. They had a pleasant breakfast in the hotel's restaurant, during which they confirmed plans for her to come with Don to Louisiana for a long weekend, right after spring semester finals. Don's father promised to have an itinerary to ensure an enjoyable stay. His wife looked at him and laughed. "We'll believe that when we see it."

"Chancey, don't pay her no mind," Emitt said. "I'm gonna type an itinerary on the computer, and we'll be ready to have a ball when you get there."

"Emitt and his computer . . . Since he bought that thing he spends hours at a time on it. I have no clue how it works, but he tracks our expenses on it, and that Internet—"

"There's a lot of good information on the Internet, honey. I made our plane reservations to come here over the Internet, remember?" he interrupted. He then turned to Chancey. "I'll have the itinerary all typed up, and I'll use the Internet to see what events will be going on during the weekend you'll be visiting."

"Okay!" Chancey said. She enjoyed spending time with Don's parents because it gave her the opportunity to get to know more about Don's background. During this visit it became apparent that Don's father had control over the family's affairs—his mother had no knowledge of their finances and allowed her husband to make the major decisions concerning her and her son.

"Just make sure you give Chancey and me enough time to get some shopping in," Glenda said.

"Good! That'll give me and my son some bonding time together," Emitt said.

"Yeah, that's right!" Don replied. "The ladies will go shopping and we'll watch a good ol' baseball game! It doesn't get any better than that!"

They all laughed while Chancey contemplated the similarities between Don and his father.

After breakfast, they drove Mr. and Mrs. Robinson to the airport and chatted until it was time for them to board the plane. Then Chancey and Don went back to his apartment, got into bed, and stayed there all day, leaving only to cook dinner. After eating, they got right back into bed and watched a movie.

It was a perfect weekend, and now it was over. She gave Don, who was still sleeping, a kiss on his muscular bicep, rolled out of bed, and headed for the shower. By the time she was dressed he had opened his eyes and was looking at her. "Good morning, my diamond." Don always told Chancey she was like a diamond in the rough—a little rough around the edges but with a little time and care, she would be fit for a solitaire. She was never sure whether or not to take that statement as a compliment. She flashed him a loving smile anyway, and began to put on her shoes. "Wake up sleepyhead," she said. "You've got to go to classes too, you know."

"I'm up." Donald yawned. He got a good look at his girlfriend. He was never thrilled with her attire. "Chancey, why are you wearing that extra-large shirt with those baggy jeans? As a matter of fact, why do you still own baggy jeans? God blessed you with a nice figure, and you should not be ashamed to show it off. Everybody knows that you're my girl, so I'm not worried about the other brothers on campus looking at you, no matter how much of your shape you show off. They all know that they can look, but I bet they'll think twice about touching."

"What's wrong with what I'm wearing? Oh, I see, you want me to dress like all those groupies who hang out at the games and at practice! That's not my style, and you know that!" she said, standing her ground.

"No, I'm not saying that you should have tits and ass exposed to the campus, but baby, you could stand to wear clothes that fit."

"Forget you, big head," she joked. "I'm just going to class. I like to be comfortable when I'm taking notes and listening to boring lectures. Nothing is more annoying than being uncomfortably dressed while taking notes from a professor speaking in a monotone voice."

Chancey had a 4.0 GPA entering college, and really didn't have to take notes in her courses. However, she did so because everybody else did. She was extremely smart and blessed with a near photographic memory. She often amazed Donald by giving him a play-by-play repeat of every move he made in each game, sometimes weeks afterward. Before she began her first year at college, she had already completed twenty-four college credit hours and tested completely out of her foreign language requirement. Most of her friends didn't know that she was actually a sophomore.

"Diamond, you can be comfortable and still look like a lady. I'm not saying that you don't look nice, but you look like a little girl, and I know that my baby is a woman. I'll tell you what, I got some extra money from Jackson and—"

"Jackson, the alumnus?"

"Yeah. Remember he took us out to eat after the first game of the season?"

"Oh, I remember him. All he talked about was football that night. He's a fanatic, but why is he giving you money?"

"Well, you know how the alums are. They just want to make sure the players worry about one thing and one thing only, and that's playing and winning football games."

"As if an education is not as important," Chancey expressed sarcastically.

Don ignored her snide remark and continued. "Jackson says I did a good job of staying focused; I helped produce two winning seasons, and I will be graduating on time. He said the alums agree that I was a major part of our team's winning a Bowl this year, and they just want to congratulate me."

"And what if the team had a losing season? Then what?" she pushed. She loved to tease him that way. They both knew what the alumni were doing was illegal. And although the treatment was nice, she wanted Don to be cautious when dealing with them.

He went on. "As I was saying, Jackson is going to give me some extra spending change, and I want to take you out Friday after class to get you a bomb-ass dress for rush. I'll get you some shoes to match and whatever else you'll need to be the classiest lady there. We'll also get your hair done. I want you to walk through those doors knowing that my diamond is outshining everybody, including your future sorors. Speaking of which, have you written your letter of intent?"

"Yes, I have written my letter, and just how much spending change is this Jackson supposed to be giving you? Baby, you know what he's doing is illegal. Anyway, I thought you liked me for me and not for my appearance."

"Chancey, slow down. The season's over. I'm about to graduate. Who's gonna care about him giving me money anyway? And about your outfit for rush—baby, you know I love you, and I do mean that. You're fine to me in whatever you wear. I just want those ladies in pink to know that their sorority will not be complete unless they have you as an addition. That is what you want, right?"

Chancey gave Don a dreamy look and a big hug. He didn't always show the greatest tact in the world, but he meant well. "You know I am dying to pledge. And you're right, when I'm accepted they won't know how they ever managed to make such a difference in the world and on campus without me." They both laughed.

"Thank you, Don. You're so good to me. I knew I fell in love with you for a reason." Chancey kissed Don on the forehead, grabbed her book bag, purse, and keys, and headed for her car.

"Baby, don't forget to make your hair appointment!"

"I won't. I love you."

"I love your fine ass too, Diamond. Now go to class and make your daddy proud," he joked.

"I will," she replied. "You'd better get over to campus soon yourself. I'll see you for lunch at the cafeteria."

"Okay, baby love," he said, as she closed the door.

SIX

The alarm clock went off at seven-thirty A.M. Cajen reached over and hit the snooze button. Just a few more minutes . . .

Nine minutes passed, and the alarm went off again. This time Cajen got out of bed and decided there was no way out of beginning this day. The first thing on her mind was that almost three days had passed since she last talked to Jason. She had left a message on his answering machine Sunday evening, but he didn't return her call. Before Friday night she had heard from him at least once a day, even though most of the time it was through notes he sent by the pledges.

Cajen was tempted to ditch her classes and stay in bed, but decided that if she was out on campus, she'd have a better chance of running into Jason. She put on her robe and shower shoes and headed for the shower. She walked through the doors of the community bathroom and stopped to use the toilet. She hurried along before the stalls were all in use, because there were only eight shower stalls and six were already filled with female students who apparently were more enthusiastic about going to class than she was.

Cajen felt a tingling, burning sensation. What is going on? she thought. She carefully wiped and went over to the shower. While in the shower, she checked to see if everything felt normal. She noticed that a little blister was growing on the lips of her vagina. Not wanting to panic or think the worst, she brushed it off as some sort of weird yeast infection.

She had a long day ahead, and rushed out of the shower and got dressed. Her first class was trigonometry, and she didn't want to be late.

Instead of going to the cafeteria to have breakfast, she stopped by the campus deli and grabbed a banana, which hit the spot. Cajen was ten minutes early for class, so she walked down the hall to the vending machine to get some juice. While deciding between orange and grape, she heard what sounded like Jason's laugh. She quickly chose orange juice, and followed the deep echo. He laughed again and then spoke, but his words weren't clear.

Cajen turned the corner and was at a stairwell, and the voice became clearer. It was Jason, and he was in the stairwell talking to two other guys. One of them said, "Jason, man, you the man!"

Jason said something she couldn't hear, and then added, "Oh, I know I'm the man." They all laughed again.

She wanted to approach them, but also wanted to hear what they were talking about.

One of them said, "You're bullshitting. Man, she all that! And she's jocking you?" he questioned.

Someone else said, "So what! She's old news, and she's all used up. She was trying to get with me last month."

"You're right," Jason said. "She ain't about shit. I heard she's been with half of the campus, but it's not my fault if she wants to slobber all over my boy, if you know what I mean. That's what freaks do, and she is definitely a freak."

Cajen couldn't believe her ears. Who were they talking about? She knew it was not her. The thought of oral sex made her nauseous. So who was this girl, and was Jason planning on having sex with her? Cajen wanted to interrupt, but she wanted to hear more. Who were they talking about?

"So what you gonna do man?" one asked.

"Use your imagination, dog!" Jason responded. They laughed some more.

Not able to take anymore, she had to interrupt. So she pulled herself together and began walking down the stairs, as if she had no idea they were there. They heard her approaching and cut their conversation. Jason looked at her as if he were seeing a ghost.

"Hi, Jason," Cajen said innocently. She recognized the other guys.

They were in his fraternity. One of them had on a cowboy hat and boots. She remembered seeing him at a campus party licking some girl's neck while they were slow dancing. He had on the same hat and boots, only that night he wasn't wearing a shirt and his pants were unzipped. Cajen thought he was gross that night, and even though he was now fully dressed, he was still disgusting. The other guy was short and clean-cut, but he had big, rusty lips. Cajen wanted badly to offer him some Chap Stick, but didn't want his lips on anything that belonged to her. She looked at them both and managed to say hello.

"Hi, Cajen," they said, with goofy grins plastered on their faces.

She realized she had left her books in her classroom and had no excuse for being in the stairwell. She felt awkward, so she decided the best way to deal with this situation was to be honest. She told Jason she was getting something to drink at the vending machine and thought she heard his voice. She could barely continue her story because Jason's fraternity brothers were eyeing her like she was a piece of meat they wanted to devour. Once she stopped talking, they looked at Jason like he was some kind of god. Then the cowboy said, "Like I said earlier, Jason, you the man." Cajen felt cheap. She wanted to turn around and walk away. How could Jason let his brothers treat her like that freak they were talking about earlier?

Perhaps Jason knew she was uncomfortable, because he told them that he would catch up with them later.

"Yeah, we'll see you tonight," they said, as they walked down the stairs. Then the one with the big lips had the nerve to turn around and shake his head and smack those chapped lips at Cajen. Yuck, she thought. But she immediately blocked him out of her mind and focused her attention on Jason. She couldn't tell if he was happy to see her, so she waited for him to speak.

"You tracking me down, sexy lady?" he asked her.

Cajen was made uneasy by that statement and wanted to make it clear to him that she was not spying. "No, I told you what happened," she responded.

"I'm just kidding. So what's new?" he asked, flashing his irresistible smile.

"You know I'm going to rush on Sunday. I'm excited about that."

"No doubt . . . no doubt," he said, while looking around every time he heard the slightest little noise. He seemed uncomfortable.

"I left a message," she managed to say.

"Oh yeah. I got it, but I've been tied up. You know, frat business."

"Yeah, I guess," she responded.

"Now stop tripping, sexy lady. You know I would've called by now if it wasn't for that."

"Yeah, I know you would have." There was something about his voice that made her feel vulnerable, but deep down Cajen suspected they were looking at their relationship through different eyes. She saw him as a potential committed boyfriend but worried that he saw her as a good time for a short time. Nevertheless, she wanted and expected more. "So when will I see you again?"

"It's hard to say."

"Oh . . ." Her heart was crushed.

He told her how hectic the rest of his week was going to be and said if he could, he'd try to squeeze some time for her late Friday or Saturday night. Then he kissed her on the cheek and said he needed to go.

With his reaction and his busy schedule, it was becoming evident that last Friday night had meant nothing to him.

Cajen walked through campus to her dormitory. The campus was beautiful—there were lots of trees, and the shrubbery around the buildings was meticulously maintained. But she wasn't aware of the beauty around her, because she was preoccupied with the encounter she'd had with Jason earlier that morning. She hoped he'd be able to squeeze some time in for her out of his busy schedule. Then she wondered if he didn't have time for her because he was spending time with that freak the guys were talking about. Is that what he wanted, someone more experienced? Cajen had no intention of being a freak like that other girl, whatever her name was, but she did want to keep Jason. There had to be another way. Wait a minute, she thought. What's happening to me? Have I actually allowed myself to fall for someone I can never have? What could be worse?

In deep thought, she didn't realize that Eric was right in front of her, showing all thirty-two of his pearly whites. He had on sweatpants and a sweatshirt with a T-shirt peeking out from underneath. He was five-eleven, attractive, intelligent, and athletic, but there was nothing about him that made her melt—at least not the way Jason did. Still, she did like Eric; he had a wonderful personality.

"Hey beautiful!" he said. "Can I walk you to your dorm?"

"Well, I have some things I have to do; I have to finish my letter of intent."

"That's right, rush is this weekend. Well, I'm on my way to the gym, and I don't have to come up. I'll just walk you to the entrance. That's if you don't mind." Eric was always polite and considerate.

"Okay, it'll give us a chance to catch up."

"It's not my fault that we haven't talked in the past couple of weeks. I'm beginning to think that we're not friends anymore."

"Now, Eric, you know that we'll always be friends."

"I hope so, Cajen, because you mean a lot to me."

Cajen was surprised to hear that from Eric. She knew he cared, but she wasn't expecting him to say so. "Well, you mean a lot to me too, Eric, and I'm glad we're friends." Eric stared at her and seemed about to say something else, but instead blurted, "Are you gonna be busy later today? Maybe we can eat dinner at the cafeteria together and talk."

"Oh, Eric, I'm not sure. I mean, I don't want to make any promises and then let you down."

"Well, we'll do it this way. Let's set a time now, and if you find out later that it won't work, just give me a call and let me know either way. I'll be in my dorm room studying after I leave the gym, and I'll wait for your call."

They approached her dormitory. Eric looked directly in her eyes; she knew how much he was hoping that she would say okay. Luckily for him there was no way she could say no. He was such a gentleman, and she needed to talk to a friend. "Okay, let's say seven-thirty, and if I can't make it I'll call."

"Okay, we'll walk over to the student center, and I'll treat."

"Thanks."

"Well, I'm gonna let you go ahead and get started on your letter. The letter of all letters. The life-changing letter," he joked. "Good luck, and if you need me to critique it, just let me know."

"I wish I could, but you know these things are supposed to be private and personal," she said, as she opened the door to her dorm. "Don't overdo it at the gym."

"I won't. But I'm looking forward to seeing you later. You know, to catch up," he said as he walked away.

Cajen changed out of her clothes into sweats and a T-shirt. Then she went across the hall to use the rest room. She experienced the same episode from the morning—a stinging irritation. She could not keep blowing this off. She had to do something. When she got back to her room she closed the door behind her, and called Student Health to ask if she could get an emergency pelvic exam. The nurse said they could squeeze her in, but it wouldn't be until four-thirty. She accepted the appointment and hung up the phone.

She looked at her clock. It was only one-forty-five. What was she going to do with herself until four-thirty? She started working on the letter of intent she had to have with her Sunday in order to be admitted through the doors of the Exclusive Pink Plush Rush. Kim, one of the members of the sorority who'd taken a personal interest in Cajen, informed her that if she wanted to be considered for the privilege of being a pledge for her sorority, her letter had to be substantive, which, in Kim's opinion, was something most college freshmen weren't capable of. Although she was distracted with the events of her day, she managed to turn on her computer and begin to work on her letter. Cajen often wondered what Kim and her sorors discussed when they sat in the cafeteria together. Their conversations always seemed so much more interesting than the ones she had in the cafeteria. Like them, Cajen longed to one day grace the campus with her pink T-shirt and pink book bag.

What will make me stand out? What will make my letter be just as good if not better than the upperclassmen who will also be writing to the sorority?

Cajen thought and wrote, and rewrote, and thought some more and rewrote again. She finally came up with what she considered a masterpiece. "Now, this has substance!" she proudly exclaimed. Then she looked over at the clock. It was already four. She couldn't believe how quickly time had passed. She'd almost forgotten her dreaded doctor's appointment.

She assured herself. It will just be a yeast infection. Or maybe it's an allergic reaction to something. Yeah, that's it. She grabbed her purse and keys and headed out the door, but Cajen's heart was heavy because deep down she knew the blister she had found while in the shower was more serious than a yeast infection.

Cajen waited in the examination room for the doctor to return with her results. For some reason, she felt the doctor was going to come back with bad news. She was relieved a female gynecologist was caring for her, because male doctors made her uneasy.

There was a knock at the door. "I'm dressed," Cajen said. Dr. Anita Mitchell walked in with the serious look that most doctors seem to have, whether they are delivering good news or bad.

"Cajen, I'm sorry, but I don't have good news. However, we can't be one hundred percent certain until we get the test results back from the lab tomorrow." She paused. Why is she pausing? What could possibly be wrong with me? It must be AIDS! I have AIDS!

Seeing the stricken look on Cajen's face, the doctor assured her, "It's not fatal, but you seem to have contracted the herpes virus."

"The what? Herpes? What . . . what is that? What's wrong with me? Virus? Oh . . . oh, no." Tears formed in Cajen's brown eyes. She could not believe the diagnosis. She had heard of herpes, but was not familiar with the ramifications of contracting the disease.

"Cajen, one out of five women has herpes. You are not going to die from this disease, but it will be annoying. Herpes comes in the form of blisters, and it's just like the common cold. When it is active, you are extremely contagious. But when it's inactive, there are no symptoms, and you are probably not. I do recommend, however, that you use a condom with your partner even if you are not having an episode, because you still may be contagious. Also, it's the nineties, Cajen, and practicing safe sex is important. It cannot only prevent annoying diseases like herpes, but also unwanted pregnancies and AIDS."

"Active, inactive, episode. You mean that this is something I'm going to have for the rest of my life? There's no medicine that I can take to make it go away?" Cajen could not fully grasp what the doctor had said. This couldn't be happening to her.

"Unfortunately, herpes is one of the few sexually transmitted diseases we do not have a cure for yet. However, it is manageable, and I will give you a prescription to get filled. You can start taking it tonight. This drug will help to shorten the time span of your episodes, and it has also been known to decrease reoccurrence. I will also give you some pamphlets to read so you can become better informed about what you're dealing with. Also, I'm going to suggest we go ahead and have you take a pregnancy test and an AIDS test."

"Why? Does herpes turn into AIDS?" This was too much for Cajen. She couldn't hold back her tears. Then she thought about Jason. He was going to cause her to die, and he didn't even love her. How could he have had sex with her without using a condom? Did he purposely give her this disgusting disease? He hadn't even called her since they'd had sex. How could she have been so stupid? Why didn't she just make him use protection?

"No, it does not mean that you have AIDS or HIV. I just think it will be a good idea, just to be safe." Dr. Mitchell looked at Cajen. She seemed concerned, more like a friend instead of a doctor. "You will need to inform your sex partner or partners, because anyone that you have had intercourse with will need to be tested."

"I only have one sex partner," she said between sniffs.

The doctor handed her a tissue and asked, "Is he your boyfriend?"

Cajen tried to wipe the tears away, but they kept coming. "Kind of, but he is the only person I've been intimate with. Dr. Mitchell, do you think he knows that he gave me her . . . herpes?"

"Well, there is a chance your boyfriend doesn't know he has herpes. There have been cases, in men especially, where there were few or no obvious symptoms. But, Cajen, that does not mean that he didn't know. How long have you two been sexually involved?"

"We were only together once. I can't believe this. What am I going to do?" Cajen stopped crying and looked at Dr. Mitchell, hoping she would tell her something that would make it all better.

"You're going to be fine. Your life is not going to end with this virus. You are going to be just fine. You will just have to make sure, in the future, to be responsible and take better precautions. Also, if you are honest about your situation, the right man will not allow this problem to affect his feelings for you." She paused. "It's really sad to say, but a large number of people on this campus have been diagnosed with herpes. Unfortunately, there are a lot of people out there who are not as cautious as they should be. Cajen, it's as simple as taking a few seconds out to grab a condom." Cajen appreciated her honesty and empathy. She did make this news a bit easier to swallow.

"Thank you."

"But I will suggest you have your boyfriend come in to be tested, and you two may need to sit down and have a long talk."

Dr. Mitchell gave Cajen the two additional tests and wrote a prescription for oral medication and a cream to use externally. She also gave her pamphlets and told her that if she had any questions, or felt she needed to talk to someone, there was a herpes hot line number on one of the pamphlets, or she could call Dr. Mitchell herself.

Cajen thanked the doctor and walked out of the office, wondering what she was going to do now.

SEVEN

Chancey came out of the dressing room to model yet another dress for Don. She had already tried on at least fifteen dresses at five different shops. None were right, but she did manage to put two on hold just in case they couldn't find anything better.

"What do you think?" She twirled around and posed with her hands on her hip.

"Un-uh!"

"I agree. To be honest, I don't like any of the styles in this shop. Let's go to Marsche's."

"Okay, that's cool, but where do you want to eat after we finish?"

"I don't know. I'm really not hungry yet," Chancey answered, and went back into the dressing room. She always felt uncomfortable in dressing rooms. Wondering if there were cameras or someone watching her undress, she never stood directly in front of the mirror while changing clothes.

"Let's go to Solomon's," Don suggested.

"Where?" she yelled from out of the dressing room.

"Solomon's." He repeated the name of the restaurant as if it were a name she heard every day.

"I've never heard of that place. Is the food any good?"

"It's the best. Stick with me, Diamond, and I'll show you nothing but the best," he joked. They both laughed.

She came out with the four dresses she had wasted her time trying on. "So, if I stay with you, I'll always have the best?"

"That's what I said." Don kissed her on the cheek.

"You and the finer things life has to offer, or a solo life filled with mediocrity. How's a girl to choose?" asked Chancey.

"You'd better choose wisely."

"In that case, lock me up and throw away the key. I'm all yours!"

Chancey put the dresses on the return rack. The sales associate asked if they wanted to see anything else, but they declined and left for Marsche's, a fashionable ladies' shop that sold dresses for every occasion. Surely they would be able to find something for a sorority rush.

While walking, Don took her hand and gave her a big smile. Excited and in an exceptionally good mood, he gave her a look that said, I'm happy to be here with you. She smiled back at him, and they both looked in the windows of the shops they passed.

At Marsche's they saw several nice dresses. Chancey picked up two. She tried on the first one. It was a long, straight brown linen dress with gold buttons down the front. The collar was wide, and the long sleeves had large cuffs with gold buttons. The dress was a classic.

"Baby, I think we just found your dress."

"You think so?"

"Yes, look at you baby. Damn!"

"You like it?"

"What? I love it. Do you like it?"

"Yeah, I think I do."

"Amen! Our search is over. Now, let's go get your accessories," Don exclaimed.

They found a nice pair of earrings at the counter, and continued shopping the mall until they found a pair of shoes and everything else to make the ensemble complete.

Don was turning out to be a good catch. In the beginning of their relationship Chancey had wondered why someone as popular and attractive as Don would want to spend so much time with her. She often asked herself why he took the time to worry about the little things that bothered her and why he spent so much time making sure their relationship continued to grow. She knew she deserved a good man, but his actions weren't typical of a star college football player.

She was eventually informed by one of his fraternity brothers that Don used to be a big-time player who juggled no less than three women at once. Toward the end of his sophomore year, his older brother, and only sibling, was killed at the age of thirty. His brother had had a steady girlfriend, but he never treated her with respect, and always joked that he would eventually settle down with her when he could no longer stay out all night and make it to work the next morning. According to one of Don's frat brothers, he really looked up to his brother. After he died, Don's entire persona changed. He broke all ties with every woman he was seeing at the time, and spent nearly a year and a half abstaining from sex. He also vowed not to get into a relationship until he found someone with whom he could be monogamous and sincere. His fraternity brother told her that Don wished his brother had settled down and had a wife and maybe a kid or two, thinking that if he had, he wouldn't have died driving home drunk after one of those wild parties he frequented. Don never talked much to Chancey about the details surrounding his brother's death. But sometimes, when she least expected it, he would mention how much he missed him and that he wished he were still alive.

Chancey knew she was the person Don needed in his life. Since his brother died, she had been the only person with whom he spent a considerable amount of time. He felt comfortable knowing she couldn't judge him for the way he used to be. And she would never know the explicit details about his past, if he had anything to do with it. He only wanted her to know the side of Don that was strong, loving, and carefree. Although Chancey knew about Don's past and about the lifestyle he and his brother had in common, she promised herself she would never bring it up until he did.

After they completed their shopping spree, they walked to Don's sport utility vehicle. It was loaded and luxurious. He had traded in his old used car and gotten it before the last official game of the season. She was never one hundred percent sure if it was a gift from his parents or those damn alumni who were always spoiling him, but she never asked. She felt that some questions are better off not asked, because she might not want to hear the answer.

Once out of the mall parking lot, Chancey reached over and kissed

Don on his cheek. "Thank you for being so wonderful. You know, I just might keep you."

"Ah, you don't mean that. You know you don't love me!" Don kidded.

"Of course I don't." Chancey played along. "How could I possibly love someone who treats me so badly?"

"I don't love you, either. There's something about you that makes it hard for me to be around you. That's why we're gonna cut the evening short—because we've already spent too much time together."

"Please, let's do. I'm getting sick just looking at you," she joked, then reached over and kissed him on his cheek again.

Don smiled at her. He enjoyed Chancey's company and had fallen in love with her because she was smart, supportive, sweet, and mature for her age. Her maturity and responsible behavior had been evident to him for some time. She'd told him that while growing up, her parents owned their own small business and spent a lot of time traveling to keep their products in the public eye. They taught her at an early age to write checks and keep up their accounting. She made sure none of the bills were late and often cared for the home and herself while they were on the road. Chancey was accustomed to making adult decisions as a child. At times she even seemed more adult than Don. Yet he seemed insistent on making decisions for her.

"So tell me more about Solomon's."

"No. You'll just have to wait until we get there to find out more about Sol-o-mon's. It's gonna take us a while to get there, so put on some nice mellow traveling music and just relax and enjoy the ride."

Solomon's was top-notch, just as Don had promised. Everyone dining in that restaurant looked like they had a million dollars in the bank. It was obvious that this was not going to be like their usual dinner dates.

"Don, this place is really nice. How did you know about it?"

"Some of the alums brought me, a few of the other players, and some other people here during my freshman year. I always promised myself that once I could afford it, and had the perfect girl to bring with me, I'd come back and enjoy the romantic atmosphere. Well, I can afford it now, and I have the perfect girl, so that's why we're here. It's kind of romantic, huh?"

"Yes, it is. Thanks for bringing me here."

"Remember what I said. If you stay with me, I'll take you everywhere I'm privileged to go."

The hostess showed them to their seats and placed menus on the table. Chancey's menu didn't have any prices on it. "Don, I don't have any prices on my menu. How am I supposed to know what we can afford to order?"

"This is a very traditional restaurant. They like to make a woman feel like she's a lady, and a lady shouldn't have to worry about prices."

"Well, I have to worry about the prices. I don't want to overorder."

"Chancey, sometimes I think you forget that in a few months I will be playing professional football. Baby, I'm guaranteed to go during the first round of the draft. I will hopefully be in the top ten picks, and it's looking very hopeful. Baby, I'll be making millions. Millions! My agent has already given me an advance. How do you think I was able to get this ride? My parents? How do you think I'm able to take you out more often and put gas in your car? The thousand dollars that Jackson gave me is just spending money. Get used to it, Diamond. In the very near future you will never have to worry about the cost of things again."

Chancey was speechless. She gave him a blank look. Momentarily, through her eyes Don was a stranger. She knew he had a great chance of making it to the pros, but she hadn't realized that people were actually going to start giving him money just because he had a good chance. She thought he was taking her out more because the season was over and he had more time. It was finally settling in that she would soon be dating a wealthy man. Chancey's parents were well-off, but they were by no means millionaires. For the first time, she was faced with the reality that Don would go away with some football team and move to some other city, which they wouldn't know until the draft. He was going to be constantly surrounded by groupies and the media. All the attention he was already getting was going to escalate.

"Chancey, you act like you're hearing all of this for the first time.

We've discussed me going pro and you visiting me for most all of the home games. That's all me and my dad talked about while he was here. Remember?"

"Don, I wasn't really listening. I was talking to your mother. I mean, I guess I knew, but it always seemed so far away."

"Well, it's getting closer every day. Your man's gonna be a professional football player. And I'm gonna have my degree too."

"I know. I'm so proud of you, but you're going to be leaving me one day."

"I'm not going to be leaving you. I'm just going to be a little farther away. And who knows, maybe I'll only be a few states over. Plus, I've been told that distance makes the heart grow fonder." He grabbed her hand from across the table. There was a pleasant silence.

"Baby, order whatever you want," Don said.

"Okay. I sure will! I'm not gonna worry about the prices, because my man is rich."

Chancey ordered grilled salmon, and Don ordered a porterhouse steak. Everything was so good. They relaxed and talked about their future together and how they were going to make their long-distance relationship work.

Instead of ordering dessert, they decided to drive back to town and rent a movie, pick up popcorn and ice cream, and spend the rest of their evening enjoying each other's company in the privacy of Don's apartment.

EIGHT

Hey, Tiara, girl. What's up?" Sandra asked, as she danced through the door into Tiara's dorm room. One of her favorite songs was blasting from her mini stereo system that sat on top of her bureau. Sandra was carrying a small bag and wearing tight black pants that stopped and cuffed at her ankle. Her rayon blouse was wrapped in the front and tied on the side, showing her navel and just a hint of cleavage. She always dressed sexily for campus parties. The look worked for her because she never wore her hair too wild and her body was so petite that nothing ever seemed to be out of proportion.

"I'm just trying to figure out what I'm gonna wear tonight. You're here early."

"Girl, my roommate was getting on my last nerve. Mindy's boyfriend is over, and they were blasting that Pearl Jam shit and smoking cigarettes. I hate to be smelling like cigarette smoke. And you know what? She only smokes in the room when he's over, and she didn't smoke at all until she met him."

"Umph!" Tiara responded.

"So I got dressed as quickly as I could, grabbed my curling iron and makeup, and came straight over here. It's okay, isn't it?"

"Of course it's okay! You know that," Tiara said. "But what kills me is when men try to be so controlling, and I hate women who change their entire lifestyles just to keep a man. If Mindy gets lung cancer, she'll only have herself to blame. Because once her boyfriend walks out of her life, she's going to be stuck with a nasty habit."

"True," agreed Sandra, "and I hope we won't still be roommates, 'cause I refuse to spend every day of my college life breathing secondhand smoke."

"But you won't have to because you'll be getting a private room next year, right? You did know they were available for second-semester sophomores in January. Why didn't you apply then?"

"My parents were so insistent on me having a roommate, at least during my first two years. I guess they figured I wouldn't get in as much trouble with a roommate. Like that makes sense. Anyway, I envy you and Gina . . . sophomores with private rooms. Why can't I be so lucky?"

"Girl, all you have to do is apply for a single in the fall. This year is almost up and next year it will be your decision. Right?"

"I hope so, but you know how my parents can be. They try to control me from home," Sandra complained. "Believe me, there will be a message on my answering machine tonight asking me to call them as soon as I get in, no matter what time. Is that ridiculous or what?"

"I couldn't begin to imagine," Tiara responded. She wanted her mother to be more responsible, but by no means did she want her to be that overbearing.

"And if I don't call them tonight, they will assume I spent the night with 'one of those nappy-headed rascals,' as my dad calls them."

"Nappy-headed what?" Tiara screamed and laughed at the same time.

"Rascals, girl!" She laughed. "They call every Friday and Saturday night like clockwork. Some nights when Mindy is in the room, she'll act like she's trying to wake me and I won't budge. She'll tell them she couldn't get me up and that I'd spent most of the night in the library studying and came home and crashed, and that she'll be sure I call them as soon as I woke up in the morning."

"Does it work?"

"Like a charm!" They both laughed and gave each other a high five.

Then, somebody knocked on the door.

"I bet it's Gina just now getting off work," Tiara said, as she answered the door. It was Gina, still dressed in her Hardee's uniform. All three girls

had part-time jobs, but she was the only one who had to work Friday
nights.

"We figured it was you."

"I just wanted to let y'all know I'm off. I'm going to take a shower,
then I'll come over here and put on my makeup. Is that cool?"

"That's cool!" Tiara and Sandra answered in unison. Gina left to go
to her room, which was right across the hall. The friends stayed on the
seventh floor of an eleven-story dormitory. The three girls were night
owls, and met their freshman year. Their friendship grew close after
forming a late-night study group. They met three to four days a week at
midnight and studied until three or four in the morning. During finals,
they didn't sleep. Although they spent a great deal of their study time gos-
siping and talking about pledging a sorority, they all managed to maintain above-average GPAs.

"I don't know what I'm gonna wear tonight," Tiara complained. She
stared into a closet full of nice clothes, most of which she'd bought with
money earned from her part-time job. Others were new and used pieces
given to her by Rhonda.

"I can't believe you. You should have had that picked out at the beginning of the week," Sandra said. "Let me see what I can hook up for
you."

Sandra helped Tiara find something to wear. "Now this will look
good on you. Plus, I've never seen you in this." It was a black miniskirt
and a tight, long-sleeve, scoop neck black top. Both still had tags on them.

"That's because I haven't worn it yet. Rhonda picked out that outfit
for me when we went shopping over the Christmas break. I haven't built
the courage to wear it yet."

"She's got good taste, and you need to be stepping out in this. Girlfriend, the winter is about over. You'd better wear it tonight because you
may not get to wear this until next winter. And who knows how much
weight you'll put on by then. I know you're familiar with the freshman
fifteen. They haven't hit you yet, but they will some time before you graduate."

"You're not the only one holding on to your shape, Miss Thang. I, too, am one of the few sophomores who still has what she came in with as a freshman," she bragged. Tiara hadn't gained any weight, mainly because she had a work/study position at the school's weight room, and worked out for thirty minutes to an hour every day after work. She was five-foot-seven and weighed 145 pounds. She was an attractive girl, and her build made her look a few years older. When she was all made up, she could pass for twenty-five or twenty-six. Her hair was cleanly shaven in the back and on the sides, which made her neck seem even longer. She stacked the top in layers going toward her face.

Her old hairdresser cut it that way before she left for school and promised her it would be a low-maintenance cut. He was right. She grew to love her short cut—she had few bad hair days.

"Are you going to try on the outfit or am I gonna have to wear it myself?"

"Okay, I'll try it on, but I'm not going to guarantee you I'll wear it." She tried on both pieces and looked at herself in the mirror." Sandra was right. Tiara looked gorgeous and extremely feminine. Her long legs looked even longer in the mini.

"Girlfriend, that looks good on you," Sandra said, and turned to look on Tiara's desk for a pair of scissors. "Now, what kind of shoes and pantyhose do you have?" She found the scissors and began to cut the tags off the new clothes.

"Well, I have some black tights and these black shoes." Tiara pulled out shoes with a thick, tall heel.

"Those are sharp. What are you waiting for? Put them on."

Tiara put on the tights and shoes. She looked like a model. She had to admit it to herself. She looked pretty good. She loved to dress and always made a fashion statement when on campus. But this time she looked good in a different way.

"I don't know why you don't dress like this more often."

"Because I feel like I'm exposing myself too much when my clothes fit too closely."

"You wear that spandex shit when you go to the gym."

"That's different."

"Whatever!"

"Whatever," Tiara sassed back. "Gina'd better hurry up!"

"That's right. If she's not here in five, we leave her." Just then Gina knocked and walked through the door. She was wearing loose black bell-bottoms and a cut-off long-sleeved top to match. The sleeves flared and hung slightly over her hands. But it was her black stacks that made the outfit sing.

"You are sharp as usual. And where did you get those shoes?" Sandra asked, and bent down to get a closer look.

"I'm not gonna tell you, because you'll go out and get the exact pair, and that would decrease the originality of mine," Gina said. "Tiara, you know that you're gonna be killin' 'em with that 'fit."

"I told you, Tiara," Sandra said. "I know what I'm talking about."

"We need to hurry up and finish getting our makeup on so we won't have to be standing at the back of the line," Tiara said, ignoring her friends' compliments.

"You're right," Gina responded, "but go on girl, anyway, with your bad self. And you don't have to say thank you, because I mean it. You're a diva tonight." They all laughed and put on their makeup and danced in the mirror while getting ready for the party.

Once their makeup and hair were perfect, they walked out of the door, leaving Tiara's room a disaster, but they looked good. Because the campus party was only about a two-minute walk from their dorm, they walked, as most students did. They were feeling good and joking and singing along the way because they all knew it was going to be a good night.

After the party, they came back to Tiara's room to recap the excitement. They joked about how all the men were checking out Tiara and how she got asked to dance more times than Gina and Sandra combined. Tiara denied their accusations, but they were telling the truth.

She was happy to have gotten so much attention, but she was not interested in any of the guys she danced with. However, there was one guy with the deepest dimples and the sexiest smile she had ever seen. She had seen him on campus before, and she thought his name was Ben, but she wasn't sure. She would have sworn he noticed her too, but he never approached her. And she was not about to approach him. She was a firm believer in men making the first move, giving her the opportunity to not appear desperate or needy. But "Dimples" was fine, and she was going to keep her eyes on him.

The girls also talked about how awestruck they were by the Greek turnout at the party; every sorority and fraternity on campus was represented in large numbers. They appreciated all the sororities, but all agreed that there was only one for them. They all had dreams of joining the "ladies in pink." The three imitated members of each organization, dancing around the room while throwing up different fraternity and sorority signs. They got in a line and tried to do the sororities' steps around Tiara's small room, but it didn't work because no one remembered the same moves.

Exhausted from the night's activities, they wound down around five-thirty. Tiara had a king-sized bed, made up of two twin beds pushed together with a king-sized egg crate foam pad on the mattresses, and they all found a spot on the huge bed and passed out in their party clothes.

Sandra was the first to wake up. It was a little after noon. "Oh no, I need to call my parents. First I need to call Mindy."

Gina looked at her and shook her head. "Let's go to Shoney's. I'm starving."

"That sounds good to me," said Tiara. "And let's stop by the mailboxes afterward because I haven't checked my mail all week."

"Neither have I. The post office is too far. Let's meet back here in about thirty minutes. I need to wash my face and brush my teeth," Gina said, frowning at the awful taste she always had in her mouth the morning after drinking alcohol. She got out of bed, put her makeup back into her bag, slid on her shoes, waved good-bye, and left.

"Mindy, did Mom call last night?" Sandra asked. "Oh, good, I can't believe it. I'm on my way to the room, but I'll be leaving to go right back out, so you and Todd don't have to worry about getting up. See ya in a sec."

Sandra hung up the phone. "Do you believe they didn't call me last night? I'd better call them to make sure that everything is all right!" Sandra put on her shoes, followed Gina's routine, and said that she'd be right back.

Tiara made her bed and picked up the remaining makeup. She had a huge piece of carpet that covered almost her entire room, but it stopped short by about two feet. She swept the part of her floor that the carpet didn't cover, which was the area close to her mirror. Then she grabbed some jeans, a sweatshirt, and her bathroom bucket, and headed to the bathroom.

The buffet was crowded with students—most had been at the party last night. Shoney's was the weekend spot. All-you-can-eat breakfast, plus students got a ten-percent discount when they showed their IDs.

"Gina, do you have everything ready for tomorrow?"

"I've been meaning to talk to you about that. I have everything ready, and I have the money, but Tiara, I don't think that I'm going to have the time that it takes to pledge. I can't quit my job, and you know the kind of hours that I work."

"Does this mean that you're not going to write this semester?" Sandra asked in an almost hopeful voice. She hated that her parents absolutely forbade her from pledging until she completed two satisfactory years of college. She hoped, somewhere deep in her heart, her friends would have to wait for her.

"I'm not sure. I mean I want to, but I'd hate to start something and not be able to finish it."

"Well, no one is guaranteed to be accepted. Both of us may write this semester and not get chosen, and then you won't have to worry about anything. But if you are chosen, it may not affect your working. Let's cross that bridge when we get to it. There may be some ways to change your schedule or switch some of your hours. Have you talked to somebody about the possibility of needing to switch hours?"

"Yeah, there's this guy I have switched hours with before, but I'm not sure that he's reliable, and I can't afford to lose my job over somebody else's negligence."

"I'm sure you'll work something out," said Sandra, "But girlfriends, you know that I hate it that y'all are going to leave me alone in the non-Greek world. What will I do without you two?"

"What do you mean?" Tiara questioned. "Greek or non-Greek, we will always be friends and nothing is going to change that."

"I needed to hear that," Sandra said.

Tiara was back in her room going through her week's worth of mail. There was a letter from her mother. She opened that first because she had only received two other letters from her mother since she had been in college. Both were short and to the point, and usually had a few dollars enclosed. This one was similar. It was a one-paragraph letter with twenty-five dollars enclosed.

> *Dear Tiara,*
>   *I'm proud of you. I know that this is not much money, but I won $100 on a scratch-off lottery ticket and I gave your brothers and sisters fifty dollars to split, and split the other fifty between you and me. Buy yourself something nice and don't be up there being all fast! Talk to you later.*
>
>   *Your momma*

"Thank you, Momma!" Tiara said out loud. "I wasn't expecting this." Then she opened the care package Rhonda sent. She sent one every month, containing all of Tiara's favorite junk foods, and sometimes there'd be money, anywhere from ten to fifty dollars. She would also include her personal favorite toiletries, which Tiara had adopted as her favorites. This care package, however, was lighter than usual, and she had already received one for the month. "What did she send this time?"

She opened the package. Inside was a dress. A nice dress and jacket. An expensive dress. She could just look at it and tell. Tiara tried it on. It was a perfect fit. She sometimes felt that Rhonda knew her better than she knew herself. It was sleeveless, camel-colored, with a simple, straight cut that came just above her knees with a short split in the back. The jacket was cut short and had a wide collar. Rhonda also sent her favorite pair of pearl earrings and a long string of pearls, which added elegance to the en-semble. In the letter that accompanied the package, Rhonda instructed Tiara to wear flesh-colored pantyhose and the camel shoes they had bought on sale a year ago. Tiara laughed to herself because she already had them on. They were a perfect match. Rhonda also instructed Tiara to return the pearl set pronto after rush.

She stared at herself in the mirror. "I look pretty damn good if I must say so myself." She took off the outfit and put on shorts and a T-shirt. She lounged on her bed, then picked up the phone and called her mother and her Big Sister, and thanked them for their gifts.

NINE

Stephanie woke up Saturday morning in bed next to Jeff. They had gone to dinner and a movie the night before. Afterward, they went back to his apartment and had drinks. After her second glass of Chardonnay, he was able to convince her to spend the night with him. Why am I still seeing this jerk? she asked herself. She looked over at him. He was knocked out. I don't like him and he can't even screw. What a wasted night. What a wasted life. Even in his sleep he looks like a jerk.

Jeff was a jerk. He was an investment banker and worked for his father's close business associate, who promised to take Jeff under his wing and teach him the ins and outs of investing. Although they were in the South, he proclaimed that he hated any city that wasn't Washington, D.C., and showed no respect for anyone who wasn't from D.C., or who wasn't in his fraternity, or didn't make or have the potential to make anything over a six-figure income.

She hated that she wasn't ready to stop seeing Jeff; he was her safety net. Although she didn't like most of his ways, she knew his family was wealthy and that he was going to receive a healthy trust fund when he turned thirty. He would be set for life, even if he chose never to work again. So she kept her negative thoughts about him to herself, but sometimes expressed them to her mother.

She quietly got out of bed and went to put on her clothes, which were scattered across the floor. As she was reaching for her underwear, she almost tripped over one of the two bottles of wine that they'd gone through the night before.

Damn! I drank too much last night, she thought. I need to get dressed and get out of here before he wakes up.

"Hey, baby doll. I know you're not leaving this early," Jeff remarked. She hated when he called her that, because she found out he called all of his previous girlfriends "baby doll." But why was she surprised? she thought. Jerks don't know how to be original. They try the same tired game on every woman they deal with, because to them pussy is pussy. It's just attached to a different face.

"Well, I have a lot to do today," she said.

He disregarded her reason. "You can't leave, because we're going to go out and get brunch and maybe come back here and do a little more of what we did last night."

"Jeff, I have to plan for rush."

"Maybe tomorrow, huh?" he asked.

"Do you ever listen to a word that comes out of my mouth? I have rush tomorrow. I've told you about rush at least three times already," she said, frustrated that he didn't remember or care.

"Oh, yeah. Is it that important?"

"What?" she asked.

"To plan. I mean. You're paying to get in anyway. You're a legacy, and you're my girl. What is there to prepare for? You're already prepared because of who you are," he whined. "Now, let's go eat."

It sometimes seemed that he never went through the college experience. Jeff graduated with honors from his parents' alma mater, Howard University, and pledged the same fraternity as his father. Yet he often acted as if Stephanie's college experiences, although similar to his, were not relevant.

"You know what? I'm going to pretend you didn't say that," she said.

"Say what?" he asked.

"Just forget it."

"Well, can we at least get a quickie in?" he begged in what he thought was his sexy voice, which fell short of its desired effect.

"I've got to go, Jeff, and I don't know when I'll be seeing you again. Bye."

She walked out of his bedroom with her shoes in hand and her pants half-zipped. She just could not get out of his condo quick enough. She was actually beginning to hate being around Jeff. There's got to be something better than this, she thought, as she slammed the door and rushed to her candy-apple-red convertible Mustang.

Stephanie got out of the tub, put on her bathrobe, went into the living room, lounged on her plush couch, and turned on the TV. An old *Love Boat* episode was playing and she tried to get into it, but it only depressed her. Everybody on those kinds of shows always seemed to be happy and in love.

She turned the television off and picked up her address book. She needed to feel special, and yearned to talk to a man who would make her smile. After going through her address book from A to Z, she could not think of one single man whom she could call, converse with, and hang up feeling good.

"What kind of fools have I been spending time with?"

She got out a piece of paper and a pen and started writing down all of the men she'd had sex with, starting in high school with her boyfriend Tim. She went on, through her freshman year in college to the present. She couldn't believe how long the list was. By the time she got to Jeff, she threw the list on the floor, laid back on the couch, and stared at the ceiling. Had she really been with that many men? What kind of person was she? Who was she? She really didn't know. She was so overwhelmed and frustrated with herself and with her life that she gave up and went to sleep.

She was awakened by the telephone. She reached over and grabbed it. "Hello!"

"Hi, Steph. What ya up to?" It was Sidney, but she didn't sound like her usual, chipper self.

"Hey, Sidney. Actually, I was taking a nap. What's wrong?"

"Nothing, really. I'm parked downstairs and figured that I'd call before I came up."

"What? Didn't you see my car parked downstairs?"

"Yeah, but I wasn't sure if you were with Jeff or not."

"Oh. I'm still in my bathrobe, but come on up."

"Okay. I just need to talk to you about something. We are good friends, aren't we? No matter what, right?"

"What's going on? Are you all right?

"I don't know."

"Come up here and talk to me!"

I decided I'm not gonna write this semester," Sidney said. Her voice sounded as if she had been crying, but Stephanie wasn't sure, because her makeup was flawless as usual and would camouflage any trace of swollen eyes.

"What?" Stephanie asked her longtime friend in disbelief. "Why not?"

"Well, the timing is not right. I'm a junior now and I do have one more year to write. Plus, when you make it in this semester you can make sure they vote me in next year."

"But, Sidney, we were supposed to do this together. I can't do this by myself. We've been planning this together for the last two semesters. You just can't give up on me like this."

"Well, Steph, you know me. I'm so quick to change my mind."

"Not about something like this. Tell me the truth, Sidney. What is really going on?"

"Steph." She paused and looked directly into her friend's eyes. "I . . . I'm pregnant."

"You're pregnant? No, that can't be right. You have been on the pill for three years. I was there when you went to the doctor to get your first prescription."

"Well, it happened, Steph. I was taking antibiotics for my sinus infection, and it apparently affected the strength of the pill. So I'm pregnant."

"By whom? You're not even seeing anybody on a regular basis. Who were you having unprotected sex with anyway?"

Stephanie had known Sidney since they were freshmen. They had a lot of the same interests, and she was the only person Stephanie felt she could really be her true self around. However, they differed in that Sidney was not into short-term relationships, and never had sex until she felt her partner was trustworthy.

Sidney paused. She looked away from her and stared at the center-piece on the coffee table. Then, after what seemed like an eternity of silence, she blurted out, "Scott."

"Scott! Scott! You're pregnant by Scott?" Stephanie could not believe what she was hearing. She used to date Scott. She had been intimate with Scott, and his name was on the list that she had compiled earlier. It had been two years since they even talked, and he was such a dog. She stopped seeing him because she found out he was also seeing a girl she had a class with. Why was Sidney seeing him, and why hadn't she told Stephanie that they were seeing each other?

"I know you're wondering why I didn't tell you about us. I was going to, but this happened. Actually, I was hoping that I would never have to tell you, because there really is no us . . . I mean there is nothing to me and Scott." She stopped talking and put her hands over her face.

Stephanie looked at Sidney and said, "I'm sorry you're pregnant, but you need to let me know just a little more about why you, my best friend, was with my ex, Scott."

Sidney began to explain. "There was a campus party about two and a half months ago. The only reason I went was because I was bored. You were visiting your grandparents in North Carolina. And as you know, I wasn't, and still am not, seeing anyone. You are basically my only friend, and you were gone. Anyway, I was trying to prove to myself that if I wanted to go out and have a good time, I didn't need to have somebody with me."

"And?" Stephanie questioned. She was only concerned with why Sidney had betrayed her.

She took a deep breath and continued. "Anyway, I had a little too much to drink and decided that I'd go to the party on campus by myself. When I got there, the only face that looked familiar was Scott's. I mean, there were other people that I knew, but . . . well, you know what I mean. We danced a couple of times, and when I realized I was at the deadest party of the year, I walked over to him—trying to be courteous—and let him know I was leaving."

"So if you were leaving," Stephanie pushed, "how did you end up sleeping with him?" At this point tears were beginning to fall. She couldn't believe she was getting this kind of news, especially the day before rush. How dare Sidney.

Feeling the hostility in Stephanie's voice, she got defensive. "Steph, I'm trying to get through this. It's not easy for me to tell you this," she said.

There was a moment of silence.

"He offered to walk me to my car. We stood by my car and talked, and he said that he had some coolers in his car and asked me if I wanted one. I said okay. I mean, I was ready to leave the party, but I wasn't trying to go to an empty apartment. Not just yet, anyway," she explained. "We sat in his car and drank. He had several. I don't know how many I had. Anyway, I woke up in his apartment, naked, lying next to him."

"Oh, so you're saying you passed out and he screwed you while you were sleeping. That's a bunch of bull, Sidney, and you know it is. Plus, why the hell did you let him drive home drunk?"

"No, that's not what I'm saying. I'm saying that it didn't even seem real. It was like a dream or something. The next day I only remembered pieces of the evening. I remember being in his apartment, but I don't even remember the ride there. It was really weird."

Stephanie was stunned. As her friend was telling her the details of that crucial night, her mind flashed back to their past conversations. Her mind flashed to them discussing how, if friends were true friends, they wouldn't, under any circumstances, see each other's ex-boyfriends. And how there were enough men on the earth that they didn't need to be recycled, at least by family and friends. Then she would flash to them discussing their plans for rush, and pledging and crossing and celebrating.

"Stephanie, we both promised never to tell anybody about what happened. I haven't even talked to him since."

Stephanie didn't respond.

"Stephanie, I am so sorry this happened. And if I could turn back time, I would have never gone to that party. I . . . I don't want this baby."

Stephanie could not find it in her heart to feel sorry for Sidney. She could only think about their plans for pledging together going down the tubes. She figured Sidney would get an abortion anyway. That was not the issue. But now Stephanie's best friend had betrayed her, and she was going to have to go into the sorority by herself with strangers.

She was so angry that she was going to walk out of the room without saying anything, but she couldn't hold back. "Sidney, how could you do this to yourself? I told you how Scott was and you slept with him anyway, knowing how he played me. How could you do this to us? I guess our friendship means nothing to you. All you care about is yourself. Now I have to go through all of this by myself. You are so selfish. I don't care what you do about your pregnancy. I really don't care."

She was tired of people being inconsiderate of her feelings. Her biological mother chose drugs over her, and Sidney chose a one-night stand over their friendship. She decided she was not going to be so trusting of people, because in the end, they always let you down. Stephanie got up, went to her bedroom, and slammed the door behind her, leaving a stunned Sidney on the couch feeling sick to her stomach. Sick because she was pregnant by someone she barely knew. Sick because she had just lost her best friend. And she felt especially sick because she didn't know what to do or where to turn to get support for her unplanned pregnancy.

TEN

Malena dressed for her date with Ray. She was convinced that tonight would determine their future together. Everything had to be just right—her outfit, her hair, her makeup, the mood—everything. Tonight was the night she was finally going to be with Ray. She was going to make sure he knew she was the only one for him. Although their date to the movies the previous weekend was their first, it was like every other time they had spent together. They kissed good night at her door. Ray couldn't come in for even a few minutes, because he had an eight o'clock class the following morning. Unlike that date, tonight would be special. They would get the opportunity to talk about the course of their relationship.

She and Tammy had gotten manicures and pedicures after class on Friday, but Malena scheduled her hair appointment for Saturday morning. Malena's hair was styled in a bob that hung just above her chin and was shorter and stacked high in the back. It was a sophisticated cut that complemented her face. She had dark chocolate brown skin, high cheekbones, pretty white teeth, and a beautiful smile, which was so outstanding that the men she dated always commented it was her smile that had attracted them to her.

Although she wanted to look appealing, she didn't want to be uncomfortably dressed, because it would hinder her from really being able to relax around Ray. She had two outfits laid out on the bed. One was a two-piece black ensemble of wide-leg pants and a jacket that crossed in a "V" in the front and tied on the side. It was classy and always looked good, and she could wear her black high-heeled shoe boots with it. The other outfit was more casual: black jeans, a spandex body suit, and a black suede jacket. She could wear her black cowboy boots with that outfit.

Malena was really into black lately because she felt it hid the eleven or so pounds she'd managed to pick up since she'd been in college. She was five-foot-five, and as a freshman she had weighed about 135 pounds. Three years later and she'd climbed two dress sizes. She had a goal, to reach what she felt was her ideal weight of 130 pounds, and she knew that once she started pledging, her diet would begin. She'd been told that most people lost at least five pounds while pledging. If she was lucky, she could shed those and lose the rest by keeping busy with all of her sorority activities.

After careful thought, she decided to dress casually, and chose the black jeans and jacket because they would help hide her waistline when she sat down. She could wait and take her jacket off when they really got comfortable. By then, he would be too close to her to be watching her waist.

As Malena put on her earrings and the finishing touches of her makeup, the door bell rang. Instantly, her stomach filled with the butterflies that always appeared whenever Ray was around. I don't have anything to be nervous about, she thought, as she walked to the door. Besides, Ray should be happy I'm spending time with him. She always made an effort to boost her self-esteem and to see the brighter side of life.

Malena held her breath, and her stomach, and opened the door. "Hi, Ray," she said casually.

"What do you mean 'Hi'? I know you can do better than that, Miss Adams. Where's my hug?" he asked.

She smiled at his excitement to see her, and put her arms around his neck. He squeezed her waist so hard that she wouldn't have to hold it in for the rest of the night. But those butterflies in her stomach started all over again. Then Ray grabbed her by the chin and gave her a sweet and gentle kiss on the lips. "So how's my favorite girl today?"

"Better now that you're here."

"That's what I want to hear. So are you ready to begin our celebration?"

"I am," she said. "So, what do you think my chances are?"

"Baby, trust me. You have all the qualities that it takes. They'll be crazy not to accept you. I mean look how good you look! You're a go-getter, you're intelligent, caring, and you are so much fun to be around."

"You're so right!" Malena agreed, pleased that Ray noticed.

"I know I am. Malena, you're always positive about everything else in your life, and you have to be just as positive about this."

"I will be," she said. "And even more so with your vote in my corner." Then she grabbed his hand and led him over to the sofa in the living room.

"Just let me get my purse, and I'll be ready to go," she said, floating to her room and almost forgetting why she went in there. I'd better get used to this good feeling whenever Ray is around, she thought.

Those butterflies actually left a good feeling in her heart. Every time he talked to her the way he did just then, she wanted to say, "Ray, honey, I love you!" and then rip off his clothes and take advantage of him. But, of course, she had to be a lady and keep her composure. So she just smiled, or hugged and kissed him. It was important to her that he respected her for who she was before she did any clothes-ripping.

She checked herself in the mirror just one more time, and grabbed her purse. Ray sat on the couch, where she'd left him, looking absolutely irresistible in his red fraternity cap and denim shirt and pants. She was glad she opted for casual.

"So are you ready to go?" he asked.

"Just waiting on you. Let's go."

Malena was under the impression that they would be going out to dinner and then back to his apartment. But Ray drove the car straight from her apartment to his.

"So, where are we going tonight, Ray?"

"Now, don't start asking questions." He looked over at her and smiled. "I told you that tonight is a celebration. You don't want to ruin it, do you?"

"Of course not. I'm just gonna relax and see what you've got planned."

"Okay, we're here," Ray said, as he parked. Malena didn't say anything as she sat there wondering what he planned. Ray got out of the car and walked around and opened her door. "Madam," he said, and motioned for her to come out. They walked to his apartment door.

"Ah . . . Lena . . . can you stay right here just for half a minute, and I'll be right back to let you in? I promise it'll only take a half a minute." He didn't wait for an answer. He quickly turned the key, let himself in, and shut the door.

"This'd better be good!" she yelled from outside the apartment door.

When Ray opened the door and let Malena in, she walked into an atmosphere that overwhelmed her. The lights were turned down low, mellow music played softly in the background, and candles glowed on his homemade dinette, which was made out of stacked egg crates, a large rectangular wooden board that was covered with a white bed sheet, and four lawn chairs. The table was set with two paper plates, plastic cups, and mixed forks and knives. Ray even had pink carnations in the middle of the table. She was touched he cared enough about her to go through all of this trouble.

He motioned for her to have a seat in a lawn chair.

"Is all of this for me?" she asked shyly, and showed him her beautiful smile.

He went to the refrigerator and didn't say a word. He brought back a bottle of white Zinfandel, and filled both plastic cups.

"Ooh la la," Malena remarked.

Ray still didn't say anything, but the look on his face let her know he was proud of himself for setting up the whole thing. He walked back to the kitchen and stirred whatever was in the saucepans. Then he looked in the oven, closed the door, and turned the oven temperature to broil. With a mysterious smile on his face, he walked back over to Malena and said, "Dinner will be ready in a matter of minutes."

"What are we having?" Malena asked, unfamiliar with the aroma coming from the kitchen.

"See, there you go asking questions," Ray said, as he sat in the lawn chair across from her. "You'll find out soon enough what's cooking. Let's make a toast."

"Okay. Shall I go first?"

"That's cool, because I have something special to say. By all means, you go first."

"Ooh!" Malena responded. "I can't wait to hear yours."

Then she held up her cup and began. "My toast is to our meeting in the bookstore and you giving me your number. And to our getting to know each other better; it's been nearly three months. And finally to tonight . . . I feel so special tonight, and I see a positive future for us, and I just want you to know that I really care about you. So this is to our future." They touched cups and took a sip. The wine was good, and the mood was right. Malena couldn't ask for anything more. Then Ray made his toast.

"It's my turn," Ray said, and held up his cup. "My toast is simply to moving forward. We've been seeing each other for a while, and I'll be graduating this May. We have been very close friends—more than friends—and we both know there's something positive between us. Malena, I want you to be my lady."

Their cups touched and they looked deeply into each other's eyes. She was floored, and her heart nearly thumped out of her chest. Ray was saying all the right things.

There was no pressure in their relationship. They just kind of spent time with each other when they could. She never asked him about anybody he was seeing, and he never asked her. She did hear once about him dancing a few too many times with some girl one night at a campus party, but she never heard anything else. Malena didn't want to go fishing for more information, because she hoped he'd never find out about her and Anthony.

And that relationship was over now—almost—and she didn't have anything to worry about. Also, she had been patient about her and Ray committing to each other, because she knew he was really close to his fraternity brothers, and that they did a lot of traveling to other campuses on the weekends. And although it killed her that they didn't spend a lot of weekends together, it wasn't so bad, because she had been seeing Anthony. Now, she hoped, everything would change. After their last date, Malena had begun to feel guilty about stringing Anthony along, so she had called him that night and broke things off.

"Malena, I know I've been spending a lot of time with the bros, plus I've been trying to finish with my master's, so I've really been studying late during the week. But now I finally see a light at the end of the tunnel, and your pretty face is there also." He smiled and actually seemed a bit nervous. He continued, "What I'm saying is that I have been offered a nice job here in the city, which I've already accepted, and I'll be staying here for sure. I will be looking for an apartment close to campus starting next week, which means I will be close to you. There are certain things that will change about me. There are certain things that are already changing. I'm just saying that I know I will have more time for our relationship. So, do you want to spend more time with me?" he asked.

"Of course I do!" Malena nearly shouted.

"Now, I do want you to pledge and experience sorority life to the fullest. And I don't want to stop you from having fun and enjoying yourself." He was saying a lot and never seemed to be at a finishing point, but he trudged on. "What I am saying is that after this semester you will have one more year left of school and you'll soon be thinking about working and where you're going to stay. I hope that you will think of me in your planning, because I want to include you in mine."

Malena was speechless. She knew tonight was going to be special, but she didn't realize that she and Ray felt the same way about each other. He was serious, maybe even more than she was. He had erased any doubts that she had about their relationship.

"So what do you think about what I said?" he asked.

"First of all, congratulations on getting a position—already. I'm so proud of you," she said, trying not to become too emotional. "Second, I am so glad to hear that you feel the way you do about me, because I definitely feel the same way about you. You have become an important part of my life, and I don't want to ever feel like we're not going to be together."

She crossed her arms on the table and leaned toward him. "I feel confident about our future together. You just don't know how happy you've made me."

"Since you're so happy, won't you come over here and show me some love?" he joked.

Malena got up and sat in his lap and pecked him on the lips. "You know, now that I know I've got you in my corner, I feel even more confident about tomorrow."

"That's my girl. You want to know something else?"

"What's that?"

"I know that I've never told you this before, but I want you to know that I love you," he said.

"Ray, I love you too," she said.

They gazed long and deep into each other's eyes. Malena knew he was sincere. She felt it in the vibe that was moving between the two of them. This was the closest she'd ever felt to him. And then he kissed her.

It was a perfect moment, interrupted only by the smell of burning food.

"What's that smell?" she asked. They both jumped up and rushed over to the oven. Ray opened the oven door to a black charcoal substance that used to be chicken. His dinner was ruined.

"Lena, you should have seen it before it burned. I called my mother and she told me what seasonings to put on it and everything." They both looked at each other. Ray had this disappointed, puppy-dog look on his face. Then they both laughed. "I'll tell you what, let's order in pizza and act like nothing about tonight went wrong." He stopped and looked deep into her eyes.

"Ooooh, that will be nice." She returned his gaze. Nothing was going to ruin their night.

After ordering the pizza, they went to his bedroom and continued their conversation about their future and hopes and aspirations. They really opened up to each other about their feelings for each other and how they thought their relationship was progressing.

They ended the night by slowly undressing and caressing and appreciating each other's sensuality. They made love and nothing else seemed to matter—not the future, not Anthony, nothing but the moment that they were sharing . . . together.

PART
TWO

*Grant me the wisdom to know when to move
forward and the patience to be calm
when I need to just be still.*

*Grant me the wisdom to accept those incidents
that are out of my control,
And give me the strength to take action
when it is necessary to take control.*

ELEVEN

The first person through the doors of the Exclusive Pink Plush Rush was Stephanie, who was embarrassed and disappointed to be the first one there. She didn't want to appear overeager. The only reason she was there so early was because once she dressed she'd made herself leave the house and head to rush before she changed her mind.

She walked over to the greeting table, which was directly to the right of the entrance. Sitting at the table was a young lady whose face wasn't familiar. "Hello," Stephanie said, hoping she didn't speak too softly.

"Hi, how are you?" The girl seemed friendly enough. Her name badge said TRACY. She instructed Stephanie to write her name, address, and telephone number in the guest book. After Stephanie filled in her information, Tracy made her a name badge to wear for the evening. She also gave her a souvenir—a small pink-tinted glass jewelry box that had the sorority's letters and SPRING RUSH engraved on a gold plate on the top.

"Thank you," Stephanie said.

"You're welcome. You can take a seat while you wait for the others to arrive. I advise you to sit in the front row to make sure you don't miss any details," Tracy suggested. Although she was cordial, Tracy didn't seem too enthusiastic about her role as greeter. "Your program will be on your seat. Now I'll need your letter of intent, references, and official transcript," Tracy said.

Stephanie almost forgot they were in her hand until she looked down and saw the package. Following her mother's instructions, she had used soft mauve paper to print her letter and references on, and she put both, along with her transcripts, in the pockets of a mauve folder. She had written her name in calligraphy on the front of the folder and placed the package in a clear mauve-tinted envelope. It really looked classy.

"Nice packaging," Tracy commented, as she received it. "You put effort into this. I hope your letter is just as good," she said, without expression.

Stephanie wasn't sure if she was supposed to be flattered or offended by that statement, but she managed to smile. Tracy didn't seem to notice that Stephanie didn't respond, because at that moment, a group of several girls showed up.

Although she was nervous, Stephanie was up to her usual interior critiquing. She scanned the room, which was a boring student center meeting room, and checked out the layout. The walls and carpet were shades of brown and tan, and there were no windows. There was a podium at the head of several chairs. Behind the podium was a huge banner that had the sorority's name and shield. She was surrounded by several chairs that were facing the podium. To the right of her, and against the wall, was a long table covered with a pink tablecloth. On the table was a cake, but Stephanie couldn't read the inscription on the cake from her chair. There were also sandwiches, and the bread was dyed pink. There were baskets filled with chips and mints and nuts. Behind the chairs for the prospective candidates was another long table on which various sorority paraphernalia was displayed. There was everything back there, from umbrellas to paddles to playing cards. If you can think of it, they have their sorority's name and colors on it, she thought. Now, I like the display. It kind of sparks excitement. However, I would have put the paraphernalia table where the hors d'oeuvres are and vice versa. Then the display would be the first thing we would see when we walked through the door, and the hors d'oeuvres would be in the back center of the room, which would encourage people to mingle while they munch.

Stephanie's thoughts were interrupted by two girls sitting beside her who were chatting nonstop.

"Can you believe today is finally here?" Malena asked Tammy.

"Yes, I can. But I miss Phil," Tammy responded.

Stephanie drifted. I wish Sidney were here with me; then I wouldn't have been the first idiot through the door, and I wouldn't be so nervous.

"How can you possibly be thinking of Phil at a time like this? Girl, put him on hold. Today could possibly change our lives forever," Malena said.

"Yeah, you're right," Tammy answered, in an uncertain voice. "People are really starting to pour in."

"That's why I told you we needed to get here early. A front-row seat gives a good impression. It shows promptness and responsibility. I can't believe that tall girl beside us beat us here. We were supposed to be first. Oh, well . . . they did a great job of making this room look festive, huh?"

"Yeah, they sure did," Tammy replied. She didn't share Malena's enthusiasm. "You know, Malena, I'm not sure I'm ready for all this . . ."

"What?" Malena asked, and then calmed herself and her voice down. "You are ready, Tammy. Your grades are in good condition and your letter was good, really good, and I should know because I proofed it personally. Stop talking crazy, girl, you're making me nervous."

Tammy didn't respond. Malena gave her a worried look and decided that now was not the time to discuss this. They were going to make a good impression, and they were both going to be accepted.

Cajen stood in line to sign in. There were four girls ahead of her. She kept repeating to herself, One in every five females has herpes. One in every five, Cajen, one in every five . . . She tried to remind herself that she wasn't the only one in the world with herpes, and was still trying to soothe herself from the shock of the information she got from the doctor. She wouldn't have come to the rush if it weren't for Kim calling her to remind her that she needed to bring her letter and transcripts, and that she might want to try to be there at least five minutes early. When Kim picked up on her hesitation, she informed Cajen that she would go to rush if she had to personally drive her.

One in every five. That means . . . She started counting from the girl at the front of the line. One, two, three, four, five. I guess I'm the one in this group of five. I wonder if anybody can tell. Her paranoia increased.

Standing behind Cajen was Chancey, and she was a nervous wreck. She looked at Cajen and asked herself, How am I gonna ever be accepted with beautiful women like her to compete with? Then she smiled and remembered how excited Donald had been when she left his apartment. He hugged her, kissed her, and encouraged her to be confident. So she decided right then and there that she would do just that. I have as good a chance as anybody else, she assured herself.

The line continued to move forward. Cajen asked herself, What am I doing here? Maybe I should just leave.

"And your name is?" Tracy asked.

"Huh?" Cajen came to her senses and realized that she was now at the front of the line.

"Your name. I need it for the badge. Hello?"

"Oh, I'm sorry. My name is Cajen, Cajen Myers. Here are my transcripts and letter of intent." Cajen handed her package to Tracy.

"Thank you. Have a seat and please wear your name tag," Tracy said, as she handed it and her souvenir to her.

"Oh, I will. Thank you." Cajen managed a fake smile and proceeded to find a seat in the back row, hoping to blend into the crowd. But she felt she stuck out like a sore thumb.

Chancey walked in after Cajen, and took a seat next to her. Because Cajen appeared as nervous as she was, she spoke. "Hi! I'm Chancey, Chancey Wright. Girl, I am so nervous I could scream."

"My name is Cajen Myers." She paused. "And I guess I'm a little nervous too."

"It's funny, but I don't know most of the girls here. Do you?" Chancey asked.

Cajen was glad that Chancey began talking to her, because it allowed her to take her mind off her new, permanent problem. "Well, some of the faces are familiar and I've passed by a lot of the girls on my way to class, but I can't say that I know anybody's name."

"What year are you?" Chancey asked.

"Oh, I'm a freshman," Cajen replied.

"I'm a sophomore. But it's my first year out of high school, so I feel like a freshman most of the time. I would have never guessed you were a freshman—you look older. I assumed sophomore or junior."

"Do you know any sorority members?"

"No. Not by name, anyway."

"Well, I know one," said Cajen. "Her name is Kim. I'll introduce you to her if she's here. I'm sure she'll come. What do you think our chances are, you know, since we really don't know them?"

"I don't know. But I would give anything to be accepted."

"So would I," said Cajen with a smile. She couldn't believe it. She was actually excited, and glad she'd met Chancey.

Why did I wait on you, Gina? You can be so slow sometimes. Now look, we're at the end of the line," Tiara complained.

"I'm sorry. Sandra met me at my door when I was coming to meet you in the lobby. I was on my way out and she begged me not to go without her. What was I supposed to do, just leave the girl crying in the middle of the hall? I felt so bad for her that I walked her back to her room and tried to calm her down."

"You know, I feel so sorry for her too. I don't understand why her parents are so strict. She's one of the nicest girls on this campus, but by the way her parents act you would think that she was failing all of her classes and sleeping with every brother on campus."

"Yeah, it's kind of sad, isn't it?"

"I don't wanna talk about it anymore, but let's just make sure we go and visit her after rush," Tiara said, and took a deep breath. "Okay, I got my letter, references, and transcripts all here. Check and make sure you have everything."

"All here and accounted for. And Tiara, I don't want to hear you fussing about anything else, 'cause here come some more girls, and that means we're no longer last. Thank you."

"You're right. But I hope we get seats, because I would hate to have to stand up through the presentation."

"We'll have seats. They always overplan for things like this."

"And just how do you know?"

"I just do!" She smiled. One eyebrow went up, and she gave a smirk that said, Now-you-know-I'm-lying.

"Girl, you are too much."

Tiara, Gina, and the few girls who were behind them finally signed in and managed to get seats, but Tiara and Gina were not able to sit together.

A line of the sorority members marched to the front of the room, singing one of their songs. After everyone stood in front of her designated seat, they ended their song and sat down.

The president stood up and walked to the podium. "Welcome to the Exclusive Pink Plush Rush. I am the president of this chapter, and I would like to begin by saying our sorority is one with deep roots. We take our vows seriously. If you are chosen, we expect you to do the same." She paused to make sure she was understood, then continued. "Yes, it's nice to socialize and wear our letters, but that is only part of the many benefits. Our sorority was founded for purposes with greater meaning. We are a sisterhood bound by our desire to better ourselves, our campus, our community, and our world." She continued to explain the goals of the sorority.

Several presenters followed. Someone gave a brief history of the organization. Another gave a list of famous members of their sorority. One presenter told of the accomplishments of the chapter, another of the accomplishments of the sorority on a national level. Other members informed the candidates of additional pertinent information about the sorority. The membership chair, who would also be the dean of pledges, reiterated the qualifications for membership, and stated in detail the kind of character they were looking for to carry on the tradition of their sorority. Included on her list was intelligence, a sincere desire to better the community, flexibility, a well-rounded personality, and confidence. The entire presentation was thorough and informative. Afterward they played a couple of games, and prizes were given away. Stephanie won a prize for being the first person present at the rush.

Next, the president returned to the podium and announced the conclusion of the formal part of the presentation, and asked that everyone stay, have refreshments, socialize, and look at the display of paraphernalia that some of the members had set up for their viewing enjoyment.

Cajen and Chancey walked over to the hors d'oeuvres table and got pieces of cake and some punch. On their way back to their seats, they were stopped by Kim. "Hi, Cajen. I'm glad you could make it."

"Yeah, me too! The presentation was really enjoyable. By the way, this is my friend Chancey."

"Hi, Chancey. I'm Kim."

"Glad to meet you."

"I think I know you. Aren't you Donald's girlfriend?"

"Yes, I am," Chancey responded, with an uncertain look. She wondered if that would be a strike against her.

"Donald is cool! We have a class together this semester, and he's always talking about how much he's in love with his girlfriend, Chancey. And here you are. You've got a good man."

"Thank you. So, Donald's always talking about me?" Chancey smiled. She was shocked, and didn't want to overdo it.

"He sure is," Kim said, and noticed someone she wanted them to meet. "Oh good, they're together. Follow me. I want you two to meet the president of our chapter and the dean of pledges. From that point, you are on your own. And make sure you mingle, mingle, mingle."

They met and chatted with the president and dean for a while. The dialogue was dry and formal. Kim, who was never at a loss for words, carried the conversation during most of their encounters. They were glad to have her with them, because although she kept saying that they were on their own, she introduced them to virtually everyone in the sorority. Both Chancey and Cajen were grateful.

Stephanie, on the other hand, knew most of the members, because she had attended several of the sorority's functions and fund-raisers throughout her years in college. She had forgotten how cool they were. Unlike a lot of the girls who were struggling to get to know them, Stephanie had no problem because several members approached her first. She was approached with comments like "It's about time you finally wrote" and "I was wondering if you were interested." She was pleased with the way they responded to her being there. Maybe they won't find out about my real mother. Maybe they won't care, she hoped.

One would have thought Tiara and Malena were trying to win a popularity contest. If there was such an award, they would have tied for a first place ribbon for "Ms. Socialite of the Evening." Neither Tammy nor Gina could keep up with them. Tammy left early, and Gina found herself talking to other candidates.

Malena knew a few of the members and chatted with them. She was introduced to others, but she took it upon herself to meet every other sorority member in the room.

Tiara, on the other hand, didn't know many of them, and personal introductions were tough, but she hung in there. Some were friendly, and others didn't seem interested. But she weathered the storm and did the best she could to be friendly and confident. Although she didn't meet every member in the room, she met all of the officers and people with influence—the big mouths, as well as some of the ones who seemed to be well-liked on campus.

The evening was long and stressful for the candidates, and everyone left that night wondering what would happen next.

TWELVE

It started at midnight. First Cajen received a telephone call, then Stephanie, Malena, Tiara, Chancey, Tammy, and two other girls. The person on the other end of the telephone was the dean of pledges, who had spoken at rush about the kind of ladies they wanted to bring into their sorority. With each call, she calmly congratulated each person for being accepted as a potential pledge, then rambled off an address and ordered each of them to be there in ten minutes—no later—and she warned them not to wear any articles of clothing of which they were fond. They were also strictly informed not to tell anyone where they were going—including their boyfriends, roommates, friends, and parents.

Both Tammy and Malena quickly dressed. Although they were going to the same place, they took separate cars to make sure they didn't break any of the instructions they were just given. Because Tiara didn't have a car, she was instructed to discreetly wait in front of her dorm for someone to pick her up. Stephanie, Chancey, and Cajen all drove their own cars. The address they were given was an apartment complex located fifteen minutes away from campus. Several seniors and graduate students lived there.

Each new pledge was frightened because no one knew what to expect, and because they knew there was no way to make it to that address in less than ten minutes. Yet they were excited because they were one step closer to becoming members of their chosen sorority.

As they got to the door, one by one they were escorted by Tracy, the girl who had signed them in at rush, through a room and past a group of the same sorority members from rush, into a dark room. Once all eight girls were inside the room, someone walked in. She closed the door behind her, turned the light on, and introduced herself. It was the dean of pledges.

"I'm your big sister Nina and am to be addressed as Dean Big Sister Nina. The first thing I want to make clear to you tonight is that whatever happens to you from this point until you cross the burning sands, and whatever you learn about this sorority's precious history and its members, will remain a secret you should keep close to your hearts for the rest of your lives. In other words, we like to keep the things surrounding our sorority a mystery to outsiders, and therefore would prefer that nobody knows anything about the way we govern our sessions and ceremonies. Am I understood?"

"Yes, Dean Big Sister Nina," most of the pledges answered.

Nina raised her right eyebrow in disapproval, but she didn't say anything about some of the pledges' failure to respond. She continued, "Everybody in this room is now considered a pledge, and you are all now line sisters."

The new pledges nodded their heads in agreement, and looked around at one another. All were beautiful, intelligent sisters. They differed in height, shape, and skin color, yet they shared the common goal of crossing over into the Greek world. Stephanie was still in full makeup but wearing jeans and a sweatshirt bearing the school's logo. Malena had on a gray sweat suit and old tennis shoes. She and Chancey had removed their makeup and contacts, and both were wearing glasses. Chancey's hair was pulled back in a long ponytail, and luckily she was wearing a baggy shirt and jeans, because she was on such a high to leave the apartment after her call that she failed to put on a bra. Tiara was wearing slacks and a blouse. She and Gina had been hanging out with Sandra all evening to cheer her up. The phone had rung as soon as she walked into her room. Tammy was wearing Philip's army T-shirt and jeans. The other girls were also dressed down in sweats. One had on a blue top and bottom, and the other a plain bright-white warm-up.

Nina had a long talk with the eight anxious girls who didn't know what was about to happen to them. After she explained what was going to take place that night, and over the next several weeks, she lined them up by height, gave them each a number from one to eight, and said, "Don't get used to your number just yet, because if as many people drop as we suspect, it's bound to change in the next few days. It will probably change before the night is over. Good luck! Also, the ladies outside of this door are no longer just regular people. They are now your big sisters. Treat them with the utmost respect and always address them as 'Big Sister' and follow their instructions to the letter T. Do I make myself clear?" she demanded.

"Yes, Dean Big Sister Nina," the line sisters answered in unison.

"Okay. Now it's time to meet your big sisters," the dean said.

The girls, lined up by height, faced the door leading to a long-anticipated private world. They were no longer individuals, but pledges who were about to experience the unknown. They didn't know what occurrences would unfold during the course of the night, not to mention during the course of the pledge period. The mystery and suspense brought with it the same kind of anxiety they used to get when they knew their parents were going to punish them.

Dean Big Sister Nina opened the door and directed them into the room filled with their new big sisters, who appeared determined to pick the new pledges' brains and their wills to see if they possessed what it took to become their sorors.

At about three-forty-five A.M., the spring line completed its first pledge session and was asked to return to the room they were in at the beginning of the evening. Nothing short of military boot camp could have prepared them for what they experienced that night. The big sisters ordered them around, yelled in their faces, and expected them to know everyone's names and entire life histories. They were learning sorority history, both old and current, and were expected to regurgitate it on the spot. There was no way they could know any of the information that was expected of them.

As they sat, their heads were spinning and everybody was uncertain about continuing with this unusual sort of initiation. To make matters worse, they could hear most of the big sisters leaving, but others were still in the front room discussing what they thought of the new pledges and naming who they thought would make it and who would drop. They also mentioned things that were important to withstanding their pledge period, such as character, strength, and a commitment to "cross the burning sands."

The dean walked into the room and sat down with the pledges to discuss with them the events of the evening. But this meeting was more intense than their first meeting. Some of the pledges were crying, others stared into space in deep thought. Their dean asked them how they felt about what just happened to them and gave each person an opportunity to state her opinion.

The girl wearing the blue warm-up commented that she didn't know any of her new sisters, and asked why the big sisters expected her to know information about them she couldn't possibly know. Everybody agreed with her question, and looked to their new dean for a justifiable answer.

Dean Big Sister Nina responded, "Life is a test. The strong survive and the weak fail. This experience is a step to prepare you for the real world after college."

"How so?" Malena asked.

"When you get into the real world you are going to have to pay bills, strive to advance in your career, decide where you're going to reside, and choose which schools are best for your children—if you decide to have children. Often you'll have to make choices based on limited information. You will have to feel your way through dark moments in life. Pledging teaches you to recognize that, and to learn to use your survival skills."

"But I thought this was supposed to be memorable and enjoyable," Tammy complained.

"Haven't you ever had an experience that seemed tough, and then looked back on it and were able to laugh?" Dean Nina asked.

"Yes," Tammy replied.

"This will be one of them," her dean responded. There was silence in the room. Then she continued, "I think all is understood."

Nobody said anything. So she gave them a moment to digest the evening and her words.

She assigned the pledges offices and told them that each person was vital to making their pledge period a success. "Stephanie, I see a strong leader within you, and we need to bring it out, so I think you should be president. Plus, you have maturity on your side."

Stephanie didn't know what to say. She had never really thought of herself as a leader, but replied, "Thank you."

"Malena, you will be vice president. I need you to know everything that Stephanie knows, if not more. You need to be able to take charge when she can't. I know it won't be a problem for you. I heard about your leadership skills from a member of your Public Relations Society."

"You did?" Malena was astonished by her dean's knowledge of her.

"Listen. To be a well-informed woman, one has to do her homework. And trust me, we have done ours."

"Yes, Dean Big Sister Nina," she responded.

"As for the rest of the offices, we'll need a secretary, treasurer, and some other officers that are not customary and work only in a pledging situation." She explained those offices and told them that they should decide midway through their meeting tomorrow who would be most capable for each of the remaining offices.

She then instructed them to write down everything they'd learned from the night's session, and to make sure they wouldn't have to relearn any of those lessons. She gave them a list of pledge dos and don'ts, sorority information, and history they would have to know inside and out to cross the burning sands, materials they would need to purchase for special projects for their big sisters, and suggestions on possible pledge fund-raisers.

She also informed them that their next meeting would be Tuesday, and advised them to decide on a private place to meet to organize and to make sure they learned as much as they could about their big sisters and everything about each other—from each pledge's favorite food, to their bra size, to when or if they had lost their virginity.

"If you are to be sisters under our sorority, you are to know everything about one another just as you would your real sister, if not more. Your pledge period is used for a number of reasons. We need to make sure you all can work together and successfully pull through almost any situation. Knowing your differences and similarities helps."

She then walked toward the door and said, "I'm going to give you five minutes to yourselves, and I'll come back in for an update. Then you'll be free to leave."

After talking to their dean, most of the pledges felt they were ready to meet the challenge of pledging. But the two girls in warm-ups told the group that they didn't know they would have to go through a pledge period in order to be accepted into the sorority.

"This is not my type of thing. I can't deal and I won't deal," said the girl in the blue sweats.

Her friend agreed. "I refuse to go through another night like this one. It won't be worth it for me."

There was silence in the room. Stephanie realized that as president of the line she needed to take charge quickly. They only had five minutes to get things accomplished, and it was being wasted by the two wimps. So she spoke up and asked, "Are you sure?"

"We're positive. I am anyway. This is just not for us. Nothing is going to change my mind. Once I leave this apartment I am not coming back. So any plans made from this point on should not include us," said the first girl.

Her friend agreed.

"Does anybody else feel the same?" Stephanie asked. She hoped anybody who was thinking about quitting would do it now.

Nobody said anything.

"Well, if the rest of you are still in this until the end, let's make plans for tomorrow. Also, let's exchange telephone numbers now." Everybody except the two friends got in a circle and discussed their class and work schedules, and came up with a meeting time. They also discussed a location to meet—Stephanie's apartment—and other possible ways of meeting without being noticed by everybody on campus.

By the time the girls had everything situated, Dean Big Sister Nina walked in and asked, "Is everything in order?"

"Yes, Dean Big Sister Nina," everybody answered, including the two girls who had already dropped line. Nobody mentioned to the dean that the girls were no longer a part of their line, because they didn't know how she would react, and didn't want to know. After such an exhausting night, they figured it would be better dealt with later.

"Good. I need a copy of that information. Also, you girls will need to be uniformed the next time we see you as a group. Stephanie, take my number down. As a matter of fact, everybody take my home and work numbers just in case anything weird happens and you need to reach me. But, Stephanie, you call me at seven-thirty A.M. today, and I will give you a list of everything the line will need to discuss and take care of. You are now free to go. Oh, yeah, Tiara doesn't have a car and will need a ride. She stays in Campton Tower. Who lives near her dorm?"

"I do," answered Cajen. "I can take her home."

"Okay. And pledges, you also need to look into carpooling so you won't be too noticeable with all of your cars parked everywhere you meet. But no more than three people per car. Am I understood?"

"Yes, Dean Big Sister Nina," they answered.

She dismissed them, and everybody walked toward their cars. All of the big sisters who were in the front room earlier were gone. The apartment belonged to Nina, so she was the only one still there. That was a relief to the worn pledges. They didn't want to face their big sisters again for a long time.

As Stephanie walked toward her car, she thought of how proud she was to be chosen president of the line. But she was also intimidated by the tremendous responsibility of caring for a line of individuals who barely knew one another. How am I going to deal with this? she wondered. Then she began to worry about how she was going to make sure she called her dean in three hours. It was almost four-thirty A.M. already, and she was exhausted. She was not a morning person and was going to need help getting up that early with so little sleep, so she decided to ask Malena for help.

She caught up with Malena, who was getting into her car. "Malena, I'm going to need your help, if you don't mind. I am not a morning person. As a matter of fact, I have been known to sleep through my alarm clock on an average morning, and this is not an average morning," she joked. "I'm scared I won't wake up early enough to call Dean Big Sister Nina, even if I set my alarm clock."

Malena smiled at Stephanie. "I don't need much sleep, plus I'm a light sleeper. I'll call you at seven-twenty-five, and I'll talk to you until seven-thirty to make sure you are alert when you call Big Sister Nina."

"Thank you so much. I owe you one."

"With the way things are looking, I'm sure that you'll have plenty of opportunities to repay the favor. Anyway, we line sisters have to stick together, right?"

"You're right. Thanks again, and I'll talk to you in about three hours."

"All right," Malena answered and got into her car. She couldn't wait to get home so she and Tammy could recap the night's events.

Stephanie walked to her car, relieved the night was over. She considered some suggestions she could give her dean about the attire she and her line sisters could wear to sessions. Then she thought as she was driving home, Who cares what we wear to session? Session is the last place to be concerned about making a fashion statement.

Unexpectedly, she began to think about Sidney, the argument they had, and the serious trouble her friend was in. I was so wrong. How could I have been so cruel? My girl needs me, probably more now than ever before, and I turned my back on her because of my own fears and insecurities. I have not been a real friend to her. What have I done?

Stephanie was disappointed with herself. She decided to fix the situation by going to talk with Sidney later that day, after her first class, to see if she could mend things between them so she would be able to help her through this tough time.

Chancey walked Cajen and Tiara to the car. "Hey, Cajen. I stay in Minor Hall. Don't you stay in the same dorm?"

"Yes," she answered.

"You think I can ride with you and Tiara to the meeting tomorrow?"

"Yeah, that'll be cool."

"Maybe we can take turns driving. Call me tomorrow at about twelve-thirty and we'll set up a meeting time."

"Remember how nervous we were earlier today?" Chancey asked.

"Yeah, and now we have so much more to be concerned with," Chancey responded.

"Ain't that the truth," Tiara added.

"Well, I think we're going to do just fine," Chancey said. "I'll see y'all tomorrow."

Cajen and Tiara pulled off and found themselves sitting in silence. Tiara was thinking about all the bits of information she had picked up that night. She had decided, when they were in the room talking to Dean Big Sister Nina, that she was going to know every piece of information that was expected of her. She refused to give her big sisters any reason not to accept her. She was also planning her study time. In addition to meeting with her line sisters and big sisters and learning her sorority history, she had to find time to concentrate on her courses, which were her primary reason for being in school. She felt overwhelmed.

Cajen felt like she was going to explode. She wasn't sure what was tugging at her most: trying to get into the sorority, living with herpes, or finding the opportunity to talk to Jason to let him know how badly he had screwed up her life. She couldn't believe he hadn't returned any of her calls. How was she going to continue pledging if she didn't talk to him and at least release some of the pressure that was quickly building up and weighing on her mind? How was any man ever going to love her with this disease? How was she ever going to allow her new line sisters to get close to her, when she didn't even want to be close to herself? She hated herself for having ran with Jason. She hated him. She decided she wasn't sure if she would even leave her room to go to class, let alone meet with her line sisters or continue this pledging ordeal.

"I hope I can survive this semester." Tiara finally broke the silence as they got closer to her dormitory.

"Huh?" Cajen asked, still preoccupied with her own mess.

"I have some difficult classes this semester. I don't know how I'm gonna maintain my GPA with everything that's going on."

Cajen hadn't given her GPA a second thought. "Yeah, I know what you mean."

"So what do you think it's going to be like?"

"What?"

"Crossing over and becoming sorors."

"You know, I can't even imagine."

"I can't either, but I'm really looking forward to it. I'm with Chancey. I think we'll make it through just fine."

"I hope so. I really do," Cajen responded, wishing Tiara hadn't broken the silence. She wasn't quite ready to get to know her just yet.

"Hey, are you okay?" Tiara asked, concerned about Cajen being so engrossed in thought.

"I'm fine. I just need to get to my bed and get some rest, you know?" Cajen replied.

"Girl, I know what you mean. I really do appreciate you dropping me off."

"Oh, it was no problem, no problem at all." Cajen drove up to the front of Tiara's dorm. There was nobody outside or in the lobby. They were both thankful for that.

"So, I guess I'll see you tomorrow?" Tiara asked, a little suspicious that Cajen might be considering dropping line.

"Yeah . . . tomorrow."

"I will see you, won't I?" she persisted.

Cajen snapped out of her trance. "Oh, yeah, I'll be there. I'm fine. It's nothing that a shower and a warm bed won't solve."

"All right, you drive safely."

"My dorm is just around the corner. I'll see you tomorrow. Remember, I'm supposed to pick you up for the meeting. Now get some rest. We're both gonna need it."

Tiara said good-bye and got her key out as she walked toward the entrance to the dorm. I wonder, she thought, how many of us will actually hold on long enough to call one another "Soror."

THIRTEEN

Malena stopped by her apartment, as planned, to pick Tammy up for the meeting with their other line sisters. She was shocked and frustrated to find Tammy lounging on the couch and watching television in a T-shirt and sweats.

"Why aren't you dressed? And why are you just sitting around like you don't have a care in the world? You know we are supposed to be at Stephanie's apartment in about fifteen minutes. Get moving!"

"I'm not going," Tammy said.

"You're not what?"

"I just got off the telephone with Philip, and we decided that my pledging would become a strain on our relationship. He told me that he's planning to ask me to marry him at the end of this semester. I want us to stay close, and I want to focus on our future together. Now is not a good time for me to be running around like a maniac, trying to please some ungrateful big sisters just to get into their sorority. Philip and I decided it would hinder our relationship, and that pledging is not worth the strain."

"So why didn't you and Philip decide that before you wrote? Why did you waste your time?"

"Well, I told him what happened last night and—"

"You did what? You told him? Tammy, I don't believe you. I don't believe we're even having this conversation. I thought being in the sorority was our dream. How can you just throw it away like this? Philip can wait."

"See, Malena, what you fail to realize is that the sorority thing was not my dream, it was yours. Now don't get me wrong, I wasn't against it. I wrote because I thought it would be something fun for us to do together, and I only wanted it if it was convenient. And you know as well as I do that getting into this sorority is going to be anything but convenient," Tammy said. Then she softened after seeing the disappointed look on Malena's face. "I'm sorry I let you down, Lena, but I have to think of what's best for me and Philip, and our future together."

Malena opened her mouth to respond, but nothing came out. It wasn't worth it. Tammy and Philip were in love, and they had their minds made up. There was nothing she could say to change that. But she had to try one more time. "Tammy, you know if you turn back now there are no chances to come back. This is it!"

"Malena, I know, and you know I support you one hundred percent, and I will help you and the rest of the line in any way I can. I do realize I'm giving up a lot, but I think the trade-off is worth it."

Tammy got up, walked over to her best friend, and hugged her. "You'll be okay, and you know I got ya' back if you need me for anything."

Malena pulled back to look Tammy directly in the eyes. "So I guess that I'm gonna have to tell everybody that you're dropping. What am I supposed to say to them?"

"You've always been good at smoothing things over. Just tell them that it's personal, and please let them know it doesn't have anything to do with them."

"What if I don't want to break the news to them? Tammy, I think you should come with me, and let them know yourself."

"You know how dramatic things would get if I told them in person. We both know that the line as a whole can't afford to have any unnecessary distractions. My being there is unnecessary, and all of the questioning will cause the meeting to run late. We can't do that to them."

"Tammy, you already did it to them . . . us."

"I know you're mad at me. If I were you, I'd be mad at me too. But I think it would be best if you told them."

Although Malena was disappointed, she couldn't argue. "Well, I guess I'd better get out of here if I want to be there on time." She walked toward the door, then turned back. "Tammy, I respect your decision. I just wish you would have made it sooner." She picked up her backpack and walked out the door. She then tried to figure out how she was going to break the news to her new line sisters that her best friend wanted to drop line because she was in love.

Malena was the last one to get to Stephanie's apartment, where the meeting was being held. When she walked through the door everybody said hello and looked past her for their other line sister.

"Where's Tammy?" Tiara asked.

"Tammy dropped."

"Why?" everybody asked in unison.

"Well, it's a long story, but she had a good reason . . . I guess."

"Hold on now!" said Cajen. "I'm sorry, but that's just not good enough. I need an excuse that's better than 'It's a long story.' I mean, is somebody gonna be dropping every day? Is that what I'm supposed to expect?"

Stephanie jumped in. "Cajen, calm down."

"I can't calm down! Tammy is the third person to drop in less than twenty-four hours, and we've only had one session. If this continues, there won't be a line. I thought about not continuing myself, but I thought about Tiara and the rest of you, and I know if I dropped it would be for selfish reasons. Does anybody else realize how much we need one another now?"

"Cajen," said Malena, "nothing could have been done to stop Tammy from dropping. She had personal reasons, and it didn't have anything to do with the line or the session last night. She did what she had to do. But Cajen, I promise you this, I have no intention of dropping line, and if nobody else can say that, I'm saying it to you right now. They're gonna have to kick me off line if they don't want me to make it. Otherwise, I plan to complete this."

"I do too," Chancey agreed. Not knowing her new line sisters well, she felt comfortable listening and absorbing everything that was said.

"And you ought to know that I can't see nothing but pink," added Tiara.

Then everybody looked at Stephanie. "I don't know why you're look-ing at me. If you only knew how much this sorority means to me, already, you wouldn't look at me like that. I'm not only doing this for me, I'm doing this for my mother and her mother. I'm not going anywhere."

"Good," Cajen said. "Because if anybody else quits, I'm out."

"And we can't let that happen," Tiara said.

A silence fell over the room, and everybody glared at one another with the same sentiment in their eyes that said, You'd better not let me down. There was a sense of security in everyone's stating they were not going to drop, but doubt still lingered in the back of everyone's mind that somebody might lose her strength or her will, and quit suddenly.

Stephanie broke the silence. "All right, now that we've established that nobody else is dropping, let's get started." She looked around to make sure she had everyone's attention. "I hate to begin this meeting on a sour note, especially after the bad news we just received, but since it's likely we're going to be meeting a lot over here, I took the liberty of adding 'Stephanie's apartment dos and don'ts' to our pledge dos and don'ts."

"What?" Tiara asked, not sure if she heard her right. Her other sis-ters felt the same way.

"Don't take it personally. I just want to make sure everybody respects my apartment. I only have three rules. Is that asking for too much?" She didn't wait for an answer. "Those rules are: When we conduct meetings over here, do not sit on my bed. Take your shoes off at the door. And make sure, please make sure, you pick up after yourselves," she said, over-articulating every word.

"Okay, Dean Big Sister Stephanie. What's up with this tyrant behav-ior?" Tiara questioned.

"Oh, no, I don't mean to offend anybody, Tiara. It's just that with five people over here every day, it's going to be tough keeping things neat. I just wanted my requests to be made known, so there wouldn't be any mis-understandings in the future. Plus, my carpet was just cleaned last month."

Tiara looked around. Stephanie's carpet was nice and plush, not like that thin plastic carpet she was used to walking on while growing up in the Indiana projects. In fact, Stephanie's entire apartment was immaculate—almost too nice for someone her age.

She had cherry wood furniture throughout, in "good as new" condition, which had been her parents' before her mother went on a decorating binge. On her walls hung matted and framed African-American art. Everything flowed and matched throughout the entire apartment, from the entrance to the bedroom to the kitchen.

"Uummp!" Tiara frowned, crossed her arms, and looked away. None of her high school friends came from homes as nice as Stephanie's apartment. She didn't know anybody else who was still in college, and few who'd graduated, who could afford to live like this. But why, she thought, does she have to be so bourgeois about her things—like we don't have any home training? I know how to be around nice things.

"Tiara, don't take it personally. We really don't know one another, and I think we need to get our pet peeves out in the open," Stephanie said.

Malena took off her shoes and said, "I understand Stephanie's wanting to keep her apartment in mint condition. I would want the same if we were using my apartment. Now, I'm not sure I understand the rule about sitting on her bed, but we have to respect her wishes. Plus, where else would we be able to meet? Since Tammy dropped, my apartment is out, and everybody else lives in the dormitories. So we have no other choice but to meet here and respect her rules. I have a pet peeve myself. I hate when people don't pull their own weight. I hate to see a lazy, trifling person who relies on everybody but herself to succeed."

"That bothers me, too," Chancey agreed.

"Now if anybody falls into that category, we're gonna have a problem," Malena explained.

"I hate when people think that just because I'm smart that I don't know how to have a good time once in a while," Chancey expressed. "My intelligence is giving me a free ride through college, and I'm grateful. I am a bit shy, and it takes me a while to warm up to people, but there's more to me than my brains—I do have a personality."

"For the record, Chancey, brains are a bonus in this camp, so don't ever think they aren't appreciated."

"Right. And as far as personality goes, I don't think you would have been accepted if your letter didn't reflect character," Stephanie added.

Malena could sense that Tiara wanted to say something but needed a push. "Now Tiara, I know there are things people do that really get to you. So go on and get it off your chest now."

"Well . . . since you insist. My pet peeve is when people feel a certain way about me or other people, who may not do things quite like they should, and they go behind their backs and talk about them like dogs, and treat them differently just because of something that they can't help or don't know. I may not have come from much, and I know I've got a lot to learn, but I don't need people looking down on me because I don't always speak correctly or use the right fork," she said, looking at Stephanie.

"That's the worst," Chancey added. "I also hate when people expect you to be something or someone you're not. I think that differences and preferences make us each unique. They add balance to the whole scheme of things." Her statement reflected her growing concern about Don's attempts to mold her into his idea of a perfect woman. She was frightened that she'd never meet his expectations.

"I hate people who are deceitful. I can't stand people who keep secrets and mislead," Cajen added, in a harsh tone. Although Cajen was talking about Jason, Stephanie secretly took it and some of the previous comments personally because of her secret about her natural mother. The room felt tense, so she quickly changed the subject and talked about some of her favorite dishes, and said they could start cooking dinner at her apartment, since they would be meeting there.

As they becoming better acquainted, they discussed more of their likes and dislikes, and started to relax, finding more in common with one another.

As that conversation began to fade, Stephanie brought up the list of items Dean Big Sister Nina gave her during their telephone conversation that morning.

Tiara began to feel kind of foolish for being upset with Stephanie, but she always felt insecure and somewhat out of place when she was around luxury, and Stephanie's apartment was the epitome of luxury. Everything was name-brand and screamed "class," just like Stephanie. Tiara thought

Stephanie could tell she wasn't accustomed to nice things, and that she didn't trust that Tiara would know how to maneuver in her apartment without breaking something. She thought that was the reason Stephanie began the meeting by dictating rules. But Tiara chose not to expose the way she really felt toward her line sisters, because she didn't know how they would react. So she made peace with Stephanie. "I'm sorry for being so defensive regarding your requests concerning your apartment."

Stephanie accepted her apology and said, "I didn't mean to come off so coldly. I'm sorry too."

"Excuse me, pledge, but rule number ten states: You're not sorry. We don't accept any person who is sorry. 'You apologize,' " Chancey said.

"What?" everybody asked in unison. They weren't sure if she was serious.

"I'm just kidding." She laughed. "But it seemed like the perfect opportunity to bring up that rule."

"Is that really one of the rules?" Cajen asked. She hadn't even looked at the first one.

"Yeah, it is. I remember seeing it last night. But is it number ten?" Tiara asked.

"Chancey, how did you know that was number ten, and how many more of those rules do you know?" Stephanie asked.

"I learned all thirty of them."

"Has anyone else memorized all of the pledge rules by heart?" Stephanie asked.

"Well, I know the first five," Malena answered. "But certainly not all thirty."

"I'm shocked, Chancey," Stephanie said. "When did you find time to learn them?"

"I just went over them this morning before I got ready for class."

"What's pledge rule number twenty-five?" Stephanie quizzed Chancey.

" 'Pledges are to always keep themselves well groomed. We cannot accept any person who does not represent her best self.' "

"Twenty-six?" Malena asked.

" 'Because of rule number twenty-five, pledges must always have their hair neat and in place, and makeup is to be worn tastefully at all times.' "

"No shit!" Tiara responded.

Chancey went through the list of pledge dos and don'ts from number one to number thirty. She knew them all. "She's quoting these rules word-for-word," Cajen responded. She had the rules in her hand and was following Chancey's responses.

"What else do you know, Chancey?" Tiara asked.

"The first two pages of the history. That's all that I had time to go over this morning." Everybody looked at Chancey in amazement. Most of them knew only a few facts, and even fewer dates.

"But how did you learn it so quickly?" Cajen asked.

"Well, I have a photographic memory, which means that I remember most things after seeing them once. But I don't like to tell too many people, you know, because of the stigma that comes with it."

"Stigma?" Malena asked.

"When I was in high school, some of the popular girls shunned me and called me 'Goody Two-shoes.' Not to mention that I had a lot of responsibilities with my family's company at an early age and didn't hang out much, so I didn't have many close friends. Now that I'm in college I don't want to be judged before you get to know the real me," Chancey explained.

"Well, what I know of you so far, I like," Stephanie said. "You're intelligent and down-to-earth. Plus you pulled Donald. Do you know how many women on this campus would pay just to have a moment of his time? You must have something right going on. What's the problem? And as far as the stigma with your memory goes, I see you as a breath of fresh air. You're just the boost we need after these last couple of days."

Everyone agreed.

Chancey had a good feeling that they were sincere. She was accepted by her new line sisters, and her intelligence was a plus to them. She was assured that she could be herself around them, and not be unfairly judged. That evening she opened up and made key contributions to their planning.

They spent an hour choosing line officers, getting the telephone numbers of all of their big sisters, and tending to other details, like setting scheduled routine meetings and group study hours, and planning a fundraiser. They decided to have a male auction. Although it would be a bit risky, they were confident they could pull it off in a way that would be pleasing to their big sisters, and be profitable.

The five girls, who didn't know each others' names before rush, were now not only working well together, but bonding. Their paths had crossed, and they all felt confident it would be a good union.

FOURTEEN

H—hello." Cajen picked up her phone after three rings. She debated whether she should answer it, because of the chance that the person on the other end could be one of her big sisters, who would probably try to get her to say something that would get her into trouble during the night's session. Plus, she and Chancey were supposed to meet downstairs at her car in less than ten minutes and she didn't want to get into a long, drawn-out conversation with someone and keep Chancey waiting.

"Hey, Cajen." Luckily it was Chancey on the other end.

"Girl, don't ever scare me like that again. I thought you were a big sister, or even worse, Dean Big Sister Nina," Cajen said.

"Nah. It's just me. I apologize for scaring you."

"We're still going to meet at my car at five-thirty on the nose, right? You know, that's eight and a half minutes from now."

"Well, that's why I'm calling. Cajen, we know each other pretty well now, right?"

"Yeah, of course. What's up?"

"You know, I actually feel like you're my real sister sometimes. It's amazing how pledging makes people closer quicker."

Cajen's heart dropped. She didn't know what Chancey was about to tell her. Did Jason talk to Donald and tell him what he gave her? And Donald in turn told Chancey? How dare he tell anybody! We haven't even discussed it ourselves yet, she thought. She forced herself to ask, "What is it?"

"Cajen, I went over to Donald's house last night, or rather this morning after the session, and spent the night. I skipped my classes today too. We just needed to spend some quality time together. I missed him so much, and I didn't think I would be able to go another day if I didn't get a chance to see him."

"I thought you were gonna tell me something else," Cajen blurted, relieved. "You deserve to spend time with him, especially after everything we've been going through. And who has to know you missed your classes? You didn't even have to tell me that part."

"Whew, I thought you would be upset."

"Girl, please!"

"Well, I kind of lost track of time, and I'm on my way now. I'll just meet you there at six, but I know everybody's gonna wonder why I didn't ride with you and Tiara. I just don't want everybody to know where I am. Can you cover for me?"

"I don't think anybody would be too upset if they found out you were spending much-deserved time with Don, but where can we say you'll be coming from? By the way, tell him I said hi and that I can't wait to meet him."

She looked over her shoulder to face him. "Don, Cajen said hi."

"Hey, Cajen! Thanks for covering for us," Don yelled in the background. He was lying in bed next to Chancey, playing with her hair while she was talking to Cajen.

"I was thinking that maybe we could say I tore one of my contacts today and had to go get a replacement, and I called to let you know. How does that sound?" Chancey was looking for an excuse. She felt guilty because her and Don's spending time together was more his idea than hers. He pressured her a little to skip her classes to spend time with him. She initially told him no, but later surprised him by showing up at his doorstep at three-thirty that morning. She felt better about her decision once he assured her that he appreciated her act of endearment, but felt guilty for not adhering to the pledgee rules and being disloyal to her sisters.

"That's fine with me. But I still think you shouldn't worry about it. I'm sure everybody will be cool about it."

"Maybe, but just this one time . . ."

"Okay, if that's how you want to deal with it, then no problem."

"Thanks, Cajen. See you at six. If I'm late, it'll be no more than five minutes."

"I'll see you then. Don't do anything I wouldn't do. Well, I'm sure you already did!" She joked. "Bye."

Cajen was relieved. Why would Jason tell Don anything that personal anyway? It wouldn't have made sense. They're not even close. "I am bugging!" she said aloud, and picked up the phone and tried to call Jason. She got his answering machine. "Where the hell is he? I'm so sick of this. I can't leave a message. I hate him! I don't even know what I'd say if I left a message. His roommate would hear it and that won't work. This entire situation is just ridiculous."

Her mood changed. She didn't feel like going to a stupid meeting tonight. She felt like a fake at times because she was holding back secrets. Tiara spilled her guts in their last session about growing up in poverty and how her mother dates a drug dealer and how there were times when her family didn't know where their next meal was coming from. *And I can't even tell anybody that I was ever involved with Jason, let alone reveal that he gave me herpes.* She slammed the phone receiver down, grabbed her keys, pledge property, and black backpack, and stormed to her car.

I hate life!" Cajen screamed, as she pulled out of the parking lot. She, as well as her other line sisters, had been spending all of their time either in class, with one another, or with their big sisters. She totally understood why Chancey needed to get away and spend some time with Don. She needed so badly to confront Jason for all of the hurt he had caused her, and after that she would need a full day to cry and release all of her pain and stress. But when was she ever going to find the time to do that?

She pulled up beside Tiara's dormitory, then watched her walk through the entrance doors and toward her car. Tiara had her black backpack over her right shoulder and was bouncing like she didn't have a care in the world. All five line sisters carried the same kind of black backpack, which were filled with matching outfits that they wore to session every night. They also kept an extra outfit that would be presentable to wear in public, just in case they didn't make it back to their dorm room after session, in addition to a comb, brush, toothbrush, and other necessities.

Tiara got in the car. She was in an annoyingly good mood. "Can you believe that we have made it three weeks without anybody dropping?" she bragged. She then realized she was sitting in the front seat; the backseat of the car, which was officially hers, was empty. "Where's Chancey?"

Cajen tried to answer, but couldn't focus because she was still in deep thought about Jason.

"I can tell by the way you're looking past me that you've got a case of the zombies. I felt that way earlier today too. But between you and me, I skipped my two-thirty class and slept until just a few minutes ago. Girl, it helped me out so much. I feel refreshed. I'm a new woman. It was the deepest sleep I've experienced in a long time," she said. "So, where's Chancey?"

"Oh, she had to pick up a new contact. She tore hers this morning. She'll meet us at Stephanie's and will probably be five minutes late." Cajen's tone was dry and her face was expressionless.

"I know you like a book and something is wrong. What's up, Cajen?"

"Nothing really. I just got a lot of things on my mind right now. That's all." While Tiara celebrated their three successfully completed weeks of pledge period, Cajen was mourning that it had been over three weeks since she had spoken to Jason. While he was enjoying his happy life, she was walking around with a secret so awful, she couldn't even share it with her new sisters. She felt close to each of them, but wondered if they would ever look at her the same way if they found out.

"I'm supposed to accept that as an answer? Cajen, we've seen each other every day, at least ten hours each day. I know most of what you're gonna say before you start talking. Just spit it out. Let it go! Let it go!" Tiara joked, trying her best to sound like a psychologist, hoping to get a laugh out of Cajen.

"Tiara, some things are just too difficult to discuss." Knowing that answer wouldn't be good enough for Tiara, she lied. "I'm having family problems. My mother got on me just before I came to pick you up. She says I don't call her as much as I used to and that she and dad are worried about me. I didn't even realize I had gone so long without talking to her." Cajen couldn't believe that she'd been lying since Tiara got into the car. But it was true that she hadn't talked to her mother in a while.

Realizing that Cajen wasn't going to expose whatever was really going on, Tiara changed the subject. "I got something that'll cheer you up," Tiara said, while pulling out a sheet of paper from her backpack. "Lots and lots of sexy, sexy fine men for the auction."

"Who did you get?" she asked, trying to sound enthusiastic.

"I can't announce the list until we get to Stephanie's."

"Thanks a lot, Tiara. That really helps my mood," Cajen said sarcastically. They sat in silence until they got to Stephanie's apartment.

Chancey pulled up at the same time they did. Good, Cajen thought. Now maybe I won't have to tell any more lies today.

"You get your contact?" Tiara asked Chancey.

"Yes, I wasn't about to wear my glasses to session tonight. I learned my lesson the last time, when everybody rode me out about how old they are. I really do need to get some new ones." Chancey had a glow on her face. She looked as relaxed as Tiara.

"Girl, you look like I feel. You sure you didn't sneak off and spend some time with your man?" Tiara questioned. Chancey didn't answer because she was speechless about how transparent she was. They were at the door, and Cajen was doing the secret knock.

Malena answered the door. "Shhh . . . Stephanie is in the kitchen talking to Big Sister Tracy on the phone. She's pissed about something."

"What's new. They're always pissed about something," Tiara commented.

They all took their shoes off at the door as they walked in, and stacked their backpacks in the hall closet.

"What's bugging her?" Chancey asked.

"I don't know, but I think she's just trying to create drama because we've been on our shit lately," Malena said.

"And you know that's right," Tiara said, and gave Malena a high five. "They can't handle the progress we've been making. I ran into Big Sister

Kim yesterday, and she said we're one of the sharpest lines that has gone through this chapter."

Stephanie covered the receiver and shushed her line sisters.

They stopped in their tracks, gave her apologetic faces, sat down in the living room, and waited for her to get off the phone. They were all quiet because they didn't want Big Sister Tracy to know they were meeting before sessions. Dean Big Sister Nina had warned them not to let their big sisters know about their meetings, for their own safety.

Stephanie hung up the phone and walked over. "I'm not gonna take her seriously, but she claims she knows what we're gonna do for our fund-raiser, and she said we need to come up with something else because it's a stupid idea."

"How would she know? Has anybody told any of the big sisters?" Malena asked.

Everybody answered, "No."

"Let's not worry about it. I think it's a ploy to make us try to change what we already have planned. We're going to continue as scheduled. Let's not change anything. And if she really knows, who cares anyway at this point?" remarked Stephanie.

"So, what's the plan for today?" Chancey asked in a calm, carefree voice.

"You look like you just came off vacation," Malena commented. "As a matter of fact, you look just like I would be looking if I just saw Ray. Did you see Donald today?"

Do I wear my emotions on my sleeve or what? she asked herself. "Well, I wasn't gonna say. Sorry, Tiara, but I did see him for a little while." Chancey confessed the half truth.

"I knew it. There's no other way to get that glow that you have," Tiara said.

"I am so jealous," Malena blurted. "I have only seen Ray once since we've been on line. How did you find the time? I need some of what you just got," she joked.

Glowing and smiling from ear to ear, Chancey said, "I'll fill you in after the meeting."

"So what are we single women supposed to do to relieve our stress?" Stephanie asked.

"I can't help you on that one, but we'll talk, Malena," Chancey said.

"Cool," Malena said.

"Okay," Stephanie interrupted. "Since none of you can produce a man worthy enough to accommodate me, let's get the business part of this meeting out of the way. Then we can do a little more bonding, like we did last night. You know, talk about all of that personal business that nobody really wants to share." She knew that she, for one, had no intentions of sharing her little secret.

"We won't meet our honorable big sisters until eleven," she joked, "so we have plenty of time to plan, study history, and just talk."

"We'll start by discussing the auction. Malena has come up with an excellent introduction for the auction—one that will blow the big sisters away. Tiara claims to have signed up the finest men on campus."

"No, honey, I ain't blowing smoke. The men I signed up are deliciously gorgeous!" Tiara interrupted.

"My bad, Miss Tiara. I stand corrected," Stephanie said, and continued. "Cajen and I have got the theme, mood, and background drafted. We even found a deejay who is going to do the introductory music for each contestant. Malena and Chancey have the promotion side of the event worked out. They have flyers and programs completed and ready to print. They also have a press release ready to send to the student newspaper. Looks like we're almost there," Stephanie said proudly. "So, Miss Tiara, who do you have signed up for the auction?"

"Thank me later, ladies, but before I let you know who the fine—and did I already say fine—brothers are that I have signed up, I have taken it upon myself to make an addition to Malena's introduction. Before anybody says anything or gets offended, Malena, the intro is all you. I just enhanced it in a way that only you and Chancey can appreciate."

"What are you talking about, Tiara?" Chancey asked.

"Well, I thought it only appropriate, since you and Chancey never find time to spend with your men, that we incorporate them in the show somehow. And I definitely didn't think y'all would want them to be auctioned off to the man-hungry females on this campus. So I said to myself, 'Self, how do we work out this little dilemma?' "

"Tiara, what did you come up with, girl?" Malena asked. "Ray hasn't said anything to me."

"Neither has Don," Chancey added.

"It's simple. Malena, you know how you said you're going to come onstage dressed like an African queen and talk about healing the ills of slavery by re-creating auctions we don't have to be ashamed of, and how we should celebrate our history and all of that other good and insightful stuff you talk about? Well, you are a queen, my dear, and should not have to walk onstage. You should be carried onstage by your humble servants, who just so happen to be Don and Ray. And after you say your monologue, they'll escort you off the stage."

"Tiara, you're a genius," Chancey said, bouncing up and down in her seat, happy to spend more time with Don.

"You're my girl and you are a genius. I mean, why didn't we think of that before?" Malena asked.

Tiara reminded them that they had a dress rehearsal the day before the show, and that Don and Ray's part in the show would allow Malena and Chancey two days to spend at least a little time with them.

"Yeah," Stephanie joined in. "Chancey, you can help coordinate the intro or something, and the four of you can at least get to do that romantic stuff like gaze into each other's eyes and whatever else you do when you're together in public."

"And who cares if we get in trouble for it, we're always 'in trouble' anyway, just because we're on line," Chancey commented.

"Ray agreed to do this?" said Malena, who was shocked that he would.

"Yeah, and so did Don. I can tell they both care about y'all. It's so sickening."

"Tiara, you just know that you got it going on, don't you? Thank you so much," Malena said.

"Yeah, Tiara, thank you," Chancey said, and gave her a hug. She was so excited that she bumped into Cajen, who was the only one not caught up in their exciting moment. Cajen was in her own zone. She actually had a pad and pen out, writing something.

"What's wrong with you?" Chancey asked. "And what are you writing?"

"I'm just working on my to-do list for tomorrow," Cajen answered.

"Don't even ask," Tiara commented. "She's been in a funk since she picked me up."

"Excuse me for not being in as good a mood as everybody else. Some people are just not fortunate enough to be chipper all the fucking time— excuse my French!" said Cajen.

"Who rained on your parade?" Stephanie asked.

"Look, I'm not in the mood to discuss anything today. I'll be fine after I sleep off the funk of this day."

"Well, looks like you're gonna be wallowing in funk for a while, because we have a long night ahead of us," Malena commented.

"Please, don't let me interrupt our meeting. I think Tiara was in the middle of telling us who she got for the auction," Cajen said, writing on her notepad.

Her line sisters looked at one another in a state of confusion. Tiara went back to talking about the auction, but her voice lacked excitement.

"I got ten brothers who said that they would do anything to help us out. Let's see, . . . Ben, Darryl, "Shaky-Shaky Please-take-me" Jason, Brian, Derrick, Tantalizing Tyrone, William "The Womanizer," David, Allen, and Malcolm. And I know I don't need to say last names because everybody knows the finest men on campus."

Cajen almost lost it. If Tiara got Jason, that meant Tiara had to have talked to him. Why is it that everybody can get in touch with him except me? Cajen thought. There is no way that I can see him on that stage. I might forget where I am and try to kill him.

"You didn't. Tiara, you are extraordinary," Stephanie complimented her.

"Well, Malena did help out. She knows what to say to the men to make them bite. I have been taking notes from her. To be all committed, that girl flirts her butt off. I just want you ladies to know that I got my eye on Brian and Ben. Anybody else is fair game."

Everybody was excited except Cajen, who was trying to figure out if she should kill Jason at rehearsal or wait until after the show.

"Cajen, after we finish with this business, you are gonna have to talk to us. I am worried about you," Malena said.

"I'm fine. I just need to use the phone."

"Cajen, what's wrong?" Chancey asked.

"I just need to use the phone." She couldn't hold her tears back anymore. She was thinking that if she could just talk to Jason tonight she could settle everything and be okay. She had to release her feelings or she wouldn't be able to continue functioning.

"Here's the phone, Cajen. But who are you calling?" Stephanie asked, as she handed her the cordless phone.

"I don't have to tell y'all everything. Just because we are on line together doesn't mean that y'all have to know every fucking thing about me and my life. I can choose to keep parts of my life private. Excuse me, I have to make a phone call."

Cajen took the phone and ran into the bathroom, slamming the door behind her, while everybody sat in silence looking at one another.

"What the hell is up with her?" Stephanie asked.

Cajen tried to call Jason. His answering machine came on. She let it play all the way through, but couldn't bring herself to leave a message. She was not going to leave the bathroom until she spoke to him. So she tried again. His frat's pledges had crossed a week and a half ago, so he wasn't at a session. "Where are you?" Cajen said so loudly that everybody in the living room could hear.

Outside the bathroom her line sisters were listening.

"What is going on?" Tiara asked.

"Chancey, you two are pretty close. Who does Cajen see?" asked Stephanie.

Chancey shrugged her shoulders. "I don't know." She was as uninformed as everybody else.

"She never mentioned having a boyfriend to us. Did she ever say anything to you?" Stephanie questioned Tiara.

"Nothing," Tiara answered.

Stephanie was concerned because she knew how much pain holding in secrets caused. She wanted so badly to reach out and help Cajen, but she didn't know what was going on with her.

Cajen tried the number again. The answering machine came on again. This time she let the machine play, but when it beeped she yelled, "I hate you!" and slammed the phone on the floor. Everybody sat in silence in the next room.

"This is gonna end right now," Stephanie said. She wasn't going to sit back and let Cajen scream into God knows who's ears. Plus, she didn't want a broken phone. She got up and tried to open the bathroom door, but it was locked. She knocked. "Cajen, open the door."

She didn't respond.

"Cajen, I know you're upset, but I can't help you if you don't let me know what's going on."

"I can handle it by myself." She picked up the phone and tried to call Jason again.

"Who are you trying to call?"

"Nobody."

"Cajen, I don't know what the fuck that bastard did to you, and I don't even know who he is, but just let us know and we'll help you get through this."

"You can't help me. There is no help for me." Cajen was sitting in the bathtub with the phone in her hands and her head leaning against the wall. She couldn't even cry anymore. She just wanted to sit in the tub and let life continue without her.

"You're right, Cajen, I can't help you. Especially when you're in there, and I'm out here. So I'm gonna let you sit in there. But Cajen, trust me when I say this, life is going to continue whether or not you participate. But if you decide to come out of the bathroom, maybe we can all figure out what we can do—not to change what has happened, but to deal with it."

Stephanie walked away from the door, and Cajen began to cry because she realized that Stephanie was right. There was no way to change what had happened. She had had no way of knowing Jason was going to give her such an awful disease. She had to let somebody know what he did to her, and if her line sisters decided she was too dirty to be on their line, at least she would be able to stop pledging and try to find Jason so she could give him a piece of her mind.

Stephanie went back to the living room. Cajen's drama brought out her own heartache over her adoption. She couldn't fight her tears because she knew that just like Cajen, she too needed to face her secrets. She needed to be woman enough to let the people in the room know she was adopted and just deal with their reaction.

"There is something I want to tell y'all about me that I haven't told anybody on this campus because I was ashamed of how it would make people look at me," Stephanie said. Cajen came out of the bathroom, but she didn't go all the way into the living room.

Stephanie continued. "Patricia and Howard Madison are not my real parents. They adopted me when I was a newborn."

"But Stephanie, if they adopted you as a newborn and raised you as their own, then they are your parents," Chancey said. "What's the big deal?"

"Well, I know who my real mother is. Her name is Helen Brown. She's a junkie, she lives in crack houses, and she's really never been a stable person. Her mother kicked her out for being pregnant with me. My parents met her through an adoption service and paid her medical fees and gave her money to keep her comfortable throughout her pregnancy . . . she basically did it for the money.

"That's deep," Tiara said, staring at Stephanie in amazement. She couldn't imagine Stephanie coming from anything that wasn't filthy rich. She initially felt a moment of satisfaction, then she realized that she and Stephanie shared the pain of abandonment.

"I don't know what parts of her I am like," Stephanie continued. "I don't know if I will one day get the urge to go out and start doing drugs. I don't know if I will be a good mother to my children. I don't know anything about myself. I don't know her, and only God knows who my real father is, or where he is. I don't know my real roots. My real grandmother died when I was about three, and I never knew her."

Like the others, Tiara looked at her as if she saw a ghost. She couldn't believe Stephanie wasn't Patricia's real daughter. From the stories Stephanie shared it seemed like they were so much alike, and were extremely close. No one would have ever known if she hadn't told them. But more than that, Tiara couldn't believe Stephanie's birth mother was a drug addict. But as unfortunate as her situation with her real mother was, it didn't change who she was as a person.

"Stephanie, at least Patricia and Howard adopted you and provided for you in ways that most people can only dream about. Plus, they love you. I understand your pain about your real mother and father, but Stephanie, you are a miracle. Your mother didn't abort you, you turned out okay, better than okay, and you have a family with enough roots to take care of any that you lost with your real mother." Tiara went on, "Sometimes I get jealous when you talk about your mother, and your grandmother and your aunts. Stephanie, they are your real family. They are who God put you with. There's nothing wrong with how you were brought on this earth. As far as I'm concerned, you are a miracle."

Tiara got on a roll and couldn't stop. "What if your mother had kept you? What kind of life would you be living right now? I doubt if you'd be in college. You are blessed. And that's a good thing. There's no other way to look at it," Tiara said, then walked over to Stephanie, who stood in front of her coffee table sobbing, and hugged her.

Malena began, "Steph, why would you think we would look at you any differently? I still see a rich, spoiled brat when I look at you." They laughed.

"But seriously, your personality doesn't change now that I know about your real mother, and your wealth sure hasn't changed. Everything about your childhood is the same. I don't understand what you're worried about. You are blessed. You should be happy. You should not be ashamed to share your story, because it is a blessing that God gave to you," Malena said.

"She's right. Patricia and Howard are that blessing, and they have shared everything they have with you as if you were their own child. To them, you are their child. You are their only child," Chancey added. "Don't you get it?"

"I think I do. But for some reason, I always thought that if I told anybody, they would see me as the child of a drug addict, and maybe not accept me. I know it sounds stupid, but I've been feeling like this all my life," said Stephanie.

"I see you as the president of this line. I see you as a strong black woman. I've admired you from the first day I met you. Nothing can change the impression I have of you," Chancey said. "I know it's been hard for you to deal with this, but when I see you tomorrow, I'm not going to say, 'Hi, Stephanie, daughter of a drug addict.' I'm gonna see my friend and line sister. And in a few weeks I will say, 'What's up, Soror Stephanie?'" Chancey said, and joined in on the group hug.

"I know that's right!" Tiara said, and sat back down. "Squash that pity party attitude, Steph. You got it going on. And all that other stuff . . . that's in the past. I say leave it there."

"I love you girls so much. Sometimes I feel like I've known all of you for years. Like y'all are the sisters I never had," Stephanie said. "Now, come back over, Miss Tiara, and join this group hug."

Stephanie felt such a relief. She felt lighter than she'd felt in years. A burden had been lifted off her shoulders. She was still crying, but they were tears of joy. "I just wish we had our missing link over here with us."

Everybody looked at Cajen, who had her head buried between her knees. She was weighing adoption versus herpes. There is no comparison, Cajen thought. Stephanie is a miracle, and I will be viewed as a whore.

The group made its way over to where Cajen was sitting on the floor. She looked up, and they had made a circle around her.

Tiara said, "We're not gonna let you out of this circle until you let us know what the hell is going on with you."

Cajen closed her eyes and said, "I can't," under her breath.

Finally Malena said, "Look, Cajen, we love your little stubborn butt. You're our little sister. But if you don't talk to us, I'm gonna be forced to . . . well, I don't know what I'm gonna do. But if somebody is messing over you, we want to make sure it stops."

Tiara added, "I'm sure this has to do with a man, and I feel personally responsible for seeing to it that no man dogs you and gets away with it."

"You won't understand, and there is nothing y'all can do to help me. It's too late," Cajen said. Her head was still buried between her knees because she couldn't face them.

"What can't we help you with?" Chancey asked. "Cajen, you have to tell us."

Cajen realized there was no way of getting out of telling them. If they think I'm gross, then who cares anyway, she thought.

She lifted her head, took a deep breath, and said, "I'll tell y'all, since you want to know so badly. But go back to where you were sitting, because I need to have some breathing room before I can talk. Plus, I don't think that I can talk with everyone staring a hole through me like I'm some kind of weirdo or something."

Relieved she was finally going to talk, they eagerly cooperated and went back to the living room, wondering what could possibly be going on with someone as young and innocent as Cajen.

She took a deep breath and started talking. "I had one boyfriend in high school. He was really good to me, and we had sex maybe four times. The first time was on our prom night. Then three times after that. I distinctly remember every time, just like it was yesterday. We broke up two weeks before college because we were going to different schools and decided that if we stayed together we would hold each other back from the full college experience. I should have never let us break up. Then my life would not be like it is now." She stopped talking and put her head on her knees again.

"So you talked to him today. What did he say to you? And why were you yelling at him?" Chancey asked, trying to figure out what was so bad about that story and why Cajen was so distraught.

"It really has nothing to do with him," Cajen responded, "but if I hadn't broken up with him, I wouldn't have met the bastard that I'm gonna kill at the auction."

"Wait a minute. Who are you talking about? 'Cause whoever it is, I got yo' back. He's outta the auction just like that," Tiara said, and snapped her fingers.

"Calm down, Tiara," Malena said. "What did the bastard do?"

"I didn't even like him at first. I wasn't even trying to like him, but he kept persisting and insisting that I give him a chance. Why didn't I trust my instincts?"

"Did he hit you, Cajen?" Stephanie asked.

"Well, no. After I got to know him pretty well, but I guess not well enough, I had sex with him and he, he . . ."

"What?" Tiara asked. She could barely sit in her seat, so she stood up to get a closer look at Cajen.

"What?" Chancey asked. "What did he do?"

"I haven't talked to him in three weeks, so I haven't even been able to confront him. I hate him. I have never hated anybody in my life. But I hate him!" Cajen said.

"Hate is so strong, Cajen," Chancey said. "What did he do to you?"

"You know what?" Cajen changed her mind. "It's not even worth talking about. Forget it. Who cares anyway?" She was literally drained and exhausted from thinking about this situation.

"Cajen!" they all yelled.

"Dang!" she sighed, and continued. "Well, after we had sex, I went to the doctor a few days later and she told me that he gave me a disease."

"So y'all didn't use a condom?" Malena asked.

"I guess not, Malena. If they did she wouldn't have a disease," Tiara said, kind of annoyed with Malena's stupid question.

"Cajen, I'm pissed for you," Stephanie said. "I've been burned myself. It's not a good situation. I cussed his ass out, and after I got treated and broke up with him, he had the nerve to try to call me to get me back. That jerk. I know how you feel. It took me a while before I could even trust being with another man. You just have to make sure that the next time you have sex the brother uses a condom," Stephanie said. "Once you give him a piece of your mind, you'll be all right."

"No, I won't be all right, because I read the literature, and there is no medicine that I can take to make herpes magically disappear! I am stuck with this disgusting shit for life," said Cajen.

They were all speechless.

Cajen wasn't expecting silence. She thought that maybe somebody would tell her she was gross, but not silence.

"Wow!" Stephanie said. This was more of a blow than she was expecting. "Who did this to you?"

She debated answering the question, then decided that since her secret was out, there was no use in holding back. "Jason Gray."

"What?" Malena screamed. "That low-down, dirty, no-good bastard!"

"Oh, he's X'd from the show!" Tiara added. She didn't know what else to say. None of them knew what to say to comfort her. They couldn't imagine themselves in her shoes, and didn't want to.

"What am I supposed to do?" Cajen began to cry. "What the fuck am I supposed to do?"

Stephanie put her arms around Cajen and said, "You're gonna be okay. You're gonna be just fine." She shook her head in disbelief. Just a few weeks ago she had made a list of all of the men that she had been with, but none of them had ever given her herpes. Cajen got herpes from her second sexual partner, she thought. She doesn't deserve that.

Chancey, as well as the other girls, was dumbfounded. "Nobody thinks badly of you, Cajen. I only hate that this happened to you."

Chancey walked over to Cajen, knelt down, and gently put her arms around her. Cajen trembled, and Chancey hugged her tighter. Cajen took a deep breath. She felt relieved to finally be able to share this with her sisters. "Tiara, don't kick Jason out of the show. I can handle it." The rest of her sisters moved closer and assured Cajen that they shared her heartache, and they too were upset at the disrespectful way in which Jason was treating her.

FIFTEEN

The five line sisters planned to meet at the auditorium an hour before the scheduled practice time, to make sure they had everything prepared so the rehearsal would run smoothly. It was important to impress Dean Big Sister Nina and the rest of their big sisters, who were skeptical about their idea of having an auction as a fund-raiser.

Stephanie and Tiara arrived early, and sat and talked in the front row. When Chancey came in, she felt like she had walked in on something, because as soon as they noticed her, they abruptly stopped talking. She didn't ask what they were talking about, because she figured if they wanted her to know, they would share it with her.

"Hey girls!" Chancey said, as she plopped down next to Tiara.

"What's up, Chancey?" Tiara responded.

"Hey girl," Stephanie said.

After a brief silence, Tiara couldn't hold it in any longer. "Chancey, I'm gonna have to fill you in later because I don't have time to start from the beginning, but we have to finish this before everybody else gets here." She looked at Stephanie and continued. "So, my friend Gina is set and ready. She knows exactly what to do."

"You didn't tell her why, did you?" Stephanie asked.

"No, of course not. Give me some credit."

"Oh good, Tiara. Cajen is going to be so grateful."

"Well, I figure it's the least I can do," Tiara said.

"But how is she gonna get out of practice?" Stephanie asked.

"Well, I'll ask her if she'll pick up the microphones for me a few minutes into practice. But I'm not gonna let her know she'll run into Jason because she may not go through with it."

"I can't take it anymore, somebody's gotta let me know what's going on!" Chancey said.

"Well, I guess we can fill you in, but you'll have to settle for the abbreviated version," Stephanie said, while looking behind her to make sure no one was coming. Then she filled Chancey in on Tiara's plan to make sure Cajen ran into Jason on his way to the rehearsal.

"What?" Chancey yelled. Just then Cajen and Malena walked in.

"Hey girls!" Malena said. While everyone else said their hellos, Cajen didn't say a word. She just waved. She was not in the mood to be away from her dorm room. It was hard enough for her to be there in the auditorium, knowing that in about an hour she was going to be in the same room with Jason. Her mind was on making it through the next hour and a half while watching him not care about how he ruined her life.

"Y'all are gonna love this intro. I went over it a million times in my head while in class today. Tammy took good notes for me so I could work on memorizing the monologue," said Malena.

"Good, Malena. How is Tammy?" Stephanie asked.

"More in love than ever."

"Good for her, but I still don't think she should've dropped line. Do you have your costume ready?" asked Stephanie.

"Yes. It's out in the car."

"Go get it!" Chancey said.

"You think I should?"

"Yes!" everybody replied in unison.

While Malena was going out the door, Stephanie noticed that Cajen looked worried about the night's practice. "Don't you worry about a thing, Cajen. Everything is going to work out just fine. Jason is not going to be in this practice tonight."

Then Tiara asked, "Cajen, do you know where that empty room is on the third floor of this building?"

"No. Is that where the microphones are?"

"No, but the entire third floor is generally empty during this time of the evening. Most night classes are held on the first and second floors."

"So, why are you telling me?"

"Because people who are informed generally make better decisions," Tiara said, hoping Cajen would remember her bit of advice when she ran into Jason.

"Why are you ragging on my decision-making skills? And what does the third floor have to do with anything?"

"Nothing, Cajen. My bad, I was just giving you a fact about this building."

"Tiara, you are bugging!" Cajen said.

Tiara didn't respond. She just bent down and looked in her book bag, and got out her folder with all of the contestant information.

Stephanie knew why Tiara had given Cajen information about the third floor being empty. She knew it was the only way to let her know where to go and talk to Jason when she ran into him on her way to pick up the microphones for the practice, without letting her know the plan. Chancey and Cajen, on the other hand, thought Tiara had lost her mind.

Stephanie stepped in, as usual, to change the subject and get to business. "All right now! Let's get started. We don't have time to talk about the third floor of this building. Dean Big Sister Nina will be here in less than an hour, and who knows who she'll bring with her." Everybody groaned at the thought of all their big sisters critiquing their rehearsal.

Stephanie continued. "I hinted to her that we would like the practice to be as closed as possible because we really want the big sisters to be surprised by our presentation tomorrow."

"So what did she say?" Chancey asked.

"Well, she said our big sisters will be able to give us constructive criticism if they come to practice and prevent us from making fools of ourselves tomorrow. But I assured her we were on top of things and she said, 'We'll see.' "

"We'll see?" Tiara shouted. "Y'all, we are gonna be bum-rushed by a gang of big sisters in a few minutes, and we're not gonna get anything accomplished tonight. The auction is gonna be all messed up tomorrow." She was worried that all their hard work would be purposely ruined by their big sisters.

"No, it won't be messed up, because no matter who comes in here tonight there is no way they can find fault in our presentation. It's going to be tasteful, entertaining, and a class act all the way around," Chancey said. "I'm not worried."

"She's right. We've got our act together. Did everybody see the backdrop Cajen and I put together?" Stephanie asked. "We have plants coming tomorrow at noon, which will add effect to the stage. Plus Mel, the deejay, is going to be here for practice. He's gonna set up everything tonight so we'll be able to practice with the music. We are way prepared."

Malena walked in with her costume in one hand and a box on her hip. Chancey ran to help her. "Are these the flyers?" she asked, as she grabbed the box from her. "I hoped you'd remember them."

Chancey walked over to her line sisters and opened the box. "Malena and I came up with a plan that will hopefully get all of us out of session tonight and allow us to do some last-minute advertising for the auction tomorrow."

"You can tell we're gonna be crossing soon, because we are all getting hip to the 'whatever it takes to get out of session' game," Tiara said.

"Oh, Malena, they look good!" Chancey said, as she pulled the flyers out of the box. "When did you find time to get our sketches on the computer?"

Malena draped her dress over a chair and explained how she'd created them on her computer earlier that morning. Because her printer was out of ink, she had called Ray, and he met her before class, took the disk to the computer lab, and printed an original. Also, he was thoughtful enough to go have copies made.

Ray met her out front when she went to get her costume. Malena took the box from him and asked him to wait until practice officially started to come in. He kissed her on the cheek and took off to grab a quick bite to eat.

"I don't know who has the better man, you or Chancey," Stephanie said, then put her hands together to send a quick prayer up. "Dear Lord, please send that same blessing my way."

"You'll get a man sooner or later," Chancey said.

"I'm hoping sooner." Stephanie pouted.

"So what's the plan for after practice?" Cajen asked in a dry tone. She wasn't the least bit interested in talk about getting or keeping a man. She had one thing on her mind—settling her problem with the man who had never been hers: Jason.

"We're going to slide these under doors in all of the girls' dormitories, and hit the two coed dorms," Chancey replied.

The line sisters finished preparing the stage. Malena went through her monologue a couple of times, and they discussed the rest of their plans for the auction. Soon it was time for the big sisters and contestants to come for the scheduled practice.

D ean Big Sister Nina and the assistant dean, Big Sister Kendra, walked through the door. The line sisters were always glad to see Big Sister Kendra because she was especially considerate of them. Like clockwork, the girls stopped what they were doing, jumped into line according to number, and began to greet their big sisters.

"Greetings, Most Honorable Big Sisters. We are so pleased to be graced by your presence. We work hard, both day and night, striving to become what you already are. May we be privileged to address you, please?" they said in unison.

Dean Big Sister Nina seemed to get a rush when they greeted her. She was cool as far as big sisters went, but she loved for the pledges to greet her. Once, she made them greet her seventy-five times before she finally granted them permission to stop greeting her. This time she responded, "No, I didn't hear any sincerity in your voices."

"Yes, you may address me," Big Sister Kendra replied. Then she looked at Nina, irritated at the power trip she'd been on since they took the new line. "Now, you know the contestants will be walking through that door at any minute, and we want them to be through all of this hazing nonsense by then so they'll be relaxed during practice."

"All right. I'll let them greet me one or two more times, and then I'll let them off the hook."

Kendra shook her head, found a row of chairs in the middle of the auditorium, and took a seat.

The pledges went through the greeting two more times, and Dean

Big Sister Nina responded, "Yes, you may address me." Then she asked, "So are you ladies ready for tonight?"

"Yes, Dean Big Sister Nina!" they replied in unison.

"We'll see about that," she smirked, and took a seat beside Kendra. "Go ahead. Break up and continue to do whatever it was you were doing before we got here. I need the secretary to come and inform me and your big sister Kendra of what we should expect to see tonight."

Cajen, who was the line's secretary, walked over to her big sisters and opened her notepad to all of the notes she had taken pertaining to the practice. She informed them of all the details that had already been taken care of, and of everything that was going to be covered in the night's rehearsal. Cajen's notes were thorough, so when she finished with her report, neither of the big sisters had any questions. They didn't even object to putting their flyers under doors in the dormitories after rehearsal, even though that meant the pledges wouldn't have to go through a physically and emotionally draining pledge session.

"Oh, yeah," Cajen remembered. "Dean Big Sister Nina, the microphones are ready to be picked up. May I have permission to get them now? We won't need them for the first part of the practice, but they will be essential for the second part."

"Number two," Nina called to Cajen. Their big sisters often switched between calling them by their line names and their line numbers. "First of all, I just want to let you know that your minute-taking skills have improved drastically. You are really developing. I'm beginning to think you just might make a fine addition to our sorority."

"Thank you, Dean Big Sister Nina," Cajen said.

"Second, you can go and pick up the microphones in a few minutes, but first there is something that I forgot to tell you and your line sisters."

Tiara heard their big sister delay Cajen, and began to worry because she wasn't sure how long her friend Gina would be able to stall Jason. She knew that when Dean Big Sister Nina got on her pedestal, she sometimes got too comfortable and dragged on and on.

"Everybody, come over here for a minute. You don't have to get in line, just come over and have a seat. Cajen, I need you to take notes."

Everyone stopped what they were doing and took seats around their big sisters.

"I hope this show runs as smoothly as it seems like it's going to, because it was difficult keeping the rest of your big sisters away from this practice, so you really have to be on top of things both tonight and tomorrow," said Dean Big Sister Nina.

The pledges were relieved that there would be no other big sisters at the rehearsal.

"Remember when I told you all to make sure you get white dresses if you don't have them?" she asked. "Does everybody have their white dresses and white shoes?"

"Yes, Dean Big Sister Nina, we all have our dresses and our shoes," Cajen responded.

"Good. You will need to go into your budgets and make sure everybody has the proper panty hose to match."

"We have those too."

"Very good."

Their dean gave them an address and a time, but left out the date. She told them not to lose the address or the time, because she would later give them only a date and they would need to put all the information together. She then asked if they had black dresses, shoes, and panty hose. When they answered yes, she informed them they would also need to make sure everyone had a black sweat suit, black socks, and black tennis shoes. She reminded them they could get cheap ones at Wal-Mart, if they didn't already have them, and suggested they use some of the money they would make from the auction. Half of the proceeds were to be donated to the charity of their choice.

They looked at one another in anguish, wondering how, with their already full schedules, they were supposed to manage to shop for sweat suits.

"Here's another address and time," she continued. "Don't confuse it with the first ones. You will be using this information before the address I just gave you, and I will later call you with a date." Big Sister Nina gave them the new location and time and told them to be in their sweat suits.

She then instructed them to be at the location at the exact time noted. She warned them that if they lost the information she just gave them, they were out of luck. Chancey always made sure to pay extra special attention to any information that had that term attached.

"Any questions?" Big Sister Kendra asked.

"No, Big Sister Kendra," the pledges responded.

"Okay, that's all," Dean Big Sister Nina said, and stretched her legs and crossed her arms. "Number two, you can go and pick up the microphones now."

Cajen put her notebook and pen in her backpack. As soon as she walked out of the auditorium and into the lobby of the building, she saw Jason talking to a girl. Her heart stopped. She panicked. She didn't know what to do. Should I talk to him now? Who is that girl? What do I do? The questions raced through her mind. Overwhelmed and unsure, she stopped dead in her tracks.

Jason looked up and saw Cajen. He was glad to see her because Gina was talking her head off about nothing and he didn't want to be rude and cut the conversation short. Now he had an excuse—Cajen.

Gina, who was cued earlier to look for Cajen, knew she was supposed to stop the conversation when she saw her walking out of the door of the auditorium. So she told Jason that she'd talk to him later. He said okay and turned and waved to Cajen.

He has some nerve. And why is he waving at me? He hasn't returned any of my phone calls. I don't believe this jerk, she thought.

"Hey, Cajen," Jason said, with a fake wide grin.

She looked over her shoulder to make sure none of her big sisters was coming through the door, and then walked over to him.

"Cajen, I'm sorry I haven't returned any of your calls," he said in a deep, mellow voice. Then he contradicted himself. "Actually, I did try to call back, several times," he explained. Then he went into some story about hearing that one year some big sisters went into a pledge's room and listened to her messages on her answering machine, and she got into trouble because of a message her boyfriend left. He assured her that he didn't want to get her into the same kind of trouble if something like that happened.

Cajen refused to fall for his story.

"So, why did you say you hated me on my answering machine? What was that all about?" he questioned.

Maybe he doesn't know, Cajen thought. Her heart started to soften. She then came to her senses and realized she still had to let him know what he had done to her. She had to let him know how irresponsible they had been and how much he had hurt her. She remembered what Tiara had said about the third floor being empty. "We need to talk, Jason."

"Well, I'm supposed to be in this rehearsal. Didn't you know I was going to be in the auction?" he asked.

"Jason, we really need to talk, and rehearsal can wait. I need to talk to you now," she demanded.

"Cajen, you trying to tell me this can't wait until later? All my boys are gonna be here in a minute, and we promised your line sister— what's her name? Tiara—that we'd be in practice, and on time."

He spoke quickly, hoping to change her mind, but Cajen was feeling the anger that had been building over the past four and a half weeks. She knew if she didn't take Jason to the third floor and talk to him, she was going to explode. Staring him right in the eyes, her right eyebrow stood at attention, "Jason, fuck practice!" she said in a low, strong voice. "I need to talk to you now."

"Damn, baby," he said, in his usual cool voice. "Is it that bad?"

"Come on," she said and started to walk, not even looking behind to see if he followed. He'd better be behind me, she assured herself.

They walked down the lobby and up the stairs to the third floor. Tiara was right. Unlike the heavy activity on the first floor, the third floor was empty. Most of the lights in the classrooms were out. It was as if they were in a different building altogether. Cajen and Jason walked midway down the hall and into one of the classrooms. He sat on the desk in the front of the room. Keeping her distance, she sat in a chair in the middle of the room.

"So what's so important that you had to drag me all the way into no-man's-land?" he asked sarcastically. "What's up?"

"I should be asking you that same question." She folded her arms and rolled her eyes.

"Cajen, it's not my fault you started pledging. I can't help it if we haven't been able to talk. You can't be mad at me for that," Jason said in a placating voice.

"You don't know, do you?" she asked. She couldn't believe it. He was acting like he still cared about her.

"Don't know what?" he questioned. "Listen, I don't have time to play games with you. Just spit it out so I can get down to the practice." He was becoming frustrated.

"Jason, after I spent the night and had sex with you, I went to the doctor a few days later and had an examination." She paused and walked over to one of the windows in the back of the classroom. "The doctor told me that I have an STD."

"An STD. Wait a minute, are you trying to say I gave you a disease?" Jason exclaimed.

"I'm not trying to say anything. I'm straight-up telling you you did," she said, and walked closer to him. Her anger gave her the strength to move into his space. "When was the last time you went to the doctor to get a checkup?"

"Well, it's been a while . . . but I haven't needed to go to no doctor." He was offended by her attitude. He had never seen this side of her.

"Well, I wish you had gone to see a doctor before you met me, because since I had sex with you, I have herpes. And I got it from you, Jason."

"Herpes . . . from me? Nah, Cajen, you didn't get nothing from me. Un-uh, I'm sorry. No sir."

She couldn't believe his nonchalant attitude. "Jason, you know I've only had sex with one other person in my life. And I haven't been with him in half a year. I've had my annual checkup since then. It wasn't until after I was with you I got herpes, and you cannot deny it, because you did give it to me," she argued. "I can't believe that you are trying to deny this." Cajen was furious. She had to sit down to calm herself.

"Look, I'm not trying to deny nothing. It's just that I don't have any symptoms, so I don't have it," Jason said.

"Do you even know what the symptoms are?"

"Well, not really." He stood up, sighed, and put his hands in his back pockets.

Cajen wasn't sure if he was going to walk out of the room, or if he was even paying attention, but she continued.

"Jason, you need to go to a doctor or a clinic, or something, because you do have herpes and you gave it to me—and God knows whoever else." She got up out of the chair. "You know what? I'm outta here, 'cause I can see I'm wasting my time with you," she said. "I just want you to know that you have completely ruined my entire life. Thanks a lot," she said, as she started toward the door. He stopped her.

"Wait." He grabbed her arm.

"Why? Why should I wait?" Cajen asked.

"Well, because I'm sorry. I'm sorry if I messed up your life. But I do want you to know I've been thinking about you since I saw you last. You have been on my mind, and I know you are mad at me, but I don't want to stop seeing you just because of this. We can work through this," he said, and stroked her cheeks with his fingers.

Cajen found some small relief in those words, because although she was upset with him, in a strange and inexplicable way she felt comforted by his still wanting her. She rationalized that if they stayed together, she wouldn't have to ever worry about being with another man and explaining that she had an STD.

Who else would want me anyway, she thought. Then she looked deep into his eyes to make sure he was sincere.

"I want you in my life, and those other girls don't mean nothing," Jason said. "Listen, when you cross, we'll talk about this again. No, as a matter of fact, let's leave this discussion in this room. Let's not talk about it again. We'll just move forward together."

Jason left Cajen speechless. She was under his spell again, and she couldn't argue.

Maybe there was no need to talk about this situation again, she assured herself. Everything was going to be all right between them.

Jason put his arms around her and said, "This don't mean nothing. We can get past all of this. I know we can." Then he pulled away to look in her eyes and asked, "Are you all right now?"

"Yeah, I'm okay," Cajen answered.

"You don't still hate me, do you? Because if you do, it won't work," Jason said, pulling her close to him again.

"I don't hate you," she whispered, as she breathed in his scent. Her anger started to dissipate and was replaced with relief. She felt that as long as he stayed with her, and she didn't have to go out into the world and face other men, she would be all right.

"Good . . . Good . . ." He hugged her.

"We need to get back downstairs." Cajen pulled away reluctantly. Although she wasn't ready to leave that room and the closeness she felt with Jason at that moment, she knew she needed to be at the rehearsal.

"Yeah, we do," he said. "Are you gonna be okay?" he asked again, and looked into her eyes.

"As long as I have you in my life I will," she responded. They hugged again. Cajen embraced him even tighter this time, convinced he truly cared about her.

"Well, I have to pick up the microphones. I'll see you in the auditorium in a few minutes. Okay?"

"Okay, beautiful," he replied.

Cajen walked into the auditorium just as they were ready to run through the entire show. Her line sisters looked at her and noticed she seemed to be in better spirits than she'd been in for some time.

"You can bring the mikes over here," Tiara said. Cajen walked over to her. "Jason's here," she whispered into Cajen's ear.

"I know," she whispered back to her, while they connected the microphones to the plugs in the stage floor. "I already talked to him."

"Are you all right?" Tiara asked. She was unsure about Cajen's emotional state, but relieved that she wasn't a wreck.

"I'm fine. I'll tell you about it later," she said, and walked off the stage past Don and Chancey.

Don told Chancey of the conversation he had had with his agent. He was excited because his agent had assured him that his chance of going in the first round of the NFL draft was great. He was even expecting him to go in the top twenty-five.

Chancey shared his excitement. "We need to celebrate the news!" she said. "I can't wait until things get back to normal. Then we can really spend time together again." She looked over her shoulder. She wasn't comfortable, because she was preoccupied with making sure her two big sisters weren't watching.

"Chancey, they're not watching us," he assured her.

"I know. I wish I could get just one little kiss from you, but I know I can't," she teased.

"You can," he said. "Wait one sec." Donald walked to a corner in the very back of the stage that was blocked from the seating area by the half-opened curtains. Once there, he motioned for Chancey to come over. She was nervous but excited. She casually walked over to him. He grabbed her and laid an extra-wet, extra-sensual kiss on her. She tried to pull away, because she didn't want anybody to see them kissing, but he wouldn't let her go. He was getting a kick out of the whole thing.

"Don," she whispered.

"Not yet, not yet. I want another one," he begged. They kissed again.

"Excuse me, lovebirds." Tiara interrupted their moment.

Chancey was so embarrassed that she jumped as far away from Don as she could.

"Did anybody else see?" she asked.

"Nah girl, but you two are steaming up the place." She laughed and walked over to center stage, where Malena and Ray were. They were discussing the best place for Ray and Don to place her for the introduction.

Every time her big sisters looked away from the stage, Ray tickled Malena on her side and she'd hit his hand. Just as Tiara got beside them, Malena hit Ray for tickling her. Unfortunately, Dean Big Sister Nina saw her.

"Malena!" she scolded. "Why are you hitting that gentleman?"

"Dean Big Sister Nina, I was not hitting him," she responded. "It was an accident. I was stretching out my arms and he was in the way, and I accidentally hit him."

Nina knew she was lying, but decided to let it slide. "Okay, Malena. But let's not forget our purpose for being here."

"No, Big Sister, I have not forgotten," she responded, and walked to the side of the stage that was blind to the audience. Ray followed, pressing his lips together to restrain the laughter.

"You're gonna get it!" she whispered, and they both laughed quietly.

Tiara walked up to the microphone and prepped everyone to begin. They went through the entire show. All the guys followed Tiara's directions and remembered their spots. They even knew when to move and turn. The music was perfect, and Malena's introduction was fantastic. Dean Big Sister Nina and Big Sister Kendra seemed pleased, almost impressed, even. The evening went well.

After the participants and Big Sisters Nina and Kendra left, and only the line sisters were in the auditorium, Tiara couldn't resist asking Cajen, "What's the deal with you and Jason?"

Cajen blushed and explained that he was outside of the auditorium when she went to pick up the mikes. She informed them that he said he didn't know he had "it," or that he had given "it" to her. And that he had apologized, assuring her that he wanted to make their relationship work. She hated the word *herpes* and vowed never to let it cross her lips again.

"And that's all that it took?" Stephanie asked incredulously.

"Well, yeah." She shrugged. "At least now I know he's not gonna leave me."

"Is that all you were worried about? Cajen, he was irresponsible. And I don't care what he says, Jason is a player, and he is not going to be faithful to you," Stephanie argued. "I've known him for three years. We came in to college together, and he has always been a womanizer. He has never taken any relationship seriously. He's gonna hurt you again. In only a matter of time, his true colors are gonna show." Stephanie hated being so hard on Cajen, but she also hated seeing her be so naïve.

"I was irresponsible too. I could have easily told him to use a condom," Cajen said. "Plus, you don't understand. If I don't stay with Jason, I won't have anybody. Who else would want me?" She put her head down. "Jason wants me, and I'm just gonna have to make it work with him."

"Cajen, you have yourself," Tiara said. "You don't need a man to define your self-worth. I haven't had a boyfriend yet. I am still a virgin, and I know I am worth a whole lot, with or without a man."

"Our situations are totally different, Tiara. How can you understand my situation?" Cajen said, glaring at her. "Plus, he was truly sincere this time, and I do still care about him. Maybe this will change him. Maybe he'll realize we need to be together—just him and me."

"Go on and live in your fantasy world, and we'll be right here when he lets you down," Stephanie replied. "Because he will let you down. Once a dog, always a dog!"

Cajen looked at Malena and Chancey, who were listening. "Do you think I'm wrong too?" she asked, hoping to find someone to understand and support her position.

"I can't live your life for you, Cajen. If you think you want to make this work with him, I'll just advise you to keep your eyes open," Malena said. "But he would have to prove himself to me over and over, and then over again. You shouldn't make it easy for him. But when it boils down to it, it's your call."

Chancey hoped she wouldn't be dragged into the conversation, because she honestly didn't know what she'd do in such a situation. But since everybody's eyes were on her, she had to answer. "I can't tell you what to do, because I'm not in your shoes. But when I think of the way he hurt you, it hurts me. And I don't know how he truly feels about you." She added, "Tonight was my first time seeing him. But I agree with Malena, you have to make that decision yourself. However, I wouldn't shortchange myself, no matter what the circumstances."

Seeing that Chancey was too considerate of Cajen's feelings to give her any straight answers, Tiara interjected, "Okay, just ask yourself, 'Is he really worth it?' Think about the things he does, not says, because a man will say anything to get what he wants—to make you feel like you're the only one for him. If he's not worth it, and I know he's not, leave him alone. Your life will continue without him."

Cajen listened to her friends' advice and acknowledged that they had valid points. But deep down she felt she was not strong enough to be without him. She was not yet ready to face her new circumstances alone. Not yet. She needed Jason to rescue her from this mess he had created. Since he said he wanted to make their relationship work, she wasn't going anywhere.

After they passed out the flyers and said good night to their sisters, Cajen asked Chancey if she and Don used protection. Chancey told her they used condoms faithfully for the first two months they started having sex, but eventually stopped. She said she started the pill once she realized their relationship was serious. Chancey said they discussed the possibility of AIDS, and both tested negative. She added that she trusted Don, and knew she would never have sex with anyone else, so she felt safe and confident they both were monogamous.

"Chancey, do you think you and Donald will get married one day?"

"I hope so. I love him so much, and I couldn't imagine being with anybody else. Just thinking about it gives me chills," Chancey responded. "But I hope he proposes to me before he goes pro. It will give me that extra bit of security I'll need before he becomes part of the fast life of professional athletes."

"I hear you. . . . You know, I think about my life and the choices I've made and the two men I've been with, and I wonder why we end up connecting with the men we choose. You know, like why did you find a godsend like Don? Why did I find Jason, of all people? And how do we know which one is the right one?"

"Well, for me it's that sweet feeling I get inside just knowing Don is a part of my life. Even when I'm not with him I feel a connection between us. I feel like his being in my life is right and meant to be. That's the only way I can explain how I know he's the right one."

"Why is it so difficult to make responsible decisions sometimes?" Cajen asked.

"I don't know. I guess making mistakes is all a part of growing up," she responded.

"But why did I have to suffer such a great consequence?" she questioned.

"You know, Cajen, I don't know. But God has a reason for everything."

"But why me?" she demanded.

"If not you, then who?" Chancey responded.

Cajen stared at her. "How could you be so cruel?"

Chancey clarified her statement. "I'm serious. We all have tough issues we have to deal with in life. This situation is just one of yours."

"I guess you're right," she responded reluctantly. "I only wish it were something else."

"Most people do," Chancey replied.

SIXTEEN

Malena's heart was racing. She and Stephanie ran around backstage to make last-minute finishes before the show. Stephanie tried to keep Malena calm by assuring her that she would do fine. Tiara was in the auditorium's tiny dressing room going over last-minute details with the men, who were dressed either in suits and ties, or nice slacks and shirts.

Chancey and Cajen sat at the entrance where they would collect either fifty cents or canned goods as admission from the eager female students, who would try to get a chance to purchase, or at least gawk at, some of the campus's most eligible bachelors.

The line sisters determined that the money earned from admission, the canned goods, and half of the money made from the actual auction would be donated to a local home for pregnant teens, who were either unwanted by their parents or who had run away from home.

While Chancey and Cajen sat at the table, waiting for the crowd, Cajen reflected on their conversation the previous evening, and decided she was no longer going to be angry and would accept her situation. She felt a sense of peace.

Two of their big sisters were approaching the table. "Why did we get door duty? We're gonna be greeting all night," Chancey moaned. Their big sisters approached and stopped in front of them.

"Hello, ladies," one said.

Chancey and Cajen jumped up and began to recite the greeting. "Greetings, Most Honorable Big Sisters. We are so pleased to be graced by your presence. We work hard, both day and night, striving to become what you already are. May we be privileged to address you, please?" They knew the greeting so well that they got through it quickly and began again before their big sisters could stop them.

"That's enough, one and two," the big sister said, calling them by their line numbers. "You'd better be glad we're in a public place, or y'all would be greetin' me until the sun decided to show up tomorrow morning. And by the way, this show better be good, 'cause if it's not, you'll never wear my letters." She and her soror broke out in laughter.

The big sister who spoke was the meanest of all their big sisters. Her line name was Attitude Adjuster. She always seemed to be the one with the attitude, and the pledges felt that she was the one who needed the adjustment. Every time they encountered her, she never said anything positive. She never showed a friendlier, softer side, no matter what the line sisters did. They often wondered if they would be able to consider her a true sister after they crossed. Most of their big sisters seemed bored by pledging them after a few weeks. But other than Dean Big Sister Nina, Attitude Adjuster was the only other one who still got a thrill from intimidating them.

"We hope you two will enjoy the show," Chancey managed.

"We'd better," Big Sister Attitude Adjuster responded. Their other big sister laughed and said, "We'll see you tonight after the auction." The two then walked into the auditorium, bragging about how the pledges were not going to get any sleep tonight.

"I can't find anything about her that I like," Cajen said.

"Yeah, but I don't think she's as mean as she comes off," said Chancey. "I think she's just fronting to keep us as edgy as she was when she was on line."

"Well, it's working."

"You're right. It is definitely working."

Their big sister Kim walked up. They loved Big Sister Kim because she wasn't into the hazing aspect of pledging as much as she was into teaching. She loved to talk and would often get off track from the topic of discussion. It did, however, work to their advantage when she would discipline them, because she would never complete a lecture.

"Don't even greet me. I don't feel like hearing it. I only want to be entertained. Please tell me I'm gonna get some entertainment. I've had a bad day," she said.

They knew they were in for a story.

She continued, "My car stopped, I had to take it to be repaired, and I took the bus back to campus. I know I could have called one of you, but I didn't have time—I had things to do. I hope there are some fine men behind those doors because I need to see something to cheer me up."

"Oh, Big Sister Kim, by the time the auction is over, you're gonna forget about everything bad that happened to you today," said Chancey.

"I hope you're right. I brought some cash with me, and I might just buy myself a servant to pamper me for a day. Now, that would really ease my mind, if you know what I mean." She winked. "I'll see you ladies later tonight. I think the crowd's coming."

Women came pouring in, and the two girls became busy with canned goods and donations.

The lights went down, the curtains opened, and Donald and Ray carried Malena onto the stage. They put her down in the center of the stage in front of the mike. She had chains around her arms and was wearing a long white dress that was ripped at the hemline. Her hair was pinned up and wrapped in a white headwrap. After a moment, she flung her arms in the air and threw her head back. Then she slowly brought her arms down and lowered her head. The deejay put on tribal music with a heavy drumbeat that blared out over the speaker system. The music was lowered and Malena began to speak:

"One hundred years ago, I was owned, possessed by another human being. I was considered property. I didn't have options . . . choices . . . freedom. *I was a slave!* I could not make decisions for myself or for my family. I was shackled and abused. I was torn from my beautiful homeland and my family was split apart! With my severed family, my stolen heritage, and my lost identity went my pride and my security. I was a slave—mind, body, and soul, until I realized one important fact: My masters could own my body, but they could never possess my spirit. It belonged to me. There were no limitations placed on my imagination, my dreams, and my hopes for you—my future. I hoped that you too would one day be free. But not just in spirit—completely free. Freer than I was ever able to be. My hope for your tomorrows gave me the courage to be strong, to withstand; the courage to demand change. You were my hope, the essence of my dreams. So don't ever forget me and my plight. Reach forward and grow upward. Move ahead. Today, let us pay homage to the progress of our race. Let us remind ourselves that we control our destiny. Let us replace the pain and suffering felt at the auction block with hope and courage. Today's auction is a celebration of our ancestors. So please join me in celebrating freedom! Freedom of choice, freedom to do, and freedom to be."

Malena bowed, and the audience cheered as the curtains closed. As she walked off the stage all of the guys told her how great she was. Then the deejay played a mellow jazz tune, and the curtains opened. Tiara stood at the microphone.

"Good evening," she said, "and thank you so much for attending our fund-raiser."

She was surprised by the number of people in the audience, and she had to take a moment to compose herself. She took a deep breath before continuing. "Wasn't the opening monologue inspiring?" she asked. The audience cheered.

"It's always good to remember from whence you came," she said, and there was more applause and nods of agreement from the audience.

"Now it's time to let loose and have a good time. And ladies, don't hold back. If you are pleased with our selection, don't hesitate to make your bids." Tiara's confidence grew. "We made sure to choose the cream of the crop," she exclaimed. The ladies cheered.

"Again, have a good time and dig deep into those designer purses. And remember, proceeds will be donated to Hope for Tomorrow, a local home for pregnant teens."

She then introduced the first guy, her personal favorite, Ben. He walked out onto the stage wearing cream slacks and a cream rayon shirt, which was unbuttoned and flowed as he walked. The ladies went wild.

"This tall, slender dream's name is Ben Jackson. He's six-foot-two and weighs in at two hundred twenty-five pounds. Ladies, he's an economics major and enjoys playing all sports. Now, Ben is a true gentleman, and says if you're lucky enough to land him that tomorrow you'll enjoy a day of his complete servitude. He'll carry your books, carry your lunch, and if your feet get tired from walking, he'll carry you."

"Wooooo!" the audience cheered.

"Can we start the bidding at ten dollars?"

"Ten dollars," some girl yelled.

"We've got ten dollars already. Can we get eleven?" asked Tiara.

"Eleven," another said.

The bidding for Ben continued until the young lady who began won with a bid of fifty-three dollars.

After she paid her money to Chancey, who was now at a table in front of the stage, Tiara introduced the next guy.

We raised six hundred forty-two dollars and fifty cents in cash and fifty-two canned goods," announced Chancey. The line sisters sat in a circle on the stage, finalizing the business part of the fund-raiser.

Stephanie suggested that they take the money by her apartment on their way to Dean Big Sister Nina's. Tiara lay on her back, gazing at the ceiling. Her mind was on her new love interest, Ben—how he had walked on stage, how handsome he had looked. She thought about their conversation right before the auction. He gave her his telephone number and asked for hers, and told her that after she crossed he'd like to take her out.

She blushed, which was unusual for her, and gave him her number. She didn't tell her line sisters because she wanted to hold on to her little secret for a little while longer. Tiara didn't notice her line sisters celebrating.

"Our days as pledges are limited," Malena said. She got up and began dancing around the stage.

"I know. Talk of having white dresses and black dresses. I smell induction ceremonies soon!" Chancey commented.

"I am so looking forward to being free!" Cajen said with a smile.

"It's good to see you smiling," Stephanie commented.

"Wait a minute. Something's wrong with this picture," Chancey said. "Tiara hasn't said a word."

"Get out of my business," Tiara joked.

"I think Miss Tiara's got herself a little crush," Stephanie said.

"I got more than a crush. I got his phone number."

"You go, girl," Stephanie said, and reached over to give her a high five.

Tiara told them about the conversation she and Ben had had before the auction, and shared that he was the first man with whom she ever felt like she could have a relationship.

Uneasy discussing her hopes for Ben and herself, Tiara changed the subject. "Can y'all believe how much money they were spending on those men?"

"Ooh, and did you see the attitude Allen's new girlfriend had when his ex-girlfriend outbid her?" Malena said.

"Ooh, she was pissed," Stephanie said.

"Which one was Allen?" Chancey asked.

"The second one out on the stage. You know, he's got the cute little dreadlocks," Tiara said.

"I missed that. But can you believe our big sisters got together and paid a hundred and thirty-five dollars for Derrick? Who did they buy him for?" Cajen asked.

"Didn't he pledge with Jason?" Stephanie asked.

"Yeah. He's fine too. I was talking to Big Sister Caren, and she told me that Derrick's interested in Dean Big Sister Nina. Y'all know she's single, right? So I bet they bought him for her," Tiara said.

"Would y'all ever do something like that for me?" Stephanie asked her line sisters.

"In a heartbeat," Tiara responded.

"Who was the girl who bought Jason?" Cajen asked. "I don't know her."

"Aw, you're talking about Shanika. We used to stay in the same dorm during my freshman year. As a matter of fact, she used to have a thing for Donald, but he never gave her the time of day, not in public anyway. But I guess she's digging on Jason now," Malena said. She was not very fond of Shanika, or the way she exploited her body by wearing clothes that always seemed at least two sizes too small.

"Donald?" Chancey was surprised. "That girl lives in our dormitory now, Cajen. But I couldn't see Don liking somebody like her."

Malena continued. "She's the kind of girl who is extremely persistent and goes out of her way to let a guy know that she's interested. And from what I hear, she doesn't have a problem pursuing brothers who are in committed relationships."

"How much did she pay?" Cajen asked.

"Let me see," Chancey said, looking over her books again. "Sixty-one dollars."

"She spares no expense, huh?" Cajen commented. "But I'm not gonna worry about it."

Nobody responded, because they knew how sensitive the whole Cajen-Jason ordeal was, and didn't want to experience another dramatic scene like the night before.

"We only have thirty minutes to get to Nina's," Stephanie said.

"What did you call her?" Chancey asked.

"Oh excuse me, Dean Big Sister Nina."

"Somebody is getting way 'laxed, but I ain't saying no names," Tiara commented.

"It's almost over," Malena said.

The girls finished cleaning the stage, grabbed their things, and closed up the auditorium. They were all mentally prepared for yet another long pledge session with their big sisters.

SEVENTEEN

"Did anybody get the newspaper?" Stephanie asked her line sisters, as she carried a box of bricks into the kitchen. "We need it to cover the floor." She put the bricks down, yawned, and stretched. Her body ached, and she craved a long hot bath.

Their big sisters had given them bricks and little lavalieres shaped in the sorority's symbol. They were to paint the bricks pink and choose one of the founders whom they felt they were most like, dedicate the brick to her, and carry the brick through the end of Hell Week, which, according to the urgency in their big sister Kendra's voice, had already begun. They spoke more with her and less with Dean Big Sister Nina ever since the night of the auction. The line sisters assumed she and Derrick had hit it off pretty well after the auction, because in the last few sessions they had with their big sisters, she wasn't as demanding as she had been during the first part of their pledge period.

Big Sister Kendra informed them that the bricks required two coats of paint, and needed to be ready yesterday. She also told them that they needed to put each person's line number on their lavalieres.

It was a Saturday morning, and the line sisters hadn't slept all night. After their big sisters left one of the biggest parties of the year, which, of course, the line sisters missed, they decided to conduct a pledge session until five-thirty A.M. The big sisters were on a high from the party, and a few were a little tipsy. The big sisters quizzed the pledges on their sorority's history and questioned them on every possible fact about one another. The pledges answered every question, and their big sisters became bored with them, so they made them stand in line for hours doing absolutely nothing. The justification was that the pledges needed to know what it felt like to be in a helpless situation that was mentally draining, unnecessary, and a waste of their time, and still function normally the following day. Their big sisters went home and got sleep afterward. The poor pledges, however, only had time to grab a quick nap because their day started at seven A.M.

"There's some newspaper in the trunk of my car," Cajen said. "I'll go get it as soon as my body lets me." She forced herself off the sofa, reached into her backpack, grabbed her keys, and went to her car.

"I'm so tired, and I'll be glad when I get my apartment back," Stephanie complained. "I can't believe Dean Big Sister Nina volunteered my place for us to move into for an entire week or longer." She yawned, sat on the floor beside the bricks, and closed her eyes for a brief moment. "I love you ladies a lot, but I'm not gonna miss any one of you when it's time to say bye, and I promise I'm gonna get a maid in here and get my carpet and upholstery shampooed. I'm gonna pamper my poor, abused apartment," Stephanie said.

Tiara, who had caught Stephanie's yawn, responded. "I hear you, girl. Some people got it like that."

She opened her eyes. "Nah, I'm sending that bill to my daddy. It will be his gift to me for crossing."

"You're saying you want us out now, but you are going to be sick when we leave, because you're gonna miss us," Malena said.

"Whatever!" Stephanie laughed.

The line sisters spent the rest of the evening painting and preparing their bricks and lavalieres. They discussed the improvements they wanted to make once they got into the sorority. They also talked about how much fun their next campus party was going to be. They would be sorority sisters and everyone would watch them and think about how exciting their lives must be as they danced their sorority steps in line around the party. They imagined they would be the envy of all non-Greek women.

The sisters talked about what they had missed most while pledging. Tiara said she missed studying with Sandra and Gina in the hall on her floor. Malena missed double-dating with Tammy. And she longed for quality time with Ray. Cajen couldn't wait to have one of those long talks with Eric that she enjoyed so much. Chancey missed Don's apartment more than her dorm room, and lying on his bed talking before class.

Although she tried otherwise, Stephanie could think only of her friendship with Sidney. That is what she truly missed. Her full days as a pledge didn't allow her time to speak with her about their previous argument and Sidney's being pregnant. She realized how much their relationship meant to her and wanted to resolve their differences.

The line sisters talked about their plans for the summer, and Stephanie invited everybody to her parents' house for a weekend when her mother would throw a party in honor of her joining the sorority. She warned them that Savannah was small, but promised that it was a beautiful city to visit. They were excited to go, and chose a weekend.

The evening flew by as they continued talking. They sang some of the sorority's songs, and practiced their sorority call. And although they were exhausted, they had an enjoyable evening. They were functioning purely off the adrenaline and the excitement of knowing that Hell Week always ended in crossing the burning sands into the Greek world.

The pledges were in Malena's car. It was five A.M., and they were leaving the worst session of their pledge period. If they hadn't known that in less than a week it would all be over, they all would have dropped line and gone back to their normal lives.

Dean Big Sister Nina instructed them to travel in one car instead of two to save time. Malena drove and Chancey was in the passenger seat. She was awake, but mentally she had checked out. She was shocked by the tremendous hazing experience she had just endured, but she was too tired to stay awake, so she zoned out. Tiara and Stephanie were passed out in the backseat. They were asleep before Malena got the car on the road. Cajen sat in the middle of her two sleeping sisters. She didn't want Malena to be the only conscious person in the car, so she kept up the conversation.

"Can you believe that session?" Cajen asked her. "I can't believe we actually made it through that chaos."

Malena didn't respond, but Cajen continued. "They had the nerve to say we all were gonna drop by the time the night was over. I guess we showed them," she said.

"They oughta know it's too late for us to turn back now," Malena said. Her tone was dry, but she was glad Cajen was talking to her, because she was sleepy.

"This has got to be Hell Week, because our big sisters are crazy. We are supposed to recite history, answer petty questions about our sincerity to join the sorority, and learn five songs by the end of the night. And just where do they get off thinking they can break our line up? We are much too tight for that. They better recognize physical hazing doesn't work either," Cajen joked. "And what about the one-eighty-degree change Assistant Dean Big Sister Kendra pulled? I never thought I'd see that side of her."

"Girl, please. Anything that happens now until we cross will not surprise me. It didn't even surprise me when Big Sister Attitude Adjuster said we'd better not go to sleep when we get to Stephanie's, and that she expects us to call her at the start of every hour and each tell her answering machine we are awake," Malena replied.

"She's psycho. I think she missed her calling. She should have become a lion tamer, or something barbaric like that, 'cause she insists on training us." She looked around. "Can you believe these wimps fell asleep on us?"

"I'm not asleep," Chancey replied, but not one bone in her body moved, and her eyes were glazed over.

"Oh, yes you are," Cajen and Malena answered in unison. They laughed.

The girls arrived at Stephanie's apartment and dragged themselves out of the car, each wondering if it was really worth it.

EIGHTEEN

O h, shit!" Cajen screamed, as she got off the phone and ran into the living room where the rest of her line sisters were going over new pieces of history and other important information about the sorority their dean conveniently forgot to give them until the end of last night's session. The girls were irritated and cursing more frequently. Even Chancey found occasion to swear.

"I just got the first of the two calls Nina told us about at the auction practice. Now get this. She said we need to be dressed in our black sweat suits and drive all the way out to Sawanee Park and be there at exactly 11:45 P.M."

"It's almost ten now. Isn't that park an hour and a half from campus?" Chancey asked.

"You're right. Anyway, then she said she wants us to park the car and walk to the large gray pavilion," said Cajen.

"What gray pavilion?" Chancey asked. She was stressed, and her right leg began to bounce as it always did when she was uncomfortable.

"Why we got to meet them all the way out there?" Tiara complained.

"Wait. That's not all." She continued. "Then she said if no big sisters show up in an hour, we are to go to the blue pavilion and call her to make sure she has already left. If she's not there, we are to call this new number she gave me for further instructions."

"They're trying to make fools of us," Malena said. She was sitting on the floor filing her fingernails. "We're gonna get to that park and nobody's gonna be there but us, sitting in the dark, looking like some damned fools, waiting to make a stupid phone call that will more than likely lead us to drive back to campus, and that's why I'm not going."

"You're probably right, but what if we don't show up and they do? What if they come out there, and we're nowhere to be found? Big Sister Nina's exact words were 'If you mess up, then you're shit outta luck,' " Tiara said.

"True, but we are forgetting one important thing. Big Sister Nina already gave us the time and the location of our second destination. What was the time and location Cajen? Wasn't it Vine something?" Stephanie asked.

"Yeah, the corner of Jackson and Vine at one A.M.," Chancey said.

"That's it exactly," Cajen confirmed.

"They won't have anything to do with us until one," Stephanie explained.

"So, they're just trying to wear us out. I'm not going," Tiara said.

"I'm not going either," Stephanie huffed. She crossed her arms and legs.

Everyone sat in silence for about five minutes. They weren't sure what their next move was going to be, but time was passing and they needed to act.

"Shit! I hate this. We have to go," Malena finally said. She put her emery board on Stephanie's coffee table and got up off the floor. They were all becoming relaxed in their treatment of the apartment.

"This is crazy," Cajen said. She got up and followed. She didn't want to go, but she, as well as her other line sisters, knew that they had no choice.

"We'll go," Stephanie said, still sitting on the couch. "But I'll tell you what else we are going to do. Chancey, how much money do we have left in the treasury?"

"What are you thinking about doing with the money?" She was protective of the line's money and wanted to make sure every penny of it was spent wisely. "We only have sixty-five dollars."

"The money is ours, right?" Stephanie asked.

"Yeah . . ." Chancey wondered where she was going with her questions.

"Well, we will only be on line for what . . . two, three more days tops."

"Well, maybe . . . maybe not," Cajen interjected.

"When was the last time that any of us sat down and ate a real meal? We have been chomping down burgers and chips and all kinds of other junk on the run. I say if we're gonna be sitting in an empty park passing time away, we think smart and make it worth our while."

"Keep going, Stephanie. I like where you're going with this," Malena said.

Knowing her idea was going to be the bright spot of their gloomy pledge period, she began to overarticulate, as she always did when she felt she had a brilliant idea. "I'm merely suggesting that we indulge ourselves in a much-deserved moonlight picnic feast."

"But what if we need the money for something else?" Chancey asked.

"You only live once," said Tiara. "I'm with Steph. Let's go for broke and stop at KFC and get a bucket of fried chicken, some mean turnip greens, cole slaw, and I say we don't stop there—let's even get corn on the cob. Then let's stop at a grocery store on our way to no-man's-land and get a pie. Why the hell not?" Tiara added.

"Y'all are crazy. What if the big sisters show up?" Cajen asked.

"What if they don't?" Malena responded.

"Let's do it!" Cajen said.

Everybody looked at Chancey who had to give permission to use the money. She held tightly to the pad she used for the accounting, and stared at it. It seemed too risky.

"Don't be a scaredy-cat!" Tiara teased.

"I am scared," Chancey admitted.

"What's the worse thing that could happen?" Stephanie said. "It's not like they want to kill us. They just want to haze us."

"Well, Big Sister Attitude Adjuster might want to kill us, but if she comes out there by herself, I think we can take her," Tiara joked.

"Chancey, get up off the cash and let's go. We're running out of time," Malena insisted.

"Okay, I'll go. But if we get caught in the park eating fried chicken, of all things, it will be our last supper, and Big Sister Attitude Adjuster and the crew won't have to kill us . . . I'll do it for her."

"That's cool. We can handle that," Tiara said.

They quickly changed into the black sweat suits and socks, grabbed their backpacks and property, slipped on their tennis shoes on the way out the door, and piled into Stephanie's car.

On the radio, an old tune was playing.

"Oh, I love that song," Cajen said.

"I do too. That's my jam," Tiara added.

They sang, and everybody knew all the words.

"Ooh!" Malena said. "This song reminds me of Ray. We danced together for the first time to that song."

Everybody sighed. The next song was an oldie too.

"What station would play that tired mess? Stephanie, why do you listen to that oldies station anyway? Sometimes I swear you act ten years older than you really are," Tiara complained.

"There is nothing wrong with my preference in music, and as far as my mannerisms are concerned, I'm not old. I'm just mature for my age. That's why I don't have a boyfriend right now. These little campus boys are just too young-acting for me. I need a real man in my life," replied Stephanie.

"Why, no matter what we're doing or where we're going, do we always end up talking about men?" Chancey asked. "We are pitiful. I know I am because I miss my Donnie-wonnie so much. We'd better hurry up and cross, because I couldn't take another week without him."

"I know how you feel. As soon as Ray and I found direction in our relationship, we were torn apart by the Attitude Adjuster and her torturous crew," Malena joked.

The girls laughed.

"Yeah, it's like my fate with Jason has been suspended. I'm just wanting to see what happens between us," said Cajen.

There was silence, but Cajen didn't say anything because she knew her sisters didn't want her with Jason, and that they were concerned about her happiness. She also knew they could never understand what she felt for him, so she decided to keep all future comments about him to herself.

hey picked up their meal and stopped by a grocery store to buy a
chess pie. Even if they were caught by their big sisters, the energy
they'd generated by carrying out a plan that was not dictated by their big
sisters would carry them through whatever they would face that evening.
The group spent the rest of their drive to the park singing, talking, and
for a change acting as if they didn't have a care in the world.

When they found the gray pavilion, they set up their picnic at one of
the tables. The girls were hungry and couldn't wait to dig in.

"Um, um, um. This chicken is finger-lickin' good. I'm so glad we did
this," Tiara said. She licked her fingers to reiterate her point.

"I just hope nobody shows up," Chancey said. She was trying to enjoy
her meal, but she was too worried about being caught.

"But you have to admit, it's good, huh." Cajen smiled and patted her
small stomach.

"Oh, it's definitely the best food I've had in seven weeks," Chancey responded.

"Let's make a toast," Stephanie suggested.

"As long as I can do the honors," Malena requested. She loved to talk,
as well as the art of ceremony.

"I would like to toast Hell Week because it's the beginning of the end.
I also toast sisterhood because I have gained four new phenomenal sisters
in my life, and I sometimes wonder how I ever made it through life without you. Y'all are my girls, and I hope we will continue to remain as close
as we are now and that we continue to stay in touch and visit each other,
even after I'm a big-time owner of a high-profile PR firm, and Chancey
and Donald become a big-time millionaire family and star in commercials and shit like that, and Tiara finally becomes an engineer and finds
the man who rocks her world, and Cajen dumps Jason's ass and moves to
New York or some big glamorous city and becomes Miss America and
has men falling over their feet trying to meet her, and Stephanie wakes up
and realizes there are good men in the world who just so happen not to be
filthy rich. Hell, you both could live off your trust fund and become a . . .
well, I don't know about him, but she'll become a professional world
shopper, shopping all across the universe. Anyway, after all that happens

I hope we'll make efforts to continue being friends and keep in touch like real sisters do."

"I'm not a shopoholic," Stephanie begged to differ.

"We follow where you're trying to go, I think," Cajen said.

"Okay, then let's toast," Malena said, and held up her cup. They touched cups and gave each other meaningful smiles. Every one of them really understood what Malena was saying underneath all her joking. They too hoped they could continue to share the special bond that had formed among them.

Their feast continued until it was time to check in with Dean Big Sister Nina. They even finished the entire chess pie Cajen had picked out. Neither Stephanie nor Tiara had ever heard of chess pie, but everybody seemed to like the sweet, eggy taste.

They found a pay phone in the blue pavilion and called Dean Big Sister Nina. She answered the phone.

"Hi, Dean Big Sister Nina. This is number five," Stephanie said. Then she began to greet, "Greetings, Most Honorable Big Sister. I am so pleased—"

"Not tonight. I'm not in the mood to be greeted. Put number two on the phone."

"Yes, Dean Big Sister Nina," Stephanie said, and handed the phone over to Cajen.

"This is number two. Greetings, Most—"

"Not right now, number two . . . Listen closely. Do you have the phone number I gave you earlier?"

"Yes, Dean Big Sister Nina."

"Call that number right now." Then she hung up. Flabbergasted, Cajen stood there and frowned, still holding the phone to her ear.

"What is she saying?" Chancey asked.

"She's not saying anything. She hung up," Cajen replied, and put the receiver on the base.

"But what did she say?" Malena asked. They circled the pay phone, waiting to hear their next step.

"She said call the number she gave us earlier."

"This is so stupid. I hate this shit," Tiara complained.

Cajen asked Chancey for another quarter, put it in the pay phone, and called the number.

"Hello," the person on the other end answered.

"Yes, I was told to call this number."

"Who is this?" the person asked. Cajen was almost sure it was Big Sister Attitude Adjuster. Static coming from the other end convinced her she was on a cellular phone.

"This is Cajen," she replied.

"Since when do you go by Cajen? Do you know who you are speaking to?"

"No. No, I do not."

"Figure it out!" The person on the other end said and then hung up the phone. Again, Cajen held the telephone to her ear, stunned. When she hung up, Stephanie asked who answered.

"I think it was the Adjuster."

"Big Sister Attitude Adjuster, oh shit," Tiara said. "What did she say?"

"I gotta call her back. I need another quarter, Chancey."

She gave her another quarter, and Cajen called back.

"Hello," the voice on the other end said again.

"Big Sister Attitude Adjuster, this is number two. Greetings, Most Honorable Big Sister—"

"Cut the shit, number two. What's the password?"

"Password?" Cajen asked, and looked around at her line sisters, confused. "I didn't know that I needed—"

"Put number one on the phone. I bet she knows the password. And tell her not to waste time greeting. This is an urgent matter."

Cajen put the receiver against her hand and whispered. "The Adjuster wants a password. We weren't given a password, but she wants to speak to you now, Chancey, and don't greet."

"Me?" Chancey squealed. Her voice was trembling.

"Girl, you better take the phone," Tiara demanded. She took the phone out of Cajen's hand and gave it to Chancey, who went through the same thing as Cajen. The Adjuster asked for a password, which she didn't know. This little ordeal continued with all of the line sisters until the phone got back to Cajen.

"Number two, did y'all figure out the password yet?"

"Well, no, Big Sister Attitude Adjuster."

"Well, that's because there is no password." The Adjuster couldn't stop laughing. "You girls are so funny. Do you have the address and the time?" She spoke in a condescending tone.

"Which one, Big Sister?"

"You don't know by now?"

"Jackson and Vine at one?" Cajen hoped she had the correct information.

"Are you asking or answering?" she questioned. "You have to be sure of yourself, number two, if you want to make it in the world. There are no handouts in life."

"I'm answering," she said in the most confident tone she could manage.

"Better. Now, BE THERE!" the Adjuster said and hung up. Cajen looked at her line sisters and asked the time.

"Twelve-fifty," Malena answered.

"We are dead!" Cajen said, and sank down on a bench.

They made it to their destination at one-forty-five A.M. Once there, they began the completion of their final weekend as pledges.

NINETEEN

Deprived of sleep, the exhausted girls were barely able to get back to Stephanie's apartment and dress in their black ceremonial outfits. They were told to take their white dresses with them. The pledges piled into the bedroom, bumping into each other as they dressed.

Dean Big Sister Nina instructed them to wear makeup, and to make sure their hair looked nice. Stephanie looked at herself in the mirror. She hadn't had a facial in weeks, her hair had not been properly cared for, and she was tired. There was no way of camouflaging the bags under her eyes, and no amount of makeup was going to make her, or her line sisters, presentable for the ceremonies.

She turned away from the mirror and informed everyone that she was in a shitty mood, and if they valued their lives, they wouldn't say a word to her. The whole pledging situation had finally gotten to her. She questioned what the big hype was all about. Her view of joining a sorority had changed. It all seemed so immature. Their big sisters were a bunch of attention starved females, power-tripping because they were in the position to give out something the pledges wanted.

Tiara was cranky and irritated too, and didn't want to continue. Earlier she tried to call her mother to check on things at home, but couldn't get through because her mother's phone had been disconnected. Although they were on the eve of their crossing, she lost her will to finish. She felt she should be spending time studying to make sure she graduated so she could take care of her family.

She was losing it. She wanted to walk out of Stephanie's apartment and back to her dorm room. The only thing keeping her there was hearing Rhonda, in the back of her mind, saying, "Tiara, if you start something, especially something that really means a lot to you, you need to finish it." So she had to stay.

Cajen and Chancey, on the other hand, were positive and beginning to feel relieved. They were tired, but managed to embrace the advice given them by their big sister Kim. She often told them that no situation, no matter how difficult it seems, lasts forever. Before you know it, it's over. With all they'd experienced, surely they could hold out for one more day.

Malena was humming a show tune from an old movie she had seen years ago. "Que sera, sera, whatever will be, will be . . ." She believed that, and was quite indifferent to their lack of sleep and the physical and mental challenges they endured. She embraced the "No pain, no gain" motto.

Her almost too pleasant attitude irked Stephanie. "Will you please stop humming that stupid song?" she snapped.

"Wait a minute. I can deal with you not wanting anybody saying anything to you, but that 'stupid song' keeps me calm," Malena said. "Now, you do what works for you, and I'll do what works for me."

"Well, if you have to sing that song, why don't you get dressed in the living room?" Stephanie snapped.

"I have no problem with that," she said, rolling her eyes. She had on a bra, panties, and panty hose. She picked up her dress, shoes, and makeup case, and walked into the living room.

"Whew, there is too much tension in this room," Cajen said, picking up her things as she walked out.

Tiara, who was disgusted with her line sisters as well as herself, didn't say a word, because she knew that whatever she said would probably not be tactful. So she sat silently, curling her hair with the curling iron. She needed a relaxer, however, and it was tough trying to make her style look good.

"Does anybody else have a problem with the tension in the room?" Stephanie challenged.

Chancey didn't say anything. She wanted to pick up her things and go to the living room, but she was too tired to move more than necessary.

The sisters continued dressing in silence. It was the most uncomfortable they'd been around each other since they first met. No one liked the mood, but there was no time to fix it.

Once she was dressed, Cajen looked at her watch. It was time to go, and she informed everyone that they needed to leave for their final ceremony.

Dressed in black from head to toe, they each carried garment bags containing white dresses and accessories. They walked out of Stephanie's apartment, realizing it would be their last time in her place as pledges. Nobody expressed it, since the mood wasn't quite right.

They put their garment bags in the trunk of Chancey's car. Malena got into the passenger side because she didn't want to be near Stephanie. Tiara sat by a window in the back, and Cajen sat in the middle—she had no choice. She only hoped Stephanie would not snap at her, because now she was in a bad mood.

The induction ceremony was private and beautiful. All of their big sisters, as well as several members of the graduate chapter, were there, and elegantly dressed in white. It was truly an enchanting sight.

After the ceremony, the five line sisters also wore white dresses, and their precious new sorority pins. Their big sisters were now their sorors, and they hugged and congratulated them and welcomed them to their exclusive sisterhood. It was like being in the twilight zone. The same ladies who were so condescending and nearly unapproachable were now reaching out to them. It would take some time for them to adjust to the change.

After individually welcoming each new soror, Nina walked to the front of the room. "To celebrate and welcome the neophytes into our sisterhood, we have planned a twofold celebration: dinner this evening and a party tonight. And, of course, because last year's line, the Inevitable Seven, are no longer neophytes, we have to celebrate their graduation to prophytes," Nina announced.

The sisters applauded, and the new prophytes were asked to stand.

Once they were seated, Nina continued. "Okay, everyone listen up, please. We rented out Bigelow Hall in the Student Center for the party. We're gonna throw the phattest coming out party this campus has ever seen. We'll all meet at my apartment for a private party where we'll teach the neos all of our steps, and we'll all learn a new one that I hear someone has made up," she said, smiling. "We'll have dinner at Ryan's Family Steak House because it's close to campus, and then we'll go to my apartment and from there we'll go to the party. First, we'll go home and rest a little. We've got a long day ahead of us, and I'm sure we can all use some rest. We'll meet up for the celebration dinner at about six-thirty."

The excited sorority sisters talked nonstop on their way back to Stephanie's apartment. Stephanie apologized for being a bitch earlier, and her line sisters forgave her. They joked about the discomfort they all felt before the ceremony. But now that they were sorors, they felt ecstatic and free. No more "Yes, big sister. No, big sister." No more greeting, no more standing in line and keeping and protecting pledge property. They were official, pinned, and there was no turning back.

Now, if only they could get some rest, all would be good.

The sisters crashed at Stephanie's apartment because they were too tired to drive back to campus. Sound asleep, no one heard the telephone ring except Cajen. Once she figured no one else was going to get it, she got out of the bed and answered.

"Hello," Cajen said.

"Hey, Soror, this is Nina."

"Oh, hi, Dean Big Sister Nina." She stopped herself because she still felt obligated to greet her.

"Girl, chill with that Dean Big Sister stuff. I'm not big sister anymore. I'm your soror now."

"My bad. I'm still programmed."

"It took me a while too, after I crossed," said Nina. They both laughed.

"I'm calling to ask you to do your last secretarial duty for the Phenomenal Five, if you don't mind."

"What's that?" Cajen asked. Even though she knew it was all over, she still felt on line.

"We changed the preparty from my apartment to Room Two Hundred in the Student Center. Girl, everybody wants to come. Some of the grad sorors even have gifts for your line. It has gotten too big for my apartment, so we reserved a meeting room."

"Really?"

"We're still gonna meet for dinner at six-thirty, but pass the word and I'll see you then. Oh, and Cajen, tell everybody to wear jeans," she said, and did their sorority call. Cajen laughed and returned the call.

She fell back on the bed and did the call again, giggling to herself. She would share the information with her sands when they woke up.

There were only a few sorors at dinner—fifteen, including the neophytes. They had the hostess put several tables together so they could all sit and chat about their expectations of the party. The president of the chapter was there, and she informed them of upcoming projects they would be involved in. Although the year was nearly over, there would be an end-of-the-semester clothes drive for a homeless shelter, and they would host a finals study hall that would run twenty-four hours a day through finals week.

After dinner, they went to the Student Center. There were several sorors there already. Most were dressed in their best party gear, and the neophytes felt awkward and out of place wearing jeans. When they walked through the door, their sisters yelled out their sorority call and walked over to the neophytes and showered them with hugs. But no one mentioned or seemed to notice that they were all underdressed. This made the neophytes feel more relaxed.

The door opened, and in walked The Adjuster, whom they now called Sheila. She carried a box.

"Can we get this show on the road?" Sheila asked.

All the neophytes looked at Sheila in astonishment. They couldn't believe she was excited to do something nice for them.

"Why are y'all looking at me like that?" Sheila asked. They continued to look at her in amazement. "What? Listen, the Big Sister Attitude Adjuster is no more. Hello, I'm Soror Sheila, and I'm cool people. I just wanted to make sure that every one of you earned these letters, 'cause I take my sorority seriously. I don't have anything against any one of you. As a matter of fact, I'm gonna cook dinner for y'all when we can get our schedules coordinated."

"Cool," Tiara said. Everybody laughed.

Nina told the five to be seated in the chairs lined up against the wall. They took a seat in order of their line numbers. It was a habit that would take a while to break. Once the line sisters were seated, they were showered with so many gifts of paraphernalia that they wouldn't have to go shopping for sorority attire and trinkets for a while. They were even given matching T-shirts, hats, and socks.

The girls changed into the matching T-shirts, which were gifts from the entire chapter. Then the prophytes put on some music and began to teach the neos the steps for the party. Tiara, Malena, and Cajen picked up the steps quickly, but Chancey and Stephanie had a tougher time.

They had a good time learning the steps and trying to stay in sync. Once they picked up the moves, their sisters joined them, and they walked in line and stepped around the room. After they learned five different steps, they rested.

Then everybody cleaned the meeting room and headed to Bigelow Hall. Because this was their coming out party, the neos didn't have to work the door admitting people. They were told to just enjoy themselves and let the prophytes do the work for a change. Before the crowd came, some of the "old head" sorors, as they called anyone who had been in the sorority more than two years, worked with them more on all the new steps that they'd learned earlier.

PART THREE

*Bless me to be a feminine woman;
the kind of woman who is virtuous and
who takes responsibility for her own
actions.*

TWENTY

By eleven P.M. Bigelow Hall was jam-packed. This was definitely not a party to be missed. All of the fraternities and sororities were "walking" (as they called stepping and dancing in line) around the party. The Phenomenal Five were in line with their sorority sisters and kept up as if they had been walking for years. Deejay Mel spun the most current hits, and the dance floor was crowded.

"Whew, this is one of the most exciting nights of my life," Tiara yelled in Cajen's ear as they left the floor.

"This has to be the party of the year," Cajen responded, while she attempted to catch her breath from dancing and sheer excitement.

"I can't believe the number of people who've congratulated me tonight. I don't even know most of them."

"Yeah, me too."

"But what set the night off was Ben asking me to save him a slow dance."

"Go, girl!" Cajen replied. She was happy for her soror, but wondered why Jason wasn't at the party. "Have you seen Jason?" she asked.

"Who?" Tiara couldn't hear Cajen, because a popular song came on and the crowd was going wild.

"Jason!" she yelled.

"Oh, no, I haven't. But he's probably around here somewhere," answered Tiara. "This party is so phat you might just be missing him." Then she noticed her friends that she hadn't talked to since rush several

165

weeks ago. "Oh, there are my girls Gina and Sandra. I'll catch up with you in a sec."

"All right. I'll catch ya later," Cajen said.

As Tiara went to talk with her friends, Cajen saw Stephanie standing by the floor, dancing. She was moving to the music and looking around like she was trying to find somebody, so Cajen walked toward her, but was stopped by Eric.

"Hey, Cajen, congratulations. You did it," he said, and stretched his arms out for a hug.

"Hey, honey!" she yelled. "Oh, and thank you. I can't believe it myself," she said as she reached to hug him.

"It seems like a year since I saw you last." He spoke in her ear so that she could hear him over the music.

"I know what you mean," she responded.

"Listen, I got a gift for you. If you're not too busy tomorrow, I'll bring it by your room," Eric said.

"Thank you, but you really didn't have to."

"Yes, I did. You wouldn't let me live it down if I didn't," he teased. "But I saw that you were on your way to talk to your girl, so I'm not gonna hold you. I'll see you tomorrow, right?"

"Okay, but call me before you come."

"Don't I always?" he asked, walking away. Cajen proceeded toward Stephanie.

"Hey, Steph, I'm going to the ladies' room, you want to go?" Cajen asked.

"Okay," she said.

"Hey . . ." Cajen tapped her on the shoulder. "Look around on the way and let me know if you see Jason."

"All right," she said, and rolled her eyes, then walked ahead of Cajen because she was taller and could see better. There was no sign of Jason on the way to the ladies' room. Inside, Cajen and Stephanie checked themselves out in the mirror to make sure their hairstyles and makeup were holding up.

"Doing our sorority walk has really caused me to perspire. I have never perspired this much at a party. But then again, I have never danced this much at a party," Stephanie said.

"But it's fun, huh?"

"It sure is. I'm already looking forward to the next party!"

"Yeah, me too." Cajen took a lipstick from her jeans pocket and freshened her lips. She asked Stephanie if she was ready to go back. She was anxious to get back out to the party to see if she could spot Jason.

"Give me a sec," Stephanie said, attempting to freshen her sweaty hair. "The party'll be over at one, right? What time is it now?"

"Twelve-thirty."

"Oh. So where are the rest of the neos?" Stephanie asked. "I want to walk some more."

"When I saw you, Tiara was talking with two of her friends. Malena and Ray were trying to outdance each other on the floor. I saw Chancey and Don. They snuck out about thirty minutes ago. You were dancing, and they didn't want to interrupt you, so she told me to tell you bye," she explained. "Girl, you look good. Now let's go!"

Stephanie inspected herself one last time and followed Cajen out to the hall. As they were walking toward the dance floor they ran into Malena and Ray.

"I've had a blast, but we're gonna call it a night," Malena said.

"One last time around the floor," Cajen said, trying to convince her to stay.

"Girl, I've overextended myself as it is. I'm gonna give it up to you single ladies."

"Couldn't hang, huh? I can't stand happy couples," Stephanie joked.

"But we love you," Malena responded, and hugged Stephanie and Cajen.

"Have fun, you lovebirds," Cajen teased. The party atmosphere was upbeat, but seeing Malena and Ray together made it tough to keep her spirits up. She couldn't believe Jason didn't make it to her coming out party, and although it wasn't mentioned on the party flyers, everybody on campus knew this party was to introduce them to the campus. Their sorors made sure to drop hints.

An up-tempo song came on, and Tiara ran over to her line sisters. "Ooh, this is my song! Let's walk."

"Cool," Stephanie said, as she grabbed Cajen's arm and pulled her onto the floor. They joined in line with six of their sorors who had already started.

When the party was over, Tiara said good-bye to her two sands and other sorors, who were engaged in a deep conversation about the differences between men who commit and those who were naturally dogs. The sisters were waiting to make sure that campus security locked up everything properly.

"Are you sure you don't want to wait for us?" Stephanie asked her. "We'll walk back to Cajen's dorm, where I'm parked, and then I'll drive you to your dorm."

"Girl, I thought you knew. Ben is waiting right outside the door for me. He's going to walk me to my dorm."

"Oh, really?" Cajen asked. "That's so sweet!" she said somewhat insincerely. She had tuned out their conversation because the discussion that her sorors, who were waiting for the security guards, were having caught her attention. One of the girls made a point that committed men were proud to be in public with their ladies, but true dogs avoided publicly showing intimacy or any proof of being linked to one particular woman. Their words went right into her heart. She knew she'd never have with Jason what Chancey and Malena had with Don and Ray.

"That's not sweet," Stephanie corrected her. "He's just trying to get his groove on. Tiara, you'd better watch out for him. And don't you move too fast. A man loves a challenge, you know?" Stephanie said.

"Okay, Momma Stephanie. But you should know me better than that. I'm still fond of my virgin status. And I'm in no hurry to change it."

"You'd better not be!"

"I'll talk to you later, Mommy. Bye, Cajen, I'm sorry Jason didn't show up," Tiara said apologetically. She tried to think of something to say to make her feel better. "Maybe something came up."

"Maybe . . ." Cajen sighed. "Bye. Have fun."

"I will," Tiara said, and walked out the door to meet Ben.

"Are they finished locking up?" Cajen asked Stephanie.

"I hope so," Stephanie replied.

Just then Tracy and another one of their sorors, Missy, came around the corner with a security officer.

"The building's all secure. You ladies can go now," the security officer said. They thanked him and walked to the door.

"Does anybody need a ride?" Tracy asked her sorors. "I can take y'all over to the dorm."

"We'll take a ride," Cajen and Stephanie responded. Their other sorors, who were still discussing men, declined. They said quick good-byes, hugged, and continued their conversation outside the building, pausing only to yell out their sorority call to the three as they walked to Tracy's car. Their sorors responded with the same.

Tracy pulled up to Cajen's dorm, hugged the neos good-bye, and pulled off. They knew she was going be a cool person to get to know.

"Cajen, can I use your phone to check my messages?" Stephanie asked.

"Yeah, but you're on your way home now, right?"

"Yeah, but I want to know now. Plus, I'm not quite ready to go to my empty apartment just yet. I already miss the pitter-patter of pledges' feet." she joked.

"We knew you would miss us!" Cajen teased. They laughed. "But I know exactly what you mean. I'm not getting to my answering machine fast enough either."

They saw a black truck with flashing hazard lights parked in front of the dormitory. "I know that's not Jason's truck!" Cajen said. But she knew it was. Who else had dark tint on the windows of a compact black truck, and a vanity plate that read "Shaky"?

"Oh, I wonder if he's looking for me," she said, trying give him the benefit of the doubt.

"I hope so, because if not, he has to answer to me personally," Stephanie said, turning up her nose. She did not like Jason and was honest about it.

"There you go again, Momma Steph. Don't you say a word either way. Let me handle it."

They got to the door of the dorm and ran right into Jason, who was also walking toward the door with his arm around Shanika, the girl who had paid sixty-one dollars to buy him at the auction. She had on Daisy Duke short shorts and a bra top that showed more than it covered. He whispered something in her ear, and she giggled and nodded her head. He looked ahead to find Cajen and Stephanie standing in front of him. Stephanie did everything she could to keep her mouth shut; she was trying to honor Cajen's wish.

"Hey, Cajen, congrats on crossing!" he said in his usual cool voice. "Oh, hi, Stephanie. Congratulations to you too." He couldn't look either of them in the eye, because he knew that if looks could kill, he would be dead instantly.

"Where are you going?" Cajen asked Jason.

"Well," he struggled.

"Well, actually . . . we're going to get a late-night snack!" Shanika butted in with a high-pitched, annoying voice. She wanted it clear to Cajen that Jason was with her. She grabbed Jason's arm to further prove her point.

"Is that so, Jason?" Cajen asked, barely acknowledging Shanika.

"Well."

"Jason, I'm hungry. Let's go," Shanika whined, while tugging at his arm.

"Here, Shanika, take the keys to my truck, and I'll meet you there."

"Okay, but don't keep me waiting too long. You know how I get when I don't get my way," she pouted, and grabbed the keys out of his hand. Cajen's blood boiled. She could not believe what she had just witnessed.

"Who the hell is she?" Cajen asked.

"Nah, nah, it's not what you think, so don't be getting all upset until you hear my side."

"You must think I'm some kind of fool, huh?"

"Nah, baby, listen. I'm just taking Shanika to get something to eat, then I'm bringing her right back and going back to my dorm, alone."

"So why didn't you come to the party? Didn't you even care?" Cajen asked.

"Baby, I got a big test on Monday, and I've been studying all weekend, so the party thing was out for me."

"Oh, but you can stop your studying for Queen Shanika."

"Listen to how you're sounding, Cajen. I'm not gonna stand here and take your nagging. If you don't trust me, how can we say we have anything?" he said, and started heading for the door.

"Jason, why are you doing this to me?" Cajen pleaded. She ran behind him and grabbed his arm as he jerked away. "I need you, Jason. Please don't leave!" she cried.

He put his hands on her arms. "I gotta go. Shanika is waiting."

"Don't you love me?" Cajen asked. He didn't say anything. He just gave her a blank look and jerked his arm away.

Stephanie couldn't bear to watch any more of this. "Cajen, fuck his trifling ass!" she said, as she grabbed Cajen's hand and tried to lead her to the elevator.

"No. Jason, answer my question," she demanded.

"Stephanie, why don't you take your friend upstairs, because she's causing a scene for no reason. I'll talk to you tomorrow, Cajen. Maybe by then you won't be so outta control," he said in a cool tone, and opened the door.

"Don't bother calling her tomorrow, and don't you ever say another word to her again . . . I mean it. Just stay out of her life, because she doesn't need anybody like you," Stephanie said.

"Answer me, Jason," Cajen yelled. But Jason didn't answer, and didn't bother to turn around as he walked out the door.

"See what you did!" Cajen turned to Stephanie. "You let him leave. I need to talk to him. I need to tell him to come back so we can finish talking," Cajen began to cry as she walked toward the door.

Stephanie grabbed her, put her arms around her, and said, "Let him go . . . it's over."

Cajen knew Stephanie was right. Jason would never love her the way she wanted and deserved to be loved. He didn't care about her, and if anything, he briefly felt guilty for what he had done to her, but not even that could make him care for or love her. She knew she couldn't make him respect her, because he didn't even respect himself. She accepted it and stopped crying, but she was still hurting inside and couldn't move. She stood at the door and watched Jason pull off with Shanika as if nothing had happened.

"Cajen, it's late and you need to get upstairs before somebody sees you down here like this."

"Yeah," she whispered. "You're right. I guess I'm lucky the lobby is empty, because I really did cause a scene."

"Yeah, you did," Stephanie said, nodding her head.

Stephanie walked Cajen to her room and stayed with her while she got all of her feelings about him off her chest. She went from needing Jason to wanting to kill him. Stephanie listened to Cajen cry, scream, cuss, and fuss her poor little self right to sleep. Once she was sure that Cajen was sound asleep, she tiptoed out the door.

TWENTY-ONE

After the party, Chancy and Don went back to his apartment for a private party of their own. He asked her to have a seat on the couch in the living room, and then ran to his room and brought back a bag filled with goodies. He set the bag beside him, got on his knees in front of her, and presented her with each of the special gifts, watching intently as she opened them.

She tore into each gift, and under the pink wrapping her surprises got progressively better and better. She was overwhelmed as she opened a gold clip with her sorority's letters. She uncovered a matching T-shirt and boxers, a book bag, custom-embroidered warm-ups, a pink leather organizer with her sorority's letters tastefully printed in the lower-right corner, and a watch. When she thought he was finished, he pulled out yet another box, stating that it was his personal favorite. She opened the box lined with Victoria's Secret paper, and inside was a pink bra and panties set.

"I want you to try that on now," he announced with a smile. "But first, tell me, did I do a good job? Do you like your gifts?"

They were special to her, and she could tell he put in a lot of time shopping. He had spent too much money, she thought.

He saw the concern on her face and assured her, "I got a good deal for purchasing so many items, and the lingerie was on sale. But, you know what, if I overspent, it's because you're worth every penny."

Chancey forgot about his overspending and clung to his sincerity. She got on the floor with him and kissed her beautiful man wherever she could find bare skin. They touched, caressed, and then moved their celebration to Don's room to complete the moment.

Chancey awoke to Don kissing her shoulder. I love this man, she thought.

"How's my Diamond this morning?"

"Refreshed, relieved, replenished, and revived!"

"Did I do all of that?" he teased.

"And then some," she responded, and reached over to hug him tightly. Their morning hugs were always passionate and filled with a feeling of closeness and oneness that neither had ever felt with anyone else. Before they untangled themselves, she kissed him on the forehead, knowing how much he loved it.

"Why don't I make breakfast for my sexy Mandingo?" she joked.

"Why don't we both cook?" he suggested. "Since you always burn the toast," he joked.

In the kitchen they prepared bacon, eggs, grits, and biscuits. Don didn't have any orange juice, so he poured two cups of Coke. They talked over breakfast and caught up on the important moments they had missed in the other's life over the past several weeks. They laughed a lot and could barely eat, because they couldn't keep their hands off each other.

"You make me happier than anyone I've ever been with," he expressed.

"I do?" her question was not for reassurance, but one leading to her real concern—his past.

"Yeah, you really do."

"So, who have you been with?" Chancey asked, looking him in the eye. She knew he had been quite a womanizer, and also remembered that Malena said Shanika had a thing for him. Although she had never asked about the women in his past because she figured talking about it would be painful for him, she now needed to know.

"Why would you ask me a question like that?"

"Well, you know about my past relationships. I want to know about yours."

"Since when, Chancey?"

"What do you mean, since when? Does it matter?"

"Oh, I see. Now that you've joined this sorority you need to know things that weren't important to you before." Donald seemed upset.

"So, do you have a problem with my joining a sorority? I thought you were happy for me."

"I am happy for you, but I didn't expect you to change."

"Change? What are you talking about? I haven't changed."

"My past never bothered you before, but I bet your sorors have been filling your head with stories about the old me," he argued, and got up from the table to look for something with which to relieve himself from the tension growing between them. He shook his head at their argument and walked to his room. She followed. He's not going to get away that easily, she thought.

Don started hanging up clothes that were draped on a chair.

"See, that's where you're wrong, Donald. Nobody has said one bad thing about you. You expect everybody to see you as this bad person or something. I don't get it."

He didn't respond, because he knew she was telling the truth. He did think the women on campus put him down whenever they had their female-to-female talks.

"Don, everybody knows you're not the same person you used to be, and they applaud you. Nobody has ever dipped into your past—at least not in a negative way."

"So, what was said?" he asked.

"Well, we were just talking about this girl, and somebody mentioned that she had a thing for you at one time. It made me curious to know who else may have had a thing for my man."

"So who were they talking about?"

"Like you said before, it doesn't matter. Right?"

"Why are you tripping?" he asked.

"Why are you tripping?" she retaliated.

"Are you gonna tell me, or what?" he asked, sitting on the chair that was now empty.

"Well, since you insist, her name is Shanika."

"Shanika Williams?" He frowned.

"I don't know her last name, but I guess that's her."

"The Shanika who lives in your dorm?"

"Yeah."

"We never dated."

"I never said you did. I said she had a thing for you. Was that the case?" she asked.

"Well, most women do," he joked. "Just kidding."

He grabbed her arm and sat her on his lap. He no longer wanted to be serious, and didn't want to have what he thought was an absurd conversation. Chancey, on the other hand, was not amused.

"So, since you had to know who I was talking about, I want to know the story."

"Baby, it's no big deal. She used to call me all the time and send me cards, and she always came to the games and waited afterward to talk to me. We went out to eat once, but I didn't have sex with her. We didn't even kiss. Plus, she's not my type."

"Oh, so where did you take her?"

"When?" he tried to play innocent, as if he didn't know what she was talking about.

"When y'all went out on a date, that's when."

"It wasn't a date. She called me one night and said she lost her ATM card and asked if I would take her to get something to eat. I wasn't doing anything, so I said okay. Plus, I wasn't seeing anybody, and at the time I didn't even know you existed."

"So, where did you take her?"

"Applebee's"

"That sounds like a date place to me."

"Now, that's why I didn't want to tell you, 'cause I knew you'd be tripping like this."

"So did you kiss her?"

"See, there you go. I told you before that I didn't."

"Did you?" She looked him directly in the eyes. She wanted a straight answer.

"I didn't, but she kissed me," he said, and gently moved her off his lap. He walked over to the closet, as if he was looking for something to wear for the day.

"That's bull!" she argued.

He sighed. "I dropped her off in front of her dorm, she thanked me for dinner and kissed me good night."

"Was it a kiss or was it a *kiss?*"

"I'm not gonna answer that question, 'cause you're starting something that has nothing to do with the here and now."

"I know it doesn't, that's why you should answer me."

"It was a regular good-bye friend kiss, Chancey. Are you happy now?"

"No, 'cause I don't want nobody kissing all over my man." Amused with his reaction, she continued the conversation, although she was satisfied when he first began to talk about it. She grinned because she really didn't care anymore, walked over to him, and put her arms around his well-toned waist.

"Diamond, you were in high school then. You didn't even know me. Plus, she don't have nothin' on you. She can't touch you with a ten-foot pole." He stopped flipping through hangers and walked her over to his bed, then got on his knees and put his arms around her waist. He liked to be level with her when he wanted her to know she had his undivided attention.

"You're right, but you're mine now. None of that stuff in your past really matters to me, but I'm gonna want to know some things from time to time."

"I bet you will," he said sarcastically.

"You're right, I will. You know what I want to know now?" she asked. "I want to know how much you love me."

"Oh, so you want to know how much I love you," he joked.

"Yeah, I do."

"I might incriminate myself if I tell you."

"Well, that's a chance you're just gonna have to take."

"Diamond, I love you more than life itself," he said in a serious tone. This man really loves me, she thought. She pulled him closer. He held her tighter and rested his head on her chest. The oneness was back.

"I love you too," she responded. He stroked her cheek, and they kissed like it was the first time.

TWENTY-TWO

Cajen woke to the thumping of loud music. Her neighbor was probably cleaning her room, since loud music in the morning usually meant her neighbor was on a cleaning spree. Unable to drift back into a peaceful sleep, she went through the events of the previous night: the preparty, dinner, the party. And then she remembered the Jason incident and how Stephanie had stopped her from chasing after him and embarrassing herself further.

"I hate myself!" she said, as she got out of bed. "But I hate Jason even more. So why is my heart still aching?" She lay back on her pillow to wallow in her misery, but was interrupted by the telephone. She quickly reached over and picked it up, hoping it was Jason apologizing for being so disrespectful.

"Hi, beautiful." It was Eric.

"Oh, hi, Eric," she said in a dry tone.

"You don't sound too good. Are you hungover?"

"No. You know I don't drink. I just have a lot on my mind."

"Well, I've been told I'm a good listener. Why don't I take you to get something to eat? I know you're hungry, and you can tell me what's going on with you. You can even hit me in the chest to let out some of your frustration. You know I've been working out, so it won't hurt me," he teased.

"I don't feel like getting out of bed," she pouted.

"Okay, I'll be over there in an hour. You don't have to wear anything formal—jeans and a T-shirt will do just fine, so be ready," he insisted.

"I guess I don't have a choice."

"No, you don't. I'll see you in about an hour . . . Bye."

"All right, but I can't promise I'll be good company."

"I'm not worried about that, because once you're around me, you'll be like a new woman. Now get dressed!" he said, and hung up the phone.

When she put the receiver on the base, the phone rang again. This time she wasn't as hopeful that Jason would be on the other end.

"Hello!" she answered.

"Hey!" Stephanie said. "Just calling to check on you. So how are you doing this morning? You hanging in there?"

"I'm okay. Sorry about last night." She felt bad for embarrassing her.

"You don't have anything to apologize for," Stephanie reassured her.

They recapped the incident and discussed how Cajen had felt when she saw Jason, concluding he wasn't worth her ruining her reputation.

"You wanna get a bite to eat, and go to the mall? I feel like I haven't been shopping in years. Maybe that'll help get your mind off Jason."

"Thank you, Steph, but Eric beat you to the punch. He's gonna be here in a little while," Cajen said. "By the way, I'm grateful that you care about my well-being and that you're still speaking to me, even after the way I behaved last night."

"You know I love you, girl. And here I was all worried about you . . . I know now you're gonna be just fine," she said. "I'll talk to you later. Do have a good time."

"I'm just going out with Eric," Cajen said. "It's not like I'm going on a real date."

"Do you realize how fine that man is?" Stephanie squealed. "I saw you talking to him at the party. He's who you should be interested in."

"Eric?"

"Yes, Eric. Your true prince is right under your nose and you don't even realize it."

"Whatever. Listen, I gotta get dressed. You still gonna go shopping?"

"Well, there's a friend I really need to visit. I was hoping to put it off, but I think I'd better deal with it today."

"Sounds serious."

"Not really. Just unfinished business. Nothing I'd feel like discussing right now."

"If it gets messy, give me a call. I owe you one," she said referring to last night's episode.

"I'll do that," she joked.

"Talk to you later?"

"Of course."

Eric met Cajen in the lobby of her dormitory. She walked down the stairs and he gave her a huge grin. She had on jeans and one of the new T-shirts she'd gotten at the party after crossing. Eric, who was in an exceptionally good mood, also had on jeans and a T-shirt. They gave each other a big bear hug and walked to his car. They didn't say much during the drive. Cajen was glad, because although it felt good being in his company, she wasn't in the mood for small talk.

"I hope you're in the mood for roast beef," Eric said, as they pulled into the parking lot of the fast food restaurant.

"You know I am."

"Noooo?" he teased, appearing surprised. Eric felt he knew her better than she knew herself. He listened and remembered everything that had the slightest meaning to her. He knew she loved sunsets, and that she was a huge tennis fan. He also knew that she had a gentle heart.

Cajen ordered her usual: a roast beef sandwich with potato cakes, a side salad with Italian dressing, and tea. Eric ordered a beef and cheddar sandwich, large curly fries, and a large Coke. They took their seats, and Cajen immediately started digging in. She didn't realize how hungry she was until she took the first bite. "Thank you, Eric. I really needed this."

"You're welcome," he replied. "So, what could possibly be going wrong with you?" he asked. "I mean, you were accepted to your dream sorority, and you just attended a party thrown for you and your girls that was off the hook. What more could you want at this point in your life?"

"Everything is not always what it seems," she said, not wanting to talk about her chaotic personal life.

"True . . . So what's up?" he asked. He hated seeing her unhappy and wanted to help.

"Eric, why do you like hanging around me?" she asked. She didn't think she'd get a satisfactory answer, but she wanted him to say something shallow so she'd have a reason to dislike him.

"That's obvious, you're a beautiful person."

"So, my physical appearance is what keeps you hanging around?"

"No, I mean you're beautiful inside and out. You have a wonderful personality, Cajen, and you are a good person with a good heart. That's why I keep hanging around," he answered. "I hope you'll one day feel about me the way I do about you."

He had never been so open about his feelings for her, and she didn't know how to react. "So what are you trying to say, Eric? Do you want to have a serious relationship with me?" She had to be blunt with him because she wanted to know exactly how he felt, so she could change his mind. He deserves better, she thought.

"Yes, that's what I'm saying. I know this might sound corny, but you are the lady of my dreams. You are everything I've ever wanted."

"No, I'm not," she said dryly. She couldn't look him in the eye, so she stared back down at the food she could no longer stomach.

"How can you tell me how I feel about you?"

"Eric, there are things about me that you don't know, which will make you change your mind about me if I ever told you."

"I doubt if you could tell me anything that would change the way I feel. That seed was planted long ago and it's going to take a lot, a whole lot, to change that. I doubt if anything could."

"Oh?" She was stuck. She couldn't think of how to change the subject, and she didn't want to continue this conversation. She tried, instead, to appear indifferent and to be as short with her words as possible.

"But it doesn't matter how I feel about you, because I know you're not into me," he said. Cajen didn't respond. "See, I told you. I was prepared for rejection. It hurts, but I was prepared," he joked. It was his way of dealing. He quickly changed the subject. "Back to the original discussion. What's bothering you?"

"It's no big deal. Let's just finish our lunch," she said, forcing a piece of potato cake into her mouth.

"Well, since you're holding out, I want to give you your gift now."

"Oh, I forgot about that."

"It's in the car," he said, and quickly eased out of his seat.

Before she knew it, Eric was back.

"For you!" He handed her a long jewelry box. "I'm not that great at wrapping, so I didn't."

"Eric, I told you that you didn't have to."

"Just open it."

She opened the box and inside was a watch with a black leather band. The face had her sorority's shield in the middle, and it was trimmed in gold.

"Thank you. It's beautiful." Her eyes widened, and she froze. She couldn't believe he had gotten her such a nice gift. She figured he would get her a hat or stationery, but never something as precious as a watch.

"A beautiful gift for a beautiful person," he said.

She looked into Eric's eyes, which was a mistake, because his sincerity caused her to cry. She couldn't handle the kindness he showed her. She was angry and disappointed with herself because she knew he had always cared about her, but instead she fell for a jerk like Jason, and look where that got her.

"Can we leave?" she asked.

"But we haven't finished eating . . . Cajen, why are you crying?" He looked confused. "I thought the gift would brighten your day."

"Let's go, please!" she insisted.

"Okay . . . but I don't understand," he said.

Before he could finish, she got up from the booth. He followed. Once outside, he asked her again why she was crying.

"You shouldn't be so nice to me."

"If it's gonna make you react like this, I'll definitely stop," Eric said.

"You don't understand. I'm not worth it."

"Cajen, why are you doing this to yourself?"

"Because, Eric, I'm not the Ms. Perfect you think I am."

"I never said you were—nobody is perfect."

"Well, I don't want to have a relationship with you."

"So, you're gonna say that without even giving it a chance?"

"A chance?" she asked.

"Yeah—I deserve at least that."

Cajen couldn't speak.

"I do, don't I?" He softened his voice.

She still didn't answer.

"Well, in that case, you are right. I don't know you," he said. He wondered aloud, "Is this what happens when people join groups—do they lose their identity and forget about the people who truly care?" He had a cold, hard look on his face. "Let's go," he said.

It frightened her. She didn't want to lose his friendship just because she was afraid to tell him she had herpes.

"Not yet . . ." she managed.

Angry and confused, Eric became defensive. "What is it now? You want to give the watch back too?"

"No," she replied. "I need to be honest with you about something."

Eric let out a long sigh, crossed his arms, and leaned against the car.

"I need to tell you something about me that's difficult to talk about."

"What is it?" His coldness started to melt.

She swallowed hard, took a deep breath, bowed her head in anticipation of how he might respond, and let it go. "I have . . . herpes," she said.

He crossed his left arm around his waist and propped his right hand on his chin, but that was all. He didn't speak, and the silence was torture for her. She couldn't determine what was going through his mind, so she looked up at him. They locked eyes, and the silence continued.

"What?" he finally responded in almost a whisper. "But how, Cajen?" he asked. "When did it happen? You didn't always have it, did you?"

"No, of course not."

"You just pledged, right? So who gave it to you, and when?"

"Before I pledged, I had sex with this guy."

"Who?" Eric appeared stunned.

"I'm not saying who, but he gave it to me, and now he's no longer interested." She laughed—if she had to tell this story one more time she was absolutely going to lose her mind.

"Why are you trying to protect the jerk? Who is he?"

Eric was angry, and Cajen knew it, but there was no way she was going to start a feud between Jason and his fraternity brothers and a solo

Eric. "Because it doesn't matter. Will you just take me back to my room now?"

"Wait a minute. I guess you think it's over just like that. You lay this on me and then you run. Cajen, be a woman and let's talk this out."

"What is there to discuss? I'm telling you so you'll know and leave me alone. Now please, just take me home."

"Is that really what you want me to do? Leave you alone?"

"You're not listening to me. I'll walk if you don't take me, it's not that far." She began to walk away from the car. Tears streamed down her cheeks. She didn't want to be Eric's new charity case.

"Cajen, why are you running from me? I didn't do anything to you! That stupid idiot that you're trying to protect is the one you should be running from."

She stopped. He was right—she was running from him. But she didn't want to force herself on him. She knew he cared about her and didn't want him to feel obligated.

"I know more about herpes than you think. I have a good friend who has it," he explained. "We've been friends since high school. Believe it or not, she got it when she was in the ninth grade. Cajen, I know that it comes and goes, and when it's not there you're just as normal as anybody else. And as you deal with it, you'll see it's not as bad as it seems to you right now. Cajen, you are still beautiful to me, inside and out," he said, and grabbed her hand. Sensing she had calmed down, he reached over and hugged her. It was a close, emotion-filled hug—just what she needed for her damaged spirit. With the understanding he showed her, she knew that whether or not they decided to be a couple everything was going to be all right between them.

TWENTY-THREE

Stephanie stepped out of the shower and wrapped an oversized, plush towel around her body. She was finally over not having her four "roommates" there, and was beginning to enjoy the freedom of having her own place again. She no longer had to share closet space, and when she thought of what to wear, she didn't have to worry about dressing like four other people. She would be an original.

After throwing on shorts and a tank top, she walked around her place to assess the damage from the wear and tear of having five girls living and working in a one-bedroom apartment. It was not in as bad a shape as she expected. However, there were bags and boxes in the living room corner that needed to be either picked up by her sands, or taken out to the trash bin. First thing Monday before class, she would call to get a maid service in to overhaul the place, and would try to find a nail salon for a pedicure and manicure. Her relaxer and facial would have to wait until Tuesday.

She drifted to how she and Sidney had always scheduled their pamper-ourselves days together. Stephanie had put it off long enough—she needed to sit down and call Sidney. While she was on line, their confrontation stayed in the back of her mind, not only because Sidney was supposed to pledge with her, but especially because of how badly they had talked to each other. Stephanie knew she had been selfish, and wanted to apologize to her in person and let her know that although she had acted harshly, she wanted somehow to be friends.

She walked over to the cordless phone to call, but was interrupted by a knock at the door. Who could this be? she wondered. She opened the door. It was Jeff. He stood there with red roses in his hand.

"Hey, baby doll, did you miss me?"

"No!" she answered honestly. She had completely forgotten about him, and was not elated to find him at her door.

"I heard that you finally crossed, so I got you flowers," he said, handing her the roses, which would have been perfectly normal, but he had to stick his foot in his mouth as he always did. "I would have gotten you paraphernalia, but I couldn't see myself going to a campus bookstore to pick out sorority nonsense. That's not my style. You know what I mean?"

She was not surprised at those words coming from his mouth. She just shrugged and walked into the kitchen to get a vase for the flowers. He walked through the door and took a seat on her couch.

"I only have forty-five minutes to visit, so let's go get a quickie in, and I'll call you tomorrow for dinner or something," he said boldly, as if what he said was law. "I know you miss me hitting your spot."

Stephanie was disgusted, and wasn't going to stand for his demanding and disrespectful attitude one second longer. She walked into the living room with the water-filled vase in her hands. "Jeff, I haven't talked to you for nearly eight weeks, and I realize I like it that way. I've got a lot of things I need to take care of today."

"Are you asking me to leave?"

"Yes, Jeff, as a matter of fact, I am."

"Oh, so you've pledged your little sorority and now you don't have time for me."

"Basically," she responded dryly.

"I'm going to give you a day or so to think about what you're doing. After all, any woman would love to have a chance with me."

"I've already thought about it, and we're over, so please leave," Stephanie said with a new strength and confidence. For the first time she didn't need to depend on Jeff or any other man to feel secure. She knew who she was and she was proud of how she had turned out, despite her birth mother's shortcomings.

"I guess that means the quickie's out," he joked.

"Listen, I have things to do," she insisted.

He smirked and responded, "I'm not surprised you're asking me to leave. You're nothing but the daughter of a broke-down junkie—you wouldn't know a good thing if it stared you in the face," he said, as he stood up and looked down at her. "But you can't help it, you were born that way."

"Get the hell outta here, you bastard!" she yelled.

"I will, because I got a date in an hour anyway, and she's a much better fuck," he said nonchalantly, and turned to walk to the door.

Stephanie was furious. She couldn't believe he had walked through her door and within minutes disrupted her peaceful afternoon. How dare he be so spiteful. Those words hurt and she was stunned. As he opened the door, she called his name.

"Jeff!"

"Yeah?" he turned around to face her.

Stephanie gripped the vase, and with all her might, hurled it forward. The water went all over his overpriced clothes, and his shoes were ruined. Before the stunned Jeff could react, she pushed him out, slammed the door, locked it, and fell against it in laughter. "Now you know how it feels to be fucked!" she yelled.

It took Stephanie a while to come off the high of drenching Jeff. She would never forget the look on his face. Her victory gave her the energy to call and try to mend things with Sidney. She picked up the phone and quickly dialed before she changed her mind.

"Hello!" Sidney answered.

"Hey, Sidney. How are you?" Stephanie asked. There was a mixture of concern and caution in her tone.

"Who is this?" Sidney asked. Although she knew it was Stephanie on the other end of the phone, she wanted her to think that it had been so long since they last spoke that she'd forgotten her voice.

"It's Stephanie."

"Oh, so what do you want?" she asked in a dry tone.

"I want to talk. I'm on my way over there."

"Huh?"

"I'll see you in a few minutes," Stephanie said quickly, and hung up the phone. She didn't want to give her a chance to say no.

Stephanie knocked on Sidney's apartment door.

"It's open," Sidney yelled from inside.

Stephanie walked in. Sidney was in the kitchen cutting up celery and carrots. Stephanie didn't immediately notice her weight gain. Sidney wore a floral-printed tent dress that fell midthigh. More concerned now with comfort than fashion, she had coordinated her look with crew socks—a different look for the usually fashionable Sidney.

In person, Stephanie realized she didn't quite know what to say. She hadn't planned any key statements. She only knew she wanted to make things right. But instead of speaking, she stared at the chopped vegetables.

"For somebody who wants to talk, you're awfully quiet," Sidney finally said, while continuing to chop. She refused to make eye contact.

"Well, I do want to talk, but I don't know where to start. It has been more than seven weeks since we last spoke."

"Oh, believe me, I know that better than you think."

"I'm sure you do," she replied. Stephanie realized this wasn't going to be easy, and that there was a good chance she would walk out of that apartment without a renewed friendship. "What I want to talk about is . . . well, what I really want to do is apologize for being such a bitch when you tried to come to me for support. I should have been there for you, but I only thought about myself and my feelings."

"As usual," Sidney blurted. She put down the knife and picked up a can of 7UP that was on the counter. She took a sip, walked over to the dining table, and sat with her back turned to Stephanie. Her feet hurt and she didn't have patience for apologies. It wasn't enough.

"Yeah, you're right, as usual. But I'd like to believe I've grown up some. I know I can't change what happened to you, or between us. I'm sorry it happened, and I wish I could take back the things I said."

"Well, don't you think it's a little too late to apologize to me now?"

"No, I don't. It's not too late. Listen, I can't lie and say that it doesn't bother me that you're pregnant by somebody I used to sleep with, because I'm still pissed off about that. But I do care about you more than I care about being angry." Stephanie sat down in the chair beside Sidney so she could look in her eyes. They always gave her true feelings away. "And I care about the well-being of your baby. And the two of you mean more to me than he ever did. I am sorry for neglecting you, your baby, and most important, our friendship."

"For the last seven weeks I've been handling things just fine by myself. I've been drinking 7UP nonstop and eating carrots and celery like crazy, because right now they are the only foods I can keep in my stomach," she said. "I've been going to class with morning sickness, and I've been spending a lot of time studying, because I realize that I'm all I got and all my baby has." Her eyes started to tear up. "So, now that you've crossed into your sorority, you started feeling good about yourself and you've been having so much fun with your new sorors that you felt guilty because you know you were wrong for the way that you treated me. Well, I don't need your guilt trip, Steph. I need a friend and that's what I thought you were. I was wrong!"

"You're right, I haven't been a friend, but I'm trying to change all of that right now. And you are right, I did feel guilty. I still do feel guilty, but not because I have new friends. I know I lost my oldest and closest friend for selfish reasons. I love you like a sister, Sidney, and I want to be there when your child is born. I want to help you prepare for the baby's arrival. I want to help you shop for baby clothes, and I want to be its godmother. I want to start where we stopped. But I understand if you don't ever want to speak to me again." She couldn't think of what else to say to convince Sidney to give her another chance.

Sidney got up out of her chair and went back to chopping her vegetables as if she hadn't heard a word that came from her ex-friend's mouth. Stephanie realized it was useless. All those years of being close and sharing their deepest secrets were over.

"I'm sorry I interrupted your day. I think I'll leave," Stephanie said softly, and got up slowly and headed for the door. She couldn't hold back her tears, and although she knew it was highly unlikely, she wanted Sidney to stop her.

"Steph, wait," Sidney said, and walked toward her. "You weren't the only one who messed up. I'm sorry too."

Stephanie was relieved. She was going to get a second chance. Her good friend was willing to talk, and hopefully, accept her back into her life.

"I'm so sorry," Stephanie managed through her tears.

"I am too," Sidney, who was also crying, said.

They hugged and apologized and promised to always be there for each other and not allow any situation to ruin their friendship. They sat down, and caught up on each other's lives. Before they knew it, it felt like old times.

TWENTY-FOUR

Tiara's alarm clock went off at eight A.M. She woke, disoriented. Her heart raced, and she was in a half-sleep, half-awake state. She was groggy and didn't want to go to class feeling that way. Then she realized it was a Sunday. She could sleep as late as she wanted. Excited, she reached over, turned the alarm clock off, laid back on her pillow, and tried to remember the events from the previous night. She found herself smiling when she relived Ben's kiss good night.

He had walked her to her dormitory, taken her hand, and said, "I didn't get a chance to congratulate you properly for crossing." Then he put his arms around her waist, pulled her close, and kissed her. Tiara could have sworn she saw fireworks. He whispered in her ear, "I'll call you tomorrow about noon to make sure you don't sleep the day away."

"Okay," she responded. She was light-headed after that kiss he laid on her.

"Well, I'll talk to you tomorrow," he said, and squeezed her hand.

Although she didn't want him to go, he began to pull away, then stopped. "Tiara, you know, I'm really glad we met," he said.

"I am too," she snapped out of her trance long enough to respond. "You're cool, and I like being around you."

"I'm glad to hear that. Maybe we can find something to get into tomorrow—that's if you want to." He looked deep into her eyes and stroked the back of her head. Slowly pulling her close, he kissed her again.

The thought of that kiss still made her blush. She flashed back to the party and the fun she and her sisters had walking in line. She jumped out of bed and started doing her favorite walk. "You were jammin' too hard last night," she said aloud, and laughed. She got back into bed, but she couldn't stop smiling. She knew it would be a while before she would have another entire day as perfect as yesterday. She wanted to savor every minute, but was interrupted by the telephone ringing.

"Hello!" she answered.

"Tiara?"

"Momma? Hey, Momma!"

"How you doing, girl? It's been so long since I heard from you. You usually be done called by now."

"Momma, I was pledging for the past seven weeks. Remember, I told you it would be a while before I would get a chance to call? Anyway, I just crossed last weekend, so I should be calling more. But I tried to call last week, and the phone was disconnected."

"Yeah, but we got it turned back on yesterday. So, you crossed? Well, congratulations, I guess. I am supposed to congratulate you, right?" her mother asked, unsure of the appropriate reaction.

"Yeah, Momma, it means I'm in the sorority now. So how's everybody doing?"

"Oh, we just fine, here. Girl, I won twenty-five dollars playing the scratch-offs at the convenience store yesterday. I was so happy, I went and bought five dollars' worth of junk food for your badass sisters and brothers."

"Momma, they're not bad," Tiara said. She wished her mother would stop reinforcing a negative image of herself and her children.

"Girl, yes they is! They just try to be on they best behavior when you home," she said, then gave the latest example of why she considered her children bad. "Man-Man and Brother were running all 'round the store yesterday. I had to threaten to call the police on them before they acted like they had some sense. But Donnell—he so sweet—was all up under me as usual. You know he's a momma's boy."

"So how are Tamika and Niece?"

"Tamika has been into her books lately, she's doing so good in school. And Niece's fast ass done gone and got this no-good, ghetto boyfriend. He always calling over here. She so gone over him that she ain't thinking about studying."

"I'm gonna have to sit down and have a talk with her when I come home. But what about you, Momma, how are you doing?"

"The same as usual. I'm thinking about dropping Charles. He get on my nerves. Sometimes he'll go three and four days without coming over and calling, and he don't return my pages. He the reason our phone got turned off. He made all these long-distance calls, and I didn't see him for a week and didn't have the money to pay the bill. He finally showed up and got the phone turned back on. He get on my nerves."

"Go on and leave him alone, Momma." Tiara wanted them to break up so badly because he was a bad influence on her brothers. He sold drugs, and he never had a steady job. He was always flashing money. Tamika once told her that whenever he wanted to be "alone" with their mother, he would pay the kids to go to the store to get candy, or pay them to go outside and play. They'd have sex and be finished by the time the children would come back in the house. Sometimes he would stay the night, and sometimes he wouldn't, depending on how much money he had in his pockets. Staying usually meant he was broke.

Tiara was convinced that the only things her brothers could learn from him were how to lie around the house and be lazy, disrespect women, and be irresponsible and unproductive. She didn't want her brothers growing up to be menaces, therefore he needed to be out of their lives.

"It ain't that easy, Tiara. He makes me feel too good—in bed. Besides, how you think I can afford a three-bedroom apartment?"

"Momma, you know you could take some night classes, and get your GED and get a job."

"Now, you know I'm too old for that nonsense. Don't try to help your momma. I'm doing just fine. I just want you to do good."

"It was just a suggestion," she said with defeat in her voice. Although Tiara loved her mother, her heart ached every time she talked to her on the phone. She so wanted a better life for her, and it was hard to let her mother be the way she was and accept it.

"That's why I sent you to school. You gonna be the first one in our entire family to get a degree, and that's all I need. Then Tamika will follow in your footsteps. Niece too fast for college."

"Don't say that, Momma. When Niece and Tamika come to visit me for a week this summer, they'll both start doing whatever it takes to come back here when they graduate."

"I hope so, but my bill is getting high. I hadn't talked to you in a while and I just wanted to make sure everything was all right."

"Everything's fine. I love you, Momma, and tell everybody I said hi and that I love them and I'll be home in about three weeks."

"Okay. Three weeks. I love you too. Bye." They hung up, and Tiara put her pillow over her face. Everything that she was smiling about earlier had faded. She had to figure out how she was going to get her family out of the Indiana slums and into better living conditions. She also wondered how to make her mother not need Charles, and how to make sure her brothers didn't end up joining gangs, or start selling drugs, or even worse, get killed before they were twenty-one. She finally concluded that she could only do what she was already doing—get her degree and get a good job that would allow her to ease the financial burden on her mother so she wouldn't need to depend on Charles, or anybody else, for survival.

To find comfort, she attempted to call Rhonda, but she got her answering machine. At the tone, Tiara yelled her sorority call and said, "Hey, Big Sister slash Soror, I can't believe you're not home. Call me later, and hug Freeman for me. Love and peace!"

She hung up the phone and decided she wasn't going to spend her day in bed mourning. There were things in life she was never going to be able to change about her mother, her family, and her past. She promised herself to accept all the things she had been ashamed of. She would accept herself as Tiara, a work in progress. Her social class wasn't as important as her loving, accepting, and allowing herself to move forward and grow. "Man, I'm beginning to sound like Rhonda," she said out loud.

She walked over to her closet to find something to wear. She wanted to be dressed if Ben called. And if he didn't, she would go do something with somebody else. There was always Gina and Sandra, and, of course, she had four new sisters to hang out with.

After showering and shampooing, she wrapped her hair and sat under the hair dryer. While under the dryer, she pampered herself with a much-needed manicure and pedicure. She then washed her face and spritzed with mineral water. Afterward, she prepared an egg mask, using only the yolk for her dry skin. Once the mask set, she rinsed her face. She ran the faucet a while to get the water as hot as possible, and soaked a washcloth under the running water, then rung it semidry and placed it on her face, allowing the steam to open her pores. It felt good. She spritzed her face again with cold mineral water. She touched her cheeks. "It feels as good as if I had gone to a spa," she said.

Once dressed, Tiara opened the latest *Essence* magazine and flipped through the pages. She was determined not to read anything dealing with her major. She loved this particular magazine. Rhonda introduced her to it and bought her a two-year subscription as part of her graduation gift. According to her big sister, *Essence* was the most complete magazine for women, from beginning to end, and she agreed.

She read two interesting articles and learned some new beauty tips, and then the phone rang. Her heart raced. *I hope it's Ben,* she wished.

"May I speak to the finest lady in Campton Tower?" It was Ben. His voice was so sexy and masculine.

"Well, if you mean Tiara, this is she."

"Hi, cutie!"

"Hi back to you," she teased. They laughed.

"So, miss, what are your plans for today?"

"Well, I'm booked solid. I already have a date with this guy . . . His name is Ben. He's all that. You couldn't even compete," she joked.

"Is that so?" he replied. "Well, that's okay because I too have a date. I'm gonna be hanging out with Tiara, and let me tell you, she is one gorgeous young lady. She's intelligent and sexy. Now I know you can't compete with that."

"I guess she wins," Tiara said.

"I guess he does too," he replied. "So what time do we meet them?"

"Well, I was hoping to see my guy soon."

"How about thirty minutes."

"Okay. See you downstairs," she said.

"Hey, dress casual," he instructed.

"All right. See you in a few."

Tiara was glad it would be a casual date. She was already dressed casually, in her sorority's paraphernalia, of course. She had on a T-shirt, jeans, and tennis shoes, which was unusual for her. But she had worn tennis shoes so much while on line that she began to appreciate the comfort.

She ran to the mirror and freshened her makeup. She was so excited. This was going to be her first real date.

Tiara met Ben in the lobby of her dormitory. He was also wearing jeans and tennis shoes. Ben was extremely attractive. He was tall, thin, and muscular, and he wore his clothes well. He was dark-skinned and had light brown eyes and perfect, bright white teeth. His hair was always perfectly trimmed close to his head, and he wore two earrings. The brother had style, which is what had initially attracted her.

"So, what's up for today?" she asked, as they walked out to his car. She couldn't imagine what they would be doing on a date that started at three.

"Well . . ." He grinned. "I wanted to take you to one of my favorite places. No, two of my favorite places."

"What are they?" she asked.

"Well, the first one is over that way." He smiled and pointed in one direction. "And the other is that way." He then pointed in the opposite direction.

"Well, I guess I'm gonna be in suspense all day. This could be fun."

"I'll tell you this much—we're going downtown."

"Okay. At least I now know you're not taking me to some foreign country," she joked.

Ben drove a used sports car. It was nothing flashy, but it was spotless. When he started the car, he quickly turned down the blasting music. They immediately engaged in light conversation. They talked about when they first met, and why they were drawn to each other. Ben told Tiara that he liked the way she took charge during the rehearsal the night before the show. "You're a strong woman, Tiara, I like that," he said. "Most girls I dated in high school were soft-spoken and weren't opinionated, at least around me. You speak your mind, that's sexy."

"Well, I've had to be strong, I grew up in the projects—survival of the fittest," she said proudly. "Now, I'm majoring in engineering. You can't be a weakling and keep a decent GPA—the classes are no joke."

"I hear you and I'm impressed," he said.

"So what about you? What's your story?"

"Well, I went to a coed private high school that was predominantly white. I got a basketball scholarship to another school, but wasn't interested in playing college ball. Since I knew I wasn't good enough to play professional ball, I didn't even bother."

"Smart decision."

"I have to take my education seriously because I'm the first in my family to attend college. Both my parents had good-paying factory jobs, but they want a degree in the family. That's where I come in," he said proudly, and took one of his hands off the steering wheel and held it up. "I'm holding my family's future in my hands."

"Tell me about it," she replied, thinking of her own responsibilities.

Downtown, they parked at a meter and began walking. Although she had been in the city for two years, she wasn't familiar with the downtown attractions, because she didn't have a car and none of her friends ever wanted to go.

They walked up to a two-story building, which housed an African-American museum.

"We're at our first stop," he announced.

"A museum?" Tiara was shocked. Ben didn't look like the museum type.

"Is this okay?" he asked, hoping she was not disappointed.

"This is perfect." She smiled. She was thrilled because she would be able to look back on her first date and say he was not only fine, but also educated and culturally aware. She couldn't wait to tell Rhonda. She would be proud.

TWENTY-FIVE

Malena walked through the door of her apartment. She hadn't been there all weekend because she had spent the last two nights at Ray's. Tammy and Philip were finishing up a late breakfast.

"Malena, am I glad to see you. Your girl here has been driving me crazy since you haven't been around. She really missed you. Are you in and out today, or are you back for good? Please say you're in," said Philip.

"Praise the Lord!" she exclaimed. "I'm back for good."

"Good, 'cause your girl, Tammy, has been a nutcase."

"Don't believe him," Tammy said, trying to defend herself while playfully kicking his leg.

"Well, I missed Tammy too," Malena said. "Especially last night. Why didn't y'all come to the party?"

"Well, we, ah . . . well, we lost track of time and were . . . well, you know," Philip stuttered.

"Gross! You two make me sick. Y'all were more interested in studying anatomy than partying with me," she joked. They laughed.

"Sorry we missed it, Malena. How was it?"

"Off the hook!"

"I knew it would be. Was Ray there?"

"Of course. We've been together all weekend. We left the party early ourselves. We were still trying to catch up."

"Gross back to you," Tammy joked.

"Ray? Yeah, he's the one you dissed my man Anthony for," Philip teased.

"See, I know you didn't go there," Malena said.

"My boy has been sick. But he's gonna be okay. He met a little cutie himself, about two weeks ago, and they've been kickin' it strong."

"That's good to hear." Malena was glad he'd found someone, because she felt bad about the abrupt way she had stopped seeing him. "I knew he wouldn't have a problem getting back into the dating game. Anthony's a good man," she added.

"What are you doing tonight, hanging out with your sorors?" Tammy asked.

"Nah, girl, we need a break from each other. It seems like we've been around one another nonstop way longer than seven weeks. I'm just gonna hang out with Ray. What are y'all doing tonight?"

"We really don't have any concrete plans."

"Well, why don't we couple up? That way Tammy and I can spend time together, and, Philip, you can meet Ray."

"Oh, good, we have so much catching up to do," Tammy said.

"Oh, Lord. I don't know if I'm going. You two will talk nonstop," said Philip.

"See, you're starting already," Tammy said, and stuck her fingers in her glass of water, then flicked water on his face. He retreated, and they started a water fight that ended with them both drenched.

Malena shook her head and walked into her bedroom, lighting candles along the way as she went into the bathroom. She filled her tub with warm water and bubbles. Then she picked out a CD that she hadn't heard in a long while and put it on. It was a variety of smooth Caribbean melodies. "Oh, now that really hits the spot," she said aloud. It seemed like it had been so long since she really had time alone. She hadn't taken a bath in ages, and showers never relaxed her the same way. She undressed and sank into the bubble bath, relaxed, meditated, and reflected on the events of the last two months.

There was a knock at the door of Malena and Tammy's apartment. "Oh, good, that's probably Ray. I'll get it," Malena said. When she opened the door Ray stood there with a single pink carnation.

"For me?" Malena asked.

"Of course. I would have gotten you a pink rose, but they were all out. Now give me some suga' and tell me I'm the man," Ray joked.

Malena put her arms around his neck and laid a juicy kiss on his lips, and in a dramatic tone said, "Ray, Ray . . . you . . . are . . . the man!" They both giggled and walked into the apartment. "Have a seat on the couch, and I'll see if Tammy and Phil are ready."

"Okay, but just one more kiss." He pulled her by the hand, hugged and kissed her, and said, "You know there's no return, don't you?"

"What do you mean?" she asked.

"You've spoiled me, and you can't undo that. You just have to keep on doing it."

"I know, and it's a shame. I've created a monster, and I don't know what to do with you now," Malena said. She walked toward Tammy's room and yelled through the door, "Let's go! Ray's here!"

"We'll be out in a second!" Tammy yelled from the other side.

"Okay!" she responded, and walked back over to the couch where Ray was sitting. "Do you want anything to drink?"

"No, I'm straight," he answered. Malena was glad he declined, because she wasn't sure whether or not they had any drinks in the refrigerator.

Tammy and Philip came out of the room wearing matching outfits—jeans and Tommy Hilfiger rugbys.

"You two are so corny," Malena said.

"Ah, you just jealous 'cause we're styling and you're not," Philip joked.

"So, where did you get those shirts from?" Malena asked.

"Philip got them from the PX on base. They were dirt cheap," Tammy answered.

"Aaaaaah, y'all look too cute," Malena said, then introduced Ray. "Philip, this is Ray."

"Hey man, what's up?" Ray said, and stood up to shake Philip's hand. "I heard a lot about you."

"I hope that's a good thing."

"No doubt, man," Ray responded.

Philip gave him a once-over, and then looked over at Malena. He said, as if it really mattered, "He's cool!"

"Oh, I already know that," she said.

"I'm starved. Let's go!" Tammy said.

"So what's the plan?" Ray asked.

"We're gonna get fast food and then see a movie."

"Cool. What's playing?"

"We don't know. We figured we could all decide what we're going to see once we get there," Malena answered.

"Sounds like a plan to me," Ray said.

They walked out and began their evening. Malena and Tammy were double-dating again, as they usually did on the weekends. Only this time, Malena was truly satisfied with the man with whom she would be spending the evening.

TWENTY-SIX

While walking to class, Cajen ran into Chancey. They did their sorority call and hugged each other.

"Hey girl," Cajen said.

"Hey yourself. You look very nice today, almost like you're glowing. What's different about you?"

"Do I seem different?"

"That's what I said."

"Well, I've got a new perspective on life, and I'm not gonna let anything that happened between me and Jason stop me from living it."

"Well, good for you, and good riddance to him," Chancey said.

"My words exactly."

"So, what about your friend, what's his name?"

"Eric?" Cajen questioned.

"Yeah, Eric."

"Well, we decided to remain friends. But we're gonna continue to take it slow and see what happens. We're both still young. But you know what? He told me he loved me, and I told him I loved him too. And Chancey, I do love him."

"Cajen, I am so happy you have a friend like Eric in your life."

"Yeah, me too."

"So, where are you headed?" Cajen asked.

"Don is parked in front of the Student Center waiting for me. He said he needed to talk."

"Did it sound like it was a good kind of talk or a bad kind of talk?"

"I'm not sure, but I don't think it's anything too bad."

"Good, because I don't want nothing but good news, at least for a little while."

"Cajen!" a familiar voice yelled from behind them.

They stopped walking and turned around. It was Jason.

"Hey, baby."

"Can I help you?" Cajen asked nonchalantly.

"Yeah, I just want to apologize for the other night. Baby, that was nothing, for real."

"Nothing! Jason, that's your problem. Nothing in life means anything to you. You couldn't care less about how you affect other people's lives, and what's even worse, you don't even care about your own life."

"So what you trying to say, Cajen? You through with me?"

"Jason, it was over between us when it began. Just do me two favors: Stay out of my life, and please, by all means, the next time you get a beautiful young lady in bed, show some respect to yourself and to her . . . use a condom!" Cajen felt a rush. The spell was broken. She wasn't letting Jason control her emotions any longer. Pleased with herself, she turned from him and walked away. Jason was speechless, and he could only stare.

Chancey rolled her eyes at him and caught up with Cajen.

"You go, girl!" she exclaimed.

"Now, that really felt good," Cajen responded, as they walked down the sidewalk toward the building where Cajen's class was held.

TWENTY-SEVEN

Chancey and Cajen parted, and Chancey walked to the Student Center. Don's car was parked in front, but he wasn't sitting in it. She found him standing in the parking lot, signing autographs for a group of professionally dressed ladies who were probably in their late thirties. Chancey waved hello to him while she put her backpack in his car, and leaned against the front of it. She was used to this routine and knew all too well that his fans weren't interested in meeting her. They were too concerned with absorbing as much attention from him as they possibly could within the time he was kind enough to share with them.

He said good-bye to the ladies and walked over to Chancey, put his arms around her, and gave her a wet kiss.

"You ready?" he asked.

"So, where are we going?"

"That's for me to know and you to find out. But first I need to blindfold you."

"You're joking, right?" she questioned.

"No, really." He pulled a gold bandanna out of his pocket and dangled it in front of her.

"I've already paid my dues as a pledge. I know you're not trying to haze me too," Chancey joked. "But seriously, I'm not putting that thing on."

"But baby, don't you trust me?"

"Of course I do."

"It's important that you don't know where we're going. I promise you'll be safe with me. Aren't you always safe with me?"

"I know I will be." She hesitated. "Okay, I'll put it on."

"Let's get in the car first." He opened the door for her and then ran over to the driver's side and got in. "Now turn around." Donald seemed so eager and Chancey didn't want to spoil his excitement, so she didn't say anything. She just smiled and turned her back to him. He put the blindfold over her eyes. "Can you see?" he asked.

"No, but we'd better hurry up and get there. I'm not gonna to be able to stay like this for long."

Don started the car and then said, "Okay, we're not going too far. Here, take my hand." He took her hand in his and rested it on his knee.

They were both silent the whole way, until finally the car stopped.

"Where are we?" Chancey asked.

"You'll find out soon enough. Now, sit tight for a second."

Donald got out and ran around to the other side of the car and opened the door.

"Okay, Diamond, now give me your hand. It's gonna be kind of a long walk. As a matter of fact, I'll carry you," he said. He picked her up piggyback-style and started walking.

He was right, they walked for quite a while. He finally put her down, and she felt grass under her feet.

"Okay, you can take it off now."

She took it off and looked around. She stood on the fifty-yard line in the middle of the school's football stadium. Chancey didn't understand where Don was going with his surprise, but Don had a look in his eyes that said he knew exactly what he was doing. He grabbed her by the hands and began talking.

"Chancey, I brought you out here because I want you to clearly understand something. Football is a huge part of my life, and pretty soon it's going to be my livelihood. You know I'll be spending a great part of my life being out here on fields all over the country, just like this one."

"I know."

"I know you do, Diamond, but do you know what comes with this lifestyle? Fans, fame, lots of travel. And you know that there'll be nights, and sometimes whole weeks at a time, that we won't see each other, especially during preseason camps."

"Don, I know. And I also know that you're probably going to go as a first round draft pick, and that you have no control over what team you'll be with or where you're going to live. And if a team suddenly decides to trade you, you're gonna have to pack up and move, no matter how much you like the city you're playing in. I know all of this. We've discussed it thousands of times." Chancey was a little irritated. She hated the thought of him leaving and wondered why he decided to choose now to remind her of all of this.

"You're right, we have, but we've only discussed how it would impact me and how I would react to that kind of lifestyle, but we never discussed how you felt about it, or how you would deal with it."

"Well, I haven't really thought about it much. I worry mostly about you leaving me at the end of the summer and starting all over without me."

"What do you mean without you?"

"I mean I know we'll still be together, but I've accepted that the changes would affect your life more than mine, at least for the next three or four years."

"But what if I don't want that?"

"What? Us to be together?"

"No, us apart," he responded. Then he got down on one knee. "Diamond, what I'm wondering is"—he reached in his pocket and pulled out a box—"will you marry me?" He opened the box, and inside was the most splendid engagement ring she had ever seen. She didn't move or respond, so Donald took the ring out of the box and placed it on her finger.

"Oh . . . baby . . . I don't know what to say," she finally voiced. "I wasn't expecting this. Not here! Not now!"

"Say yes!"

This was exactly what Chancey hoped for, but she hesitated. "Well . . ."

"Listen, I'm not talking about getting married tomorrow or next month. I'm talking about a year from now. It'll give me a chance to feel out my first year in the NFL, and it'll give you a chance to be with your new sorors and finish up another year of school. Plus you'll be taking summer classes, right? After you transfer to where I'll be, maybe it won't take you four full years to graduate. Chancey, you know how smart you are. But after our year apart, Diamond, I want you to be my wife." Donald was more sincere than Chancey had ever seen him.

"Donald, there's something that I want to discuss with you—I've wanted to for some time, but I never knew how."

"What is it, baby?"

"Well . . ." She wasn't sure how to put it, but decided to be honest. "I don't like it when you act as if you're my father. After all, I am a grown woman."

He laughed. "So, you noticed. I was hoping you wouldn't."

"What do you mean you were hoping I wouldn't? I can't help but notice. I can't marry you if you have to feel like you own me."

"I don't want to own you, Diamond," Donald said, shaking his head. "I saw this growing up and promised myself I wouldn't repeat my father's behavior with my mother. Your independence is one of the reasons that I love you. I know that you will be able to help me make wise decisions, and I know that you will have my back when it comes to finances and any other important decisions concerning us."

"But—"

"Listen, I know I can be forceful, but I love you and I'm willing to work on it, baby. Even if it means you pointing it out to me every time I step out of the boundaries that we can set together."

"But what about the way I dress? Don, I am not one of those glamorous model types. I won't ever be. Will you ever accept that?"

"You're beautiful to me. I love you just the way you are. That's why I want to marry you. So?"

Chancey's head was spinning. She had always felt in her heart that she and Don would eventually marry, and the sincerity and love she saw in his eyes helped to quell any doubts she had.

"Oh, my God!" she gasped, as the full weight of the decision she was about to make hit her.

"Will you answer me?" he begged.

"I can't believe you! I was not expecting this, not today. I'm not even dressed appropriately. I'm wearing a T-shirt!"

"You look like a diamond to me. So, will you?"

"What, are you crazy? Of course I will. Yes! Yes, I will marry you, Donald Robinson," she said, and pulled him close to her and kissed him passionately.

TWENTY-EIGHT

H ello!" Tiara said, answering her telephone.

"Hey, Soror." It was Rhonda.

"Rhonda, hi! I've been trying to get in touch with you since I crossed."

"I know. I got all your messages. Congratulations! Be expecting something in the mail in the next couple of days."

"Oh, thank you! What is it?"

"Patience, my child. You'll see when it gets there," she joked.

"So, where have you been?" Tiara asked.

"I've been working on this huge project. I've been working late every night and most of the weekend. But you know I can't miss church for work, and I made that clear to my boss before we started, so he didn't give me a hassle. We finally finished two days ago, and the big presentation was yesterday. We made that company a whole lot of money. I took off today, and I'm gonna take Monday off too."

"Well, good for you."

"And poor Freeman, he's been so mad at me. It got to a point that when I walked through the door those late nights, he didn't run up to me and lick me as he usually does. He'd walk into the next room. But you know he loves his mommy. I called him, and when he came running, I gave him a doggy treat. Then he forgot he was mad and jumped all over me."

"Girl, you love that dog, don't you?"

"Yeah, he's the son I'll probably never have."

"Oh, please. You still have time."

"I hope I do. So, how are you feeling? You know, with crossing and all?"

"I feel good. No, I feel great. You didn't tell me I was gonna be this excited."

"I thought you knew," Rhonda joked. "I'm so proud of you. I knew you could do it. You are really growing up to be something special."

"Thank you."

"I mean it. And when you come and visit, we'll have a slumber party and stay up all night exchanging line stories. But I don't know if you can handle my stories, because I had some crazy big sisters."

"I can't wait to hear them. But guess what."

"What?"

"I have a date tonight."

"Oh my goodness. I can't believe it. With whom?"

"This guy named Ben. And girlfriend, he is too fine."

"Tell me more."

"Believe it or not, I met him when I was on line. He was in the auction that we had as a fund-raiser. He fell for me instantly."

"My, aren't we conceited."

"Oh, I'm not conceited, just convinced."

"I hear ya!" Rhonda said, laughing.

"We're supposed to go to a movie that's playing in the Student Center. It's a sneak preview."

"Do you like him?"

"Of course I do."

"Well, I know how tough you are on men, so I had to ask."

"Actually, I like him a whole lot."

"Well, good. I'm glad to hear it. Now I'll have some exciting stories to look forward to, but just make sure you take it slow with him."

"You know I will. I haven't changed that much! Well, I'm gonna finish getting ready, and I'll talk to you in a few days."

"Okay. Have fun tonight."

"I will."

Tiara met Ben in the lobby of her dormitory.

"Hey, you," he said.

"Hey."

"Oooh, you look nice," he commented. And she did—she wore a bodysuit, loose-fitting jeans, and black shoe boots with an extremely high heel.

"Thank you."

"So, do you want to skip the movie altogether and go back to my room and get close?" he asked.

"No." She brushed off his advance. "I really want to see the movie."

"We can see that movie anytime."

Tiara knew she needed to set the pace for their relationship and wanted to set boundaries early on. "And we can go back to your room anytime, right?" she looked him directly in his eyes.

"You're right. There's no need to rush."

"Yeah, 'cause if you're in a hurry, you got the wrong lady," she announced.

"No hurry. Trust me, no hurry at all," he responded.

"Cool. Now let's go see this movie."

"After you," he said, and opened the door and followed her out.

TWENTY-NINE

"Hey, Soror."

"Hi, Mommy," Stephanie said in her mushy little-girl voice, pleased that her mother had called her. She spoke to her parents that way when either she hadn't heard from them in a while, or she wanted something.

"How's my beautiful little girl?"

"I'm good," she gushed.

"Well, you're really not a little girl anymore. You're a lady and you've grown up, and you're following in the footsteps of some amazing women," her mother said. "You must come home soon. Remember that your aunts, some of your cousins, and I will be throwing you a celebration party."

"Ooooh, good. I'll be home in a few weeks, and I'm gonna bring some of my sands with me. I can't come home next weekend because I'll be attending my first chapter meeting. I'll call you back with a definite date."

"It's exciting, isn't it?"

"Yes, it really is, Momma."

"You know what? You're really going to be able to affect a lot of lives through your service in our sorority. A lot of people don't give sororities and fraternities enough credit for the work they do in the community, but we really do make a difference."

"Well, we've already raised money for a homeless shelter for pregnant teens, and I never knew that place ever existed before now. It's really close to the school."

"Really?"

"Yeah, and we're gonna have a clothes drive on campus at the end of the semester."

"I am so proud of you."

"You're proud of me?"

"Of course I am. I just don't know why you waited so long."

"I don't either, but I love my sands. They're a good group of girls."

"So how's your love life?" her mother asked.

"Better."

"And who are you seeing now?"

"Nobody."

"But I thought it was better."

"Well, it is . . . because I'm not wasting my time anymore with jerks who happen to have money. I've decided to be more selective about the men with whom I spend my precious time. I don't want to get pregnant before I'm ready, or catch a disease. So, right now I'm spending time appreciating and getting to know me, and when the right man comes along, it won't be rushed. I won't have to be fake, and I won't be frustrated or confused. And, as you always tell me, I'll know when he's the right one."

"Sounds like my daughter is really growing up."

"Well, it was bound to happen eventually," she joked. "So where's Daddy?"

"He's taking a shower. He just got in from playing golf. We're getting ready to go out for a late lunch. We're dating again."

"What?"

"We're going to a jazz set tomorrow evening, and not just because anybody who's anybody is going to be there, but because we enjoy each other's company again, and we want to enjoy jazz together."

"Didn't you always?"

"Yeah, we did, but sometimes you forget how precious each other's company truly is until something special reminds you again."

"So what reminded you?"

"One of your daddy's old friends and his wife renewed their wedding vows and invited us to attend. It was so special and it reminded us of what we have."

"Oh, Mommy, that's so sweet."

"You'll have the same thing one day too."

"I'm sure I will," Stephanie replied. "Kiss Daddy for me, and have a wonderful evening tomorrow night."

"I love you, Steph."

"I love you too, Mommy," she said.

Stephanie was happy and relieved. Her parents were still her model for a good relationship. They weathered the tough times and appreciated the good. Although she worried that they were growing apart, she realized they were simply evolving. This made her feel better about taking her time in the relationship game so she could have what they did.

THIRTY

"Let's move in together!" Ray announced. He and Malena were lying in his bed. They had spent the night at his apartment, and stayed up all night watching movies they'd rented. She was still half asleep, but Ray had been up for a while, thinking of the best way to ask her to move in with him.

"What are you talking about? It's Saturday morning, our day to sleep in, and you're playing games with me," Malena said with her eyes still closed. She was not ready to wake up, especially to Ray joking.

"What, you think I'm not serious?"

"Are you?" She sat up.

"I wouldn't ask if I wasn't serious."

"Ray, I'm flattered, but why do you want to move in together now?"

"Economics. See, I've been thinking about it, and from what Tammy and Philip said when we went out with them last weekend, they're gonna get married. Tammy will move out by the beginning of the semester and you'll be in need of a roommate. Getting a one-bedroom will be costly for you. It would save us both money if we got a place together, off campus. I'll begin my new job at the end of the semester, and I've started apartment hunting. I already found a nice place near campus, and I would love to have you live there with me, you know, and kind of give the place a lady's touch."

Malena was shocked. She couldn't believe what she was hearing. He was being so insensitive about such a serious step. "Ray, it's cool that you want to save money and all, but that is not a good enough reason for me to want to move in with you." She cared about Ray, but didn't want to be thought of as mere convenience.

"Baby, that's not the only reason. I care about you, you know that. I love you and, well, I'm starting a new life and I want you there with me."

"I will be there."

"So, you don't want to move in with me?"

"I didn't say that. I just think we should move in together for the right reasons, and I'm not sure economics will cut it. Plus, I always thought I'd be married before I moved in with a man."

"Well, I'm sure we'll get married . . . one day. But I don't think we're really ready for that yet. Do you?"

"No . . . I, for one, am not ready. The thought of marriage, especially while I'm still in school, scares me."

"So what would be the wrong reasons to move in together, since neither of us is ready for marriage?"

"Economics, period. Economics doesn't determine the quality of the relationship."

"I didn't mean to hit you with it like that. I just wanted to make moving in with me seem appealing to you."

"You are appealing to me. Being with you is what's important to me. Making such a major step is gonna take time."

"Well, the semester is almost over, and I'm gonna need an answer soon so I can figure out what I need to do."

"So, are you demanding an answer?" Malena asked, offended by his approach.

"No, I'm not. I thought you'd be happy that I want something more permanent for us, but I guess I was wrong," he said, defending himself.

"I just don't want to feel pressured. You've apparently been thinking about this for some time. I would like the same amount of time to do likewise."

"There is no pressure. Look, just forget it. It was just a thought. Let's scratch it. Let's just pretend I never said anything." Ray got out of bed and put on his pants.

"Oh, so you're leaving now," Malena said dryly.

"I got things I need to do."

"So, the conversation is over just like that?" Malena argued. She was shocked that he would drop a bombshell and run off before a fair discussion.

"Yeah, it is. I tried to surprise you, hoping to make you happy, and you took it the wrong way. But I have other things to do. You can stay in bed if you want, but I'll be in the kitchen studying."

"Ray! Wait!" Malena shouted. "I am happy that you asked. I'm just shocked, and that doesn't mean shocked in a bad way. I'm surprised. I just need time."

"How long?"

"Give me two weeks. Is that cool?" she asked. Malena was a bit turned off. She always thought out major steps in her life, and she didn't want anyone to cause her to move hastily.

"All right. You got two weeks, but I won't take no for an answer," he said, and walked out of the room.

Malena lay there, stunned. She would have never guessed Ray would want such a commitment. After all, they had only been seeing each other for a little more than four months. She wasn't sure what she wanted to do, but she was sure she didn't want to lose him.

THIRTY-ONE

S pending all day with everybody today kind of reminds me of the good ol' days when we were on line," Chancey said.

"What do you mean, the good ol' days?" Stephanie replied. "Those days weren't good, and it was just last month that we crossed." The girls had spent the entire Sunday together. They met early that morning at Chancey and Cajen's dormitory and went to church. Afterward, they attended their first sorority chapter meeting. Now they were all at Stephanie's apartment preparing dinner. They chipped in and stopped by the store on their way to Stephanie's and picked up salad and dressing, spaghetti, sauce, ground beef, and garlic bread.

"So, who's cooking, because y'all know I'm not the one," Tiara joked.

"I will," Malena said.

"I'll help," Cajen added.

"So, Miss Tiara, what's going on with you and Ben?" Stephanie asked.

"We're still taking it slow. But you know what's so messed up? Now I understand why Chancey and Malena are always going around looking all googly-eyed. Love is some powerful shit."

"So, you're in love, Tiara?" Stephanie asked.

"Not yet, but I'm enjoying getting there."

"She's gone!" Malena joked, and everybody laughed. "Now, if you want to hear some news, check this out." Everybody stopped and waited to hear what she had to say. "Ray asked me to move in with him." She wasn't going to mention it at first, but she knew her sands were always willing to give advice regardless of whether she wanted it or not, and she really needed it.

"What?" Stephanie yelled.

"When?" Cajen asked.

"So what did you say?" Tiara asked.

"I didn't give him an answer," said Malena.

"You mean you didn't say yes?" Chancey asked.

"No, I didn't. It's a big step. How do I know he won't want to keep us that way permanently? I do want to get married one day."

"You're right. So did you tell him that?" Tiara asked.

"Well, no, but only because I don't want to get married for at least another two years. I want to wait until after I graduate and get my career established," Malena said. "I didn't want him to think I was hinting around about getting married anytime soon. Plus, the thought of getting engaged is scarier than moving in together—to me anyway."

"Well, it sounds to me like you just answered your own question," Stephanie said.

"What do you mean?"

"If you don't like it, you can always move out. I'll even open my apartment to you if you need it, provided, of course, you'll look for a new place to stay immediately afterward."

"Don't pressure yourself, Malena," Tiara added. "You two are a good team, and Ray is going to love you no matter what you decide. Just make sure you have peace with your decision."

"You're right, there shouldn't be any pressure," Malena said.

"I like Ray, so don't go back and forth with him, it could cause some serious strain to you, and him. I say make a decision and stick by it," Cajen suggested.

"So, what do you think, Chancey?" Malena asked. "Sitting over there all quiet. What's on your mind."

She laughed sneakily because it was hard to hold her own news in. "Do what's best for you. And don't allow us to influence your decision. After all, what do we really know?"

"You're right about that," Tiara said.

"I'm sure I won't lose him if I say no, so I'm gonna say yes. As a matter of fact, I'm gonna call him now. Steph, can I use the phone in your room?"

"Of course. But then who's gonna cook?"

"I'll help," Chancey said, and got up out of her chair and walked to the stove next to Cajen.

"So, have you heard from Jason since that night we saw him with that girl?" Stephanie asked Cajen.

"Who? Please, I have definitely moved on. Jason is old, old, old news."

"That's good to hear," Stephanie said.

Chancey dropped the spaghetti into the water that Malena had put on. "Yeah, I'm so proud of her, we saw him the other day when she was going to class, and she told him a thing or two."

Cajen was preparing the beef and the spaghetti sauce. "Yeah, I had to let him know that he was an ultimate loser and I didn't have time for his game—the jerk."

"That's what I'm talking about. He's definitely old news," Tiara added.

"I don't mind making spaghetti." Cajen changed the subject and stirred the sauce into the browned beef. "It's easy and it's so inexpensive." Then she said, as if talking to herself, "Eric likes spaghetti."

"Oh, yeah, Eric," Stephanie gushed. "So what's going on with you two?"

"We're just friends."

"Yeah, right. 'Eric likes spaghetti,'" she said in a dreamy voice, gently mocking Cajen.

"No, seriously. I mean, we do care a lot about each other, but we're playing it slow, extremely slow."

"Well, I have an announcement." Stephanie interrupted the flow of the conversation. She stood up and posed. "I'm fine, sexy, single, and proud of it! Excuse the interruption, but I just wanted to make that point clear." Everybody laughed.

Malena walked back into the kitchen. "He wasn't in, so I left a message on his machine. Maybe he's out getting some things for our new apartment."

"Ooooooh!" They teased.

"Just think, y'all are going to be living together," Tiara said. "That's major."

"Y'all are so silly. Don't even start. So what did I miss while I was on the phone?"

"Nothing really," Chancey said. "We were just talking about men, as usual."

"Why do we always talk about men every time we get together? There's got to be something more important in life," Malena said, and picked up a large bowl for the salad, then went through Stephanie's cabinets to find bowls and plates.

"You're definitely right," Chancey said. "But before we change the subject, I have to say one thing that involves men. Well, my man in particular."

"Of course, it wouldn't be right if you didn't," Tiara joked, and everybody looked at Chancey, waiting to hear something mushy about how sweet Donald is or what nice thing he did for her.

"Well, last weekend, Cajen, remember when I told you Don was waiting at the Student Center for me because he wanted to talk?"

"Yeah, what did he say?" Cajen asked.

"Well, he blindfolded me and took me to the football stadium."

"Why?" everybody asked, trying to figure out where Chancey was going with this story.

"I know. It didn't make sense to me either, at first, but then . . ." She took her hand and held it out so that everybody could see her beautiful engagement ring. "He asked me to marry him!" she screamed.

Cajen, who was standing next to her, put her hands over her mouth and yelled, "Oh, my God!"

"Oh, my goodness!" Malena said, and she ran over to Chancey, grabbed her hand, and admired her ring along with everyone else. Then they hugged and congratulated her.

"Wait a minute," Tiara said. "Why are you just now saying something?"

"Well . . ." Chancey said, shrugging her shoulders. "I'm telling you now."

"So, did you two set a date?" Stephanie asked.

"Sometime next year. Probably midsummer, but we didn't set a definite date."

"Are you sure you're ready for this?" Stephanie was concerned for her. Chancey seemed too young for marriage.

"Girl, you know I'm an old soul," Chancey joked.

"You're right about that," Tiara added.

"And Don's life is getting ready to take off. I want to be along for the ride. I always hoped he'd ask me to marry him before his life changed, so I've had time to think about my decision," Chancey said. "We'll be engaged for a year, so that gives me time to change my mind if the NFL turns him into a stranger. But I love him, and I think we're meant to be."

"That's a mature answer," Stephanie said, and smiled at her sister. "That means we have a year to plan the wedding." Stephanie was sure she would be the coordinator. "That's plenty of time. Have you chosen your colors yet?"

"Yes, Momma Stephanie," Chancey said. "I've always dreamed of my colors being pale pink and summer white, and of course I'll want all of you to be in the wedding. Plus, I'm gonna need help addressing and sending out all the invitations. You know Don knows everybody in the world. But it'll be a long while before we'll even get to that stage of the planning."

"It'll be here before you know it," Malena said

"You're right. After we're married, I'll transfer and do my final year in whatever city he'll be."

"So that means that in a year or so you'll be moving away?" Cajen asked in a disappointed tone. She looked at Chancey with sadness. She wasn't ready to lose her new friend.

"Yes, you're right, but that doesn't mean we won't keep in touch," Chancey responded.

"But you can't leave, not yet," Cajen said. She was getting misty-eyed.

"I promise we'll keep in touch."

"You'd better. We made a pact, remember?" Malena asked.

"But that's a full year from now. We'll have plenty of good quality time together," Chancey responded.

"Let's not get started, because I'm not in the mood to cry, and if we don't change the subject, I'm going to. Please, let's postpone this drama for after the wedding," Tiara said.

"Right, Tiara, let's change the subject. We have so much to look forward to with the upcoming semester," Stephanie said.

"Well, we can always talk about the stepshow and homecoming in the fall," Malena said.

"And don't forget the chapter meetings and all the fund-raisers we'll be doing," Chancey added.

"And we're gonna have a million and one 'men talks' in the next year," Tiara added.

"But you know what?" Cajen asked. "I can't think of a better group of intelligent, sophisticated, strong, beautiful, and I can go on and on, women I'd want to share those experiences with!"

"Tell it, girl!" Malena joked.

"You left out classy," Stephanie added.

"But seriously, Cajen's right. I'm so glad we all met and that we all pledged together. I'm really gonna miss y'all when I move," Chancey said.

"You ladies can sit here and start this mushy stuff if you want to, but I'm getting ready to chow down on this spaghetti," Tiara said. She picked up a fork and plate from those that Malena set out, and piled her plate with spaghetti. Everyone followed her lead.

The young ladies spent the rest of the evening indulging in their spaghetti dinner and engaging in the same kinds of discussions good friends have when they come together to enjoy one another's company.

A CONVERSATION WITH TAJUANA "TJ" BUTLER

Did you pledge a sorority, and if so, how does the process in <u>Sorority Sisters</u> mirror your own?

Yes, I did. I joined my sorority in 1990. *Sorority Sisters* mirrors my pledge process in that I was fortunate enough to be brought into the sorority by young ladies who didn't abuse the procedure. I will admit that some of what occurred during my pledge process was ridiculous and/or unnecessary; however, there were definite instances where I learned from my big sisters. Also, like the characters in *Sorority Sisters,* I bonded with my line sisters and established a true sisterhood with them that has grown with time.

How do you feel about hazing?

I write honestly about the pledge experience in *Sorority Sisters,* but I do object to hazing. There have been numerous examples of "bad pledging" found on campuses. And increasingly there have been cases where pledges were injured or even killed as a result of hazing. Individuals and groups have acted irresponsibly. Because of that the process had to be altered. If it means saving a life or preventing unnecessary injury, I am all for the new changes.

I entered into Greek life before hazing became illegal. I included that aspect of joining a sorority in my novel because, although the process has often been abused, it did exist and was at one time a major part of becoming a member of a Greek organization. In *Sorority Sisters,* I chose to write about a situation in which pledging was handled with respect and therefore a successful procedure. If more people took responsibility for their own actions, the reality of a fun and memorable experience of pledging would still exist. I feel good that people who read *Sorority Sisters* will have the opportunity to vicariously experience the process without the threat of injury or harm.

Which character in the book most closely resembles you, if any?

I am fond of each of the characters, probably because each of them has a bit of me in them.

Why did you write this book?

Sorority Sisters is an accumulation of everything good and bad that I witnessed both first- or secondhand while I was in college. I wrote it a year or two after I graduated. I always say I didn't choose the story, the story chose me. I just allowed all of my thoughts and feelings from that time to be processed and come alive in the form Malena, Stephanie, Chancy, Tiara, and Cajen.

What is next for you?

I've been blessed with an abundance of opportunities. I am currently sorting through them all to make solid decisions. For sure is the release of my second novel, *Hand-me-down Heartache*. Also, I am working on my third novel. In addition I am developing sitcom story lines, taking acting classes, and interning in the area of television production. I guess I'm in a learning stage. I'm excited about my possibilities. I'm sure that when he's ready, God will help me to bring it all together.

Are you going to write a sequel?

A sequel to *Sorority Sisters* has definitely been brewing in the back of my mind.

Sisterhood is an ongoing theme in your writing, both with this book as well as your poetry collection, <u>Desires of a Woman</u>. Describe what sisterhood means to you and how it has manifested itself in your own life.

I have been blessed to share my life with two incredible women, my sisters, Kim and Tracy. They are supportive, loving, and blatantly honest. We disagree and argue often, but as we've grown older we have realized that a lot of times our arguments arose from our wanting the other to become better. I would have not had the courage to venture out and try new things without their support. Because of them sisterhood means to me unconditional friendship. I am a firm believer that if you don't have a family or if yours isn't nearby, God will give you one. Sometimes that family comes in the form of groups and organizations. The sorority was that for me while I was in college.

READING GROUP GUIDE

The following questions are intended to enhance your group's discussion of *Sorority Sisters*.

1. Although sororities have social and charitable functions, they are fundamentally based on the power of sisterhood. How does Tajuana Butler illustrate this in *Sorority Sisters*? What role does the pledge period play in creating these bonds of sisterhood? What makes them so strong they last almost for life?

2. Each of the women enters the pledge period with different expectations, motivations, and circumstances. How do these change from the beginning of the pledge period to the end? What do the women learn about themselves and one another?

3. Both Stephanie and Cajen share secrets they feel will cause others to look down on them, yet both suffer more by harboring the secrets than revealing them. How do Stephanie and Cajen change after telling their secrets to their line sisters? Which is harder, keeping a secret or sharing it?

4. After the pledge period ends, Chauncey's boyfriend, Don, proposes and she accepts. Although she is technically a sophomore, Chauncey is still the same age as most freshmen; is she right to agree to marry Don at such an early age? Will she miss anything by changing schools to be with him? Would you do the same?

5. The Big Sisters want to test their pledges' commitment to joining the sorority. What do they hope to achieve by subjecting them to the arduous pledge process? Although the hazing the line sisters endure seems mild, what kind of hazing isn't right?

6. When Stephanie's best friend becomes pregnant by her ex-boyfriend, Stephanie doesn't bother asking many questions and nearly ends their friendship. Did Sidney's encounter with Scott sound consensual? Is Stephanie overlooking this when she becomes angry with her?

7. Cajen pays a price for her brief relationship with Jason but emerges from the experience stronger and more mature. Why couldn't she see Jason for what he really was? Are men like him common on campus? What happens to them?

To print out copies of this or other Strivers Row
Reading Group Guides, visit us at www.atrandom.com/rgg

8. Of the eight women chosen to be on line three eventually drop out. What is the difference between the women who drop out of the line and those who stay? What kind of woman is drawn to join a sorority?

9. Tiara comes from a disadvantaged background and seems more mature than her fellow line sisters. How does her background influence the choices she makes? In some ways Rhonda is more of a mother to Tiara than her own, where would Tiara be if she didn't have Rhonda?

10. Malena faces the difficult task of disentangling herself from a relationship that isn't too bad but not very good, either. After she meets Ray on campus, she is sure about leaving Anthony. What is the difference between the two men? Does she know what she really wants?

11. Stephanie grew up in a wealthy and loving family but feels deeply insecure about her past. Why does she have such a hard time accepting the fact that she is adopted? Should parents tell their children that they are adopted or not?

12. In some ways the unnamed college in *Sorority Sisters* is a typical college campus, with its mix of athletes, scholars, and students from all backgrounds. How do the line sisters reflect this? How is college life different from a young person's life before and after the experience?

ABOUT THE AUTHOR

TAJUANA "TJ" BUTLER is the founder of Lavelle Publishing and is also a writer, poet, and public speaker who lectures on sisterhood at colleges throughout the United States. *Sorority Sisters* is her first novel. She has published a collection of poetry entitled *The Desires of a Woman: Poems Celebrating Womanhood*. She is originally from Kentucky, where she attended the University of Louisville. Her second novel, *Hand-me-down Heartache*, will be published by Villard Books in fall 2001. She lives in Los Angeles. You can visit her website at www.tjbutler.com.